EMERSON'S
NATURE

Origin, Growth, Meaning

SECOND EDITION, ENLARGED

Edited by

MERTON M. SEALTS, JR.

University of Wisconsin-Madison

and

ALFRED R. FERGUSON

Late of University of Massachusetts-Boston

SOUTHERN ILLINOIS UNIVERSITY PRESS
CARBONDALE AND EDWARDSVILLE
FEFFER & SIMONS, INC.
LONDON AND AMSTERDAM

LIBRARY OF CONGRESS
CATALOGING IN PUBLICATION DATA

Sealts, Merton M., Jr., comp.
  Emerson's *Nature*.

  Bibliography: p.
  1. Emerson, Ralph Waldo, 1803–1882. Nature.   2. Nature in literature—Addresses, essays, lectures.   I. Ferguson, Alfred Riggs, joint comp.   II. Emerson, Ralph Waldo, 1803–1882. Nature. 1836.   III. Title.
PS1613.S4   1979   191   78-13945
ISBN 0-8093-0891-6
ISBN 0-8093-0900-9 pbk.

ACKNOWLEDGMENTS
Grateful acknowledgment is made to the Ralph Waldo Emerson Memorial Association and to Columbia University Press, Harvard University Press, and Houghton Mifflin Company for permission to reproduce and reprint in Part 1 of this volume material from Emerson's journals, lectures, and correspondence.
  The Correspondence of Emerson and Carlyle, edited by Joseph Slater. New York and London: Columbia University Press, 1964. © Copyright 1964 by Columbia University Press.
  The Early Lectures of Ralph Waldo Emerson, edited by Stephen E. Whicher, Robert E. Spiller, and Wallace E. Williams, vols. I and II. Cambridge: Harvard University Press, 1959; The Belknap Press of Harvard University Press, 1964. © Copyright 1959, 1964 by the President and Fellows of Harvard College.
  The Journals of Ralph Waldo Emerson, edited by Edward Waldo Emerson and Waldo Emerson Forbes. 10 vols. Boston and New York: Houghton Mifflin Co., 1909–1914. © Copyright 1909, 1910, 1911, 1912, 1913, 1914 by Edward Waldo Emerson.
  The Journals and Miscellaneous Notebooks of Ralph Waldo Emerson, edited by William H. Gilman, Alfred R. Ferguson, Merrell R. Davis, Merton M. Sealts, Jr., Harrison Hayford, et al., vols. I–VI. Cambridge: The Belknap Press of Harvard University Press, 1960–1966. © Copyright 1960, 1961, 1963, 1964, 1965, 1966 by the President and Fellows of Harvard College.
  The Letters of Ralph Waldo Emerson, edited by Ralph L. Rusk. 6 vols. New York: Columbia University Press, 1939. © Copyright 1939 by the Ralph Waldo Emerson Memorial Association.
  The illustrations in Part 1 of this volume are reproduced by courtesy of The Houghton Library, Harvard University.

PREFACE

From its publication in 1836 until the present day, Emerson's first book, *Nature*, has provoked sharp disagreement. Among his contemporaries, some thought it "mere moonshine," others praised it as a "prose poem" or "the effusion of a prophet-like mind," and still others attacked it on doctrinal grounds, as disseminating "infidel and insidious poison." To Emerson's present-day interpreters, commonly less concerned with measuring its departures from orthodoxy than with weighing its literary merits, *Nature* appears variously as "a fundamentally unsatisfactory piece of work" (R. P. Adams); a "sober-sided rhapsody," stiff, naïf, and over-elaborate, yet an "extraordinary" production (Stephen Whicher); and "our primal book" in a major American literary tradition (Jonathan Bishop). Part 2 of the present volume, which samples representative comments on *Nature* made between 1836 and 1967, reveals how wide the divergence has been over how to read such a work—whether as doctrine or mysticism, philosophy or poetry.

This book about a book is dedicated to an idea that Emerson himself was fond of quoting—in *Nature* and elsewhere—from George Fox, the seventeenth-century Quaker: " 'Every scripture is to be interpreted by the same spirit which gave it forth,' is the fundamental law of criticism." The approach followed in Part 1, "Origin and Growth of *Nature*," will therefore take the reader not to Emerson's numerous "teachers"—Plato, Plotinus, Plutarch, Montaigne, Bacon, Swedenborg, Goethe, Wordsworth, Coleridge, and Carlyle, to name a few whose influence on his early thought has been intensively studied—but to his own writing of 1832–1836: the journals and lectures which were the seed-bed both of *Nature* and of later addresses and essays. Recent scholarly editions of these materials provide a firm basis for the current reevaluation of Emerson by those seeking neither to justify him nor dismiss him but to meet him on his own terms, in his own spirit, as a writer of unusual power. It is our working with Emerson manuscripts in editing volumes IV and V of *The Journals and Miscellaneous Notebooks of Ralph Waldo Emerson* that led us to think of assembling in this book the 1836 text of *Nature*, the primary materials from which it was drawn, and pronouncements about it by critics from Emerson's time down to the present day. We hope that the reader, in approaching *Nature* for himself, will share our pleasure in following the course of Emerson's engrossing self-discovery as he set down his developing conceptions of nature and of *Nature*.

A further word about texts is in order here. Modern study of Emerson and his writings has been greatly facilitated by the publication of major editions of his collected works, correspondence, and manuscripts. His son, Edward Waldo Emerson, edited the *Complete Works* (1903–1904) and, in collaboration with Waldo Emerson Forbes, the *Journals* (1909–1914). These editions, long standard, are now being superseded by a more complete scholarly edition of *The Journals and Miscellaneous Notebooks* (1960–), a shorter reader's edition (in preparation), and a scholarly edition of the works (also in preparation). *The Early Lectures* (1959–) are in progress. Supplementing the basic collection of *Letters* (1939) and *The Correspondence of Emerson and Carlyle* (1964, replacing Charles Eliot Norton's edition of 1883), a gathering of additional letters is also in preparation by Professor Eleanor Tilton.

The following abbreviations are used throughout this volume to refer to standard published editions:

CEC   *The Correspondence of Emerson and Carlyle,* edited by Joseph Slater. New York and London: Columbia University Press, 1964.

EL   *The Early Lectures of Ralph Waldo Emerson,* edited by Stephen E. Whicher, Robert E. Spiller, and Wallace E. Williams. Cambridge: Harvard University Press, 1959; The Belknap Press of Harvard University Press, 1964– .

J   *The Journals of Ralph Waldo Emerson,* edited by Edward Waldo Emerson and Waldo Emerson Forbes. 10 vols. Boston and New York: Houghton Mifflin Co., 1909–1914.

JMN   *The Journals and Miscellaneous Notebooks of Ralph Waldo Emerson,* edited by William H. Gilman, Alfred R. Ferguson, Merrell R. Davis, Merton M. Sealts, Jr., Harrison Hayford, et al. Cambridge: The Belknap Press of Harvard University Press, 1960– .

L   *The Letters of Ralph Waldo Emerson,* edited by Ralph L. Rusk. 6 vols. New York: Columbia University Press, 1939.

W   *The Complete Works of Ralph Waldo Emerson,* edited by Edward Waldo Emerson. 12 vols. Boston and New York: Houghton Mifflin Co., 1903–1904.

Preparation of this volume was assisted by a grant to Mr. Sealts by the Research Committee of the Graduate School, The University of Wisconsin—Madison.

MERTON M. SEALTS, JR.
ALFRED R. FERGUSON

ADDENDUM, 1979

Two additional abbreviations are used in material added in the Second Edition:

CW   *The Collected Works of Ralph Waldo Emerson,* Alfred R. Ferguson, General Editor, 1971–1974. Volume I: *Nature, Addresses, and Lectures.* Introductions and Notes by Robert E. Spiller; Text Established by Alfred R. Ferguson. Cambridge: The Belknap Press of Harvard University Press, 1971.

YES   *Young Emerson Speaks: Unpublished Discourses on Many Subjects by Ralph Waldo Emerson*. Edited by Arthur Cushman McGiffert, Jr. Boston: Houghton Mifflin Co., 1938; reprinted, Port Washington, N.Y.: Kennikat Press, Inc., 1968.

As in the original edition, Part 2 of this volume standardizes all citations of Emerson's writings within individual essays, using the abbreviations listed here. All references to *Nature* itself are to the text printed on pp. 5–37 below. Wherever possible, reference is made to the edition of *The Journals and Miscellaneous Notebooks* currently in progress, cited by volume number and page. The original pagination of articles and books reprinted or excerpted in Part 2 is indicated in brackets within the present text. The spelling and punctuation of these selections have been retained, except for one point of styling: where smaller type is used to indicate quoted material, the terminal quotation marks also used by some nineteenth-century authors or printers have been silently omitted. Other adaptations made for the present volume have been recorded in initial footnotes to individual selections.

MMS

This edition of *Emerson's "Nature"*
is dedicated to the memory of
Alfred Riggs Ferguson (1915–1974)

CONTENTS

The Later Nineteenth Century, 1862–1898   111

Recent Criticism, 1930–1967   129

Scholarship of the 1970's   175

ILLUSTRATIONS

1. ORIGIN AND GROWTH OF NATURE

NATURE.

"Nature is but an image or imitation of wisdom, the last thing of the soul; nature being a thing which doth only do, but not know."

PLOTINUS.

BOSTON:

JAMES MUNROE AND COMPANY.

M DCCC XXXVI.

Title page of the 1836 edition of *Nature*

NOTE ON THE TEXT

This volume reprints the 1836 text of *Nature* with the following emendations by the present editors:

Page and line	Reading	1836 reading
10.5	classes:	classes;
13.31	man is	man, is
14.4	seen, comes	seen comes
14.19	beauty is	beauty, is
14.23	architect, seek	architect seek
15.6	particular spiritual facts	particular facts [*corrected by RWE in presentation copies*]
15.7	spirit	spirits [*corrected by RWE in presentation copies*]
19.38	foregone	forgone
20.4	are affected	is affected
22.25	conspicuous	conspic-/ous [*at line-division*]
24.40	vision	vis-/sion [*at line-division*]
24.41	portrait	protrait
32.27	lays	lay
34.25	achievement	achievements

Some of these emendations parallel revisions in the 1849 text; some embody corrections made in 1856 and later. (Page references are to the text as it appears in the present volume.)

We have made no attempt either to regularize punctuation or to modernize such archaic words or spellings as "befal" (8.14), "cotemporaneous" (17.15), "chuse" (23.8), "connexion" (25.22–23, 28.13), "befals" (28.34), "baulks" (30.30), "opake" (34.38), or "cobler's" (35.33), all of which are representative of Emerson's usage in 1836 though changed in later editions. Nor have we corrected errors in quotations from Shakespeare (18.22, 26.7—where "ARIEL" should read "PROSPERO"), George Herbert (32.33), and Plato (33.21–22—where Emerson mistakenly interpolated phrasing from Aristotle).

A list of verbal (substantive) revisions made by Emerson for the edition of 1849 is given below, pp. 68–71.

The original pagination of the 1836 edition of *Nature* is indicated in brackets within the present text.

128

The Scholar works with invisible tools to invisible ends.
So passes for an idler or worse; brain sick; defenceless
to idle carpenters, masons, & merchants, that having
done nothing most laboriously all day pronounce on him
fresh for spoil at night. Character founded on natural
gifts as specific as rare as military genius: the power
to stand beside his thoughts, or, to hold off his thought at arm's length
& give them perspective; to form il più bell' uno, he
studies the art of solitude (see above p. 60) he is gravelled
in every discourse with common people (J 1833 p 119)
He shows that to be infinite wh. you had thought exhausted (See above p. 60) There is a real object in nature
to wh. y. grocer turns, y. intellectual man (J 1833 p 137)
                        praestantia novrat
        Plurima, mentis opes amplas, subjectore fervans
        Omnia vestigans sapientum dicta reperta.
                        Empedocles de Pythagora   Laërtius
                                                    II. 271
So Bacons globe of crystal & globe of matter
The Thinker like Glauber keeps what others throw away
He is aware of Gods way of hiding things in light.
Also he knows all by one (See above p 117)
Set men upon thinking & you have been to them a god. All history
is poetry; the globe of facts whereon they trample is bullion
to y. scientific eye. Meanest life a thread of empyrean light
Scholars converts for them y. dishonored facts
which they lean, into trees of life; their daily
routine into a garden of God by suggesting y. principle which classifies y. facts. We build the
sepulchers of our fathers: Can we never behold
the Universe as new and feel that we have a
stake as much as our predecessors

(The Houghton Library, Harvard University)

PLATE I

At Concord, January 22–23, 1836, Emerson begins formulating what became the
Introduction to Nature (Journal B, p. 128, in JMN, V, 116–117; in the present
text, see pp. 5; 42, item 13; 46).

INTRODUCTION.

OUR age is retrospective. It builds the sepulchres of the fathers. It writes biographies, histories, and criticism. The foregoing generations beheld God and nature face to face; we, through their eyes. Why should not we also enjoy an original relation to the universe? Why should not we have a poetry and philosophy of insight and not of tradition, and a religion by revelation to us, and not the history of theirs? Embosomed for a season in nature, whose floods of life stream around and through us, and invite us by the powers they supply, to action proportioned to nature, why should we grope among the dry bones of the past, or put the living generation into masquerade out of its faded wardrobe? The sun shines to-day also. There is more wool and flax in the fields. [6] There are new lands, new men, new thoughts. Let us demand our own works and laws and worship.

Undoubtedly we have no questions to ask which are unanswerable. We must trust the perfection of the creation so far, as to believe that whatever curiosity the order of things has awakened in our minds, the order of things can satisfy. Every man's condition is a solution in hieroglyphic to those inquiries he would put. He acts it as life, before he apprehends it as truth. In like manner, nature is already, in its forms and tendencies, describing its own design. Let us interrogate the great apparition, that shines so peacefully around us. Let us inquire, to what end is nature?

All science has one aim, namely, to find a theory of nature. We have theories of races and of functions, but scarcely yet a remote approximation to an idea of creation. We are now so far from the road to truth, that religious teachers dispute and hate each other, and speculative men are esteemed unsound and [7] frivolous. But to a sound judgment, the most abstract truth is the most practical. Whenever a true theory appears, it will be its own evidence. Its test is, that it will explain all phenomena. Now many are thought not only unexplained but inexplicable; as language, sleep, dreams, beasts, sex.

Philosophically considered, the universe is composed of Nature and the Soul. Strictly speaking, therefore, all that is separate from us, all which Philosophy distinguishes as the NOT ME, that is, both nature and art, all other men and my own body, must be ranked under this name, NATURE. In enumerating the values of nature and casting up their sum, I shall use the word in both senses;—in its common and in its philosophical import. In inquiries so general as our present one, the inaccuracy is not material; no confusion of thought will occur. *Nature*, in the common sense, refers to essences unchanged by man; space, the air, the river, the leaf. *Art* is applied to the mixture of his will with the same things, as in a house, a [8] canal, a statue, a picture. But his operations taken together are so insignificant, a little chipping, baking, patching, and washing, that in an impression so grand as that of the world on the human mind, they do not vary the result.

NATURE.

CHAPTER I.

To go into solitude, a man needs to retire as much from his chamber as from society. I am not solitary whilst I read and write, though nobody is with me. But if a man would be alone, let him look at the stars. The rays that come from those heavenly worlds, will separate between him and vulgar things. One might think the atmosphere was made transparent with this design, to give man, in the heavenly bodies, the perpetual presence of the sublime. Seen in the streets of cities, how great they are! If the stars should appear one night in a thousand years, how would men [10] believe and adore; and preserve for many generations the remembrance of the city of God which had been shown! But every night come out these preachers of beauty, and light the universe with their admonishing smile.

The stars awaken a certain reverence, because though always present, they are always inaccessible; but all natural objects make a kindred impression, when the mind is open to their influence. Nature never wears a mean appearance. Neither does the wisest man extort all her secret, and lose his curiosity by finding out all her perfection. Nature never became a toy to a wise spirit. The flowers, the animals, the mountains, reflected all the wisdom of his best hour, as much as they had delighted the simplicity of his childhood.

When we speak of nature in this manner, we have a distinct but most poetical sense in the mind. We mean the integrity of impression made by manifold natural objects. It is this which distinguishes the stick of timber of the wood-cutter, from the tree of the poet. [11] The charming landscape which I saw this morning, is indubitably made up of some twenty or thirty farms. Miller owns this field, Locke that, and Manning the woodland beyond. But none of them owns the landscape. There is a property in the horizon which no man has but he whose eye can integrate all the parts, that is, the poet. This is the best part of these men's farms, yet to this their land-deeds give them no title.

To speak truly, few adult persons can see nature. Most persons do not see the sun. At least they have a very superficial seeing. The sun illuminates only the eye of the man, but shines into the eye and the heart of the child. The lover of nature is he whose inward and outward senses are still truly adjusted to each other; who has retained the spirit of infancy even into the era of manhood. His intercourse with heaven and earth, becomes part of his daily food. In the presence of nature, a wild

7

delight runs through the man, in spite of real sorrows. Nature says,—he is my creature, [12] and maugre all his impertinent griefs, he shall be glad with me. Not the sun or the summer alone, but every hour and season yields its tribute of delight; for every hour and change corresponds to and authorizes a different state of the mind, from breathless noon to grimmest midnight. Nature is a setting that fits equally well a comic or a mourning piece. In good health, the air is a cordial of incredible virtue. Crossing a bare common, in snow puddles, at twilight, under a clouded sky, without having in my thoughts any occurrence of special good fortune, I have enjoyed a perfect exhilaration. Almost I fear to think how glad I am. In the woods too, a man casts off his years, as the snake his slough, and at what period soever of life, is always a child. In the woods, is perpetual youth. Within these plantations of God, a decorum and sanctity reign, a perennial festival is dressed, and the guest sees not how he should tire of them in a thousand years. In the woods, we return to reason and faith. There I feel that nothing can befal me in [13] life,—no disgrace, no calamity, (leaving me my eyes), which nature cannot repair. Standing on the bare ground,—my head bathed by the blithe air, and uplifted into infinite space,—all mean egotism vanishes. I become a transparent eye-ball. I am nothing. I see all. The currents of the Universal Being circulate through me; I am part or particle of God. The name of the nearest friend sounds then foreign and accidental. To be brothers, to be acquaintances,—master or servant, is then a trifle and a disturbance. I am the lover of uncontained and immortal beauty. In the wilderness, I find something more dear and connate than in streets or villages. In the tranquil landscape, and especially in the distant line of the horizon, man beholds somewhat as beautiful as his own nature.

The greatest delight which the fields and woods minister, is the suggestion of an occult relation between man and the vegetable. I am not alone and unacknowledged. They nod to me and I to them. The waving of the boughs [14] in the storm, is new to me and old. It takes me by surprise, and yet is not unknown. Its effect is like that of a higher thought or a better emotion coming over me, when I deemed I was thinking justly or doing right.

Yet it is certain that the power to produce this delight, does not reside in nature, but in man, or in a harmony of both. It is necessary to use these pleasures with great temperance. For, nature is not always tricked in holiday attire, but the same scene which yesterday breathed perfume and glittered as for the frolic of the nymphs, is overspread with melancholy today. Nature always wears the colors of the spirit. To a man laboring under calamity, the heat of his own fire hath sadness in it. Then, there is a kind of contempt of the landscape felt by him who has just lost by death a dear friend. The sky is less grand as it shuts down over less worth in the population.

"Standing on the bare ground, — my head bathed by the blithe air, & uplifted into infinite space, — all mean egotism vanishes. I become a transparent Eyeball." *Nature, p. 13.*

PLATE II

At Cincinnati, January 12, 1839, Christopher Pearse Cranch illustrates Emerson's "transparent eye-ball" passage in *Nature* (see p. 8).

[15]

CHAPTER II.

COMMODITY.

WHOEVER considers the final cause of the world, will discern a multitude of uses that enter as parts into that result. They all admit of being thrown into one of the following classes: Commodity; Beauty; Language; and Discipline.

Under the general name of Commodity, I rank all those advantages which our senses owe to nature. This, of course, is a benefit which is temporary and mediate, not ultimate, like its service to the soul. Yet although low, it is perfect in its kind, and is the only use of nature which all men apprehend. The misery of man appears like childish petulance, when we explore the steady and prodigal provision that has been made for his support and delight on this green ball which floats him through the [16] heavens. What angels invented these splendid ornaments, these rich conveniences, this ocean of air above, this ocean of water beneath, this firmament of earth between? this zodiac of lights, this tent of dropping clouds, this striped coat of climates, this fourfold year? Beasts, fire, water, stones, and corn serve him. The field is at once his floor, his work-yard, his play-ground, his garden, and his bed.

> "More servants wait on man
> Than he'll take notice of."———

Nature, in its ministry to man, is not only the material, but is also the process and the result. All the parts incessantly work into each other's hands for the profit of man. The wind sows the seed; the sun evaporates the sea; the wind blows the vapor to the field; the ice, on the other side of the planet, condenses rain on this; the rain feeds the plant; the plant feeds the animal; and thus the endless circulations of the divine charity nourish man.

[17] The useful arts are but reproductions or new combinations by the wit of man, of the same natural benefactors. He no longer waits for favoring gales, but by means of steam, he realizes the fable of Æolus's bag, and carries the two and thirty winds in the boiler of his boat. To diminish friction, he paves the road with iron bars, and, mounting a coach with a ship-load of men, animals, and merchandise behind him, he darts through the country, from town to town, like an eagle or a swallow through the air. By the aggregate of these aids, how is the face of the world changed, from the era of Noah to that of Napoleon! The private poor man hath cities, ships, canals, bridges, built for him. He goes to the post-office, and the human race run on his errands; to the book-shop, and the human race read and write of all that happens, for him; to the court-house, and nations repair his wrongs. He sets his house upon the road, and the human race go forth every morning, and shovel out the snow, and cut a path for him.

[18] But there is no need of specifying particulars in this class of uses. The cata-

logue is endless, and the examples so obvious, that I shall leave them to the reader's reflection, with the general remark, that this mercenary benefit is one which has respect to a farther good. A man is fed, not that he may be fed, but that he may work.

[19]
CHAPTER III.

BEAUTY.

A NOBLER want of man is served by nature, namely, the love of Beauty.

The ancient Greeks called the world κοσμος, beauty. Such is the constitution of all things, or such the plastic power of the human eye, that the primary forms, as the sky, the mountain, the tree, the animal, give us a delight *in and for themselves*; a pleasure arising from outline, color, motion, and grouping. This seems partly owing to the eye itself. The eye is the best of artists. By the mutual action of its structure and of the laws of light, perspective is produced, which integrates every mass of objects, of what character soever, into a well colored and shaded globe, so that where the particular objects are mean and unaffecting, the landscape which they compose, is round and [20] symmetrical. And as the eye is the best composer, so light is the first of painters. There is no object so foul that intense light will not make beautiful. And the stimulus it affords to the sense, and a sort of infinitude which it hath, like space and time, make all matter gay. Even the corpse hath its own beauty. But beside this general grace diffused over nature, almost all the individual forms are agreeable to the eye, as is proved by our endless imitations of some of them, as the acorn, the grape, the pine-cone, the wheat-ear, the egg, the wings and forms of most birds, the lion's claw, the serpent, the butterfly, sea-shells, flames, clouds, buds, leaves, and the forms of many trees, as the palm.

For better consideration, we may distribute the aspects of Beauty in a threefold manner.

1. First, the simple perception of natural forms is a delight. The influence of the forms and actions in nature, is so needful to man, that, in its lowest functions, it seems to lie on the confines of commodity and beauty. To the body and mind [21] which have been cramped by noxious work or company, nature is medicinal and restores their tone. The tradesman, the attorney comes out of the din and craft of the street, and sees the sky and the woods, and is a man again. In their eternal calm, he finds himself. The health of the eye seems to demand a horizon. We are never tired, so long as we can see far enough.

But in other hours, Nature satisfies the soul purely by its loveliness, and without any mixture of corporeal benefit. I have seen the spectacle of morning from the hilltop over against my house, from day-break to sun-rise, with emotions which an angel might share. The long slender bars of cloud float like fishes in the sea of crimson light. From the earth, as a shore, I look out into that silent sea. I seem to partake its rapid transformations: the active enchantment reaches my dust, and I dilate and conspire with the morning wind. How does Nature deify us with a few and cheap elements! Give me health and a day, [22] and I will make the pomp of emperors ridiculous. The dawn is my Assyria; the sun-set and moon-rise my Paphos, and unimaginable realms of faerie; broad noon shall be my England of the senses and the understanding; the night shall be my Germany of mystic philosophy and dreams.

Not less excellent, except for our less susceptibility in the afternoon, was the charm, last evening, of a January sunset. The western clouds divided and subdivided themselves into pink flakes modulated with tints of unspeakable softness; and the air had so much life and sweetness, that it was a pain to come within doors. What was it that nature would say? Was there no meaning in the live repose of the valley behind the mill, and which Homer or Shakspeare could not re-form for me in words? The leafless trees become spires of flame in the sunset, with the blue east for their background, and the stars of the dead calices of flowers, and every withered stem and stubble rimed with frost, contribute something to the mute music.

[23] The inhabitants of cities suppose that the country landscape is pleasant only half the year. I please myself with observing the graces of the winter scenery, and believe that we are as much touched by it as by the genial influences of summer. To the attentive eye, each moment of the year has its own beauty, and in the same field, it beholds, every hour, a picture which was never seen before, and which shall never be seen again. The heavens change every moment, and reflect their glory or gloom on the plains beneath. The state of the crop in the surrounding farms alters the expression of the earth from week to week. The succession of native plants in the pastures and roadsides, which make the silent clock by which time tells the summer hours, will make even the divisions of the day sensible to a keen observer. The tribes of birds and insects, like the plants punctual to their time, follow each other, and the year has room for all. By water-courses, the variety is greater. In July, the blue pontederia or pickerel-weed blooms in [24] large beds in the shallow parts of our pleasant river, and swarms with yellow butterflies in continual motion. Art cannot rival this pomp of purple and gold. Indeed the river is a perpetual gala, and boasts each month a new ornament.

But this beauty of Nature which is seen and felt as beauty, is the least part. The shows of day, the dewy morning, the rainbow, mountains, orchards in blossom, stars, moonlight, shadows in still water, and the like, if too eagerly hunted, become shows merely, and mock us with their unreality. Go out of the house to see the moon, and 't is mere tinsel; it will not please as when its light shines upon your necessary journey. The beauty that shimmers in the yellow afternoons of October, who ever could clutch it? Go forth to find it, and it is gone: 't is only a mirage as you look from windows of diligence.

2. The presence of a higher, namely, of the spiritual element is essential to its perfection. The high and divine beauty which can be loved [25] without effeminacy, is that which is found in combination with the human will, and never separate. Beauty is the mark God sets upon virtue. Every natural action is graceful. Every heroic act is

also decent, and causes the place and the bystanders to shine. We are taught by great actions that the universe is the property of every individual in it. Every rational creature has all nature for his dowry and estate. It is his, if he will. He may divest himself of it; he may creep into a corner, and abdicate his kingdom, as most men do, but he is entitled to the world by his constitution. In proportion to the energy of his thought and will, he takes up the world into himself. "All those things for which men plough, build, or sail, obey virtue;" said an ancient historian. "The winds and waves," said Gibbon, "are always on the side of the ablest navigators." So are the sun and moon and all the stars of heaven. When a noble act is done,—perchance in a scene of great natural beauty; when Leonidas and his three hundred martyrs consume one day in [26] dying, and the sun and moon come each and look at them once in the steep defile of Thermopylæ; when Arnold Winkelried, in the high Alps, under the shadow of the avalanche, gathers in his side a sheaf of Austrian spears to break the line for his comrades; are not these heroes entitled to add the beauty of the scene to the beauty of the deed? When the bark of Columbus nears the shore of America;—before it, the beach lined with savages, fleeing out of all their huts of cane; the sea behind; and the purple mountains of the Indian Archipelago around, can we separate the man from the living picture? Does not the New World clothe his form with her palm-groves and savannahs as fit drapery? Ever does natural beauty steal in like air, and envelope great actions. When Sir Harry Vane was dragged up the Tower-hill, sitting on a sled, to suffer death, as the champion of the English laws, one of the multitude cried out to him, "You never sate on so glorious a seat." Charles II., to intimidate the citizens of London, caused the patriot Lord Rus-[27]sel to be drawn in an open coach, through the principal streets of the city, on his way to the scaffold. "But," to use the simple narrative of his biographer, "the multitude imagined they saw liberty and virtue sitting by his side." In private places, among sordid objects, an act of truth or heroism seems at once to draw to itself the sky as its temple, the sun as its candle. Nature stretcheth out her arms to embrace man, only let his thoughts be of equal greatness. Willingly does she follow his steps with the rose and the violet, and bend her lines of grandeur and grace to the decoration of her darling child. Only let his thoughts be of equal scope, and the frame will suit the picture. A virtuous man is in unison with her works, and makes the central figure of the visible sphere. Homer, Pindar, Socrates, Phocion, associate themselves fitly in our memory with the whole geography and climate of Greece. The visible heavens and earth sympathize with Jesus. And in common life, whosoever has seen a person of powerful character and happy genius, will have re-[28]marked how easily he took all things along with him,—the persons, the opinions, and the day, and nature became ancillary to a man.

3. There is still another aspect under which the beauty of the world may be viewed, namely, as it becomes an object of the intellect. Beside the relation of things to virtue, they have a relation to thought. The intellect searches out the absolute order of things as they stand in the mind of God, and without the colors of affection. The intellectual and the active powers seem to succeed each other in man, and the

exclusive activity of the one, generates the exclusive activity of the other. There is something unfriendly in each to the other, but they are like the alternate periods of feeding and working in animals; each prepares and certainly will be followed by the other. Therefore does beauty, which, in relation to actions, as we have seen, comes unsought, and comes because it is unsought, remain for the apprehension and pursuit of the intellect; and then again, in its turn, of the active power. Nothing divine dies. All [29] good is eternally reproductive. The beauty of nature reforms itself in the mind, and not for barren contemplation, but for new creation.

All men are in some degree impressed by the face of the world. Some men even to delight. This love of beauty is Taste. Others have the same love in such excess, that, not content with admiring, they seek to embody it in new forms. The creation of beauty is Art.

The production of a work of art throws a light upon the mystery of humanity. A work of art is an abstract or epitome of the world. It is the result or expression of nature, in miniature. For although the works of nature are innumerable and all different, the result or the expression of them all is similar and single. Nature is a sea of forms radically alike and even unique. A leaf, a sun-beam, a landscape, the ocean, make an analogous impression on the mind. What is common to them all,—that perfectness and harmony, is beauty. Therefore the standard of beauty is the entire circuit of natural forms,—the totality of nature; [30] which the Italians expressed by defining beauty "il piu nell' uno." Nothing is quite beautiful alone: nothing but is beautiful in the whole. A single object is only so far beautiful as it suggests this universal grace. The poet, the painter, the sculptor, the musician, the architect, seek each to concentrate this radiance of the world on one point, and each in his several work to satisfy the love of beauty which stimulates him to produce. Thus is Art, a nature passed through the alembic of man. Thus in art, does nature work through the will of a man filled with the beauty of her first works.

The world thus exists to the soul to satisfy the desire of beauty. Extend this element to the uttermost, and I call it an ultimate end. No reason can be asked or given why the soul seeks beauty. Beauty, in its largest and profoundest sense, is one expression for the universe. God is the all-fair. Truth, and goodness, and beauty, are but different faces of the same All. But beauty in nature is not ultimate. It is the herald of inward and eternal beauty, and is [31] not alone a solid and satisfactory good. It must therefore stand as a part and not as yet the last or highest expression of the final cause of Nature.

CHAPTER IV.

LANGUAGE.

A THIRD use which Nature subserves to man is that of Language. Nature is the vehicle of thought, and in a simple, double, and threefold degree.

1. Words are signs of natural facts.
2. Particular natural facts are symbols of particular spiritual facts.
3. Nature is the symbol of spirit.

1. Words are signs of natural facts. The use of natural history is to give us aid in supernatural history. The use of the outer creation is to give us language for the beings and changes of the inward creation. Every word which is used to express a moral or intellectual fact, if traced to its root, is found to be borrowed from some material appearance. *Right* originally means *straight; wrong* means *twisted. Spirit* primarily means *wind; trans-*[33]*gression,* the crossing of a *line; supercilious,* the *raising of the eye-brow.* We say the *heart* to express emotion, the *head* to denote thought; and *thought* and *emotion* are, in their turn, words borrowed from sensible things, and now appropriated to spiritual nature. Most of the process by which this transformation is made, is hidden from us in the remote time when language was framed; but the same tendency may be daily observed in children. Children and savages use only nouns or names of things, which they continually convert into verbs, and apply to analogous mental acts.

2. But this origin of all words that convey a spiritual import,—so conspicuous a fact in the history of language,—is our least debt to nature. It is not words only that are emblematic; it is things which are emblematic. Every natural fact is a symbol of some spiritual fact. Every appearance in nature corresponds to some state of the mind, and that state of the mind can only be described by presenting that natural appearance as its picture. An enraged [34] man is a lion, a cunning man is a fox, a firm man is a rock, a learned man is a torch. A lamb is innocence; a snake is subtle spite; flowers express to us the delicate affections. Light and darkness are our familiar expression for knowledge and ignorance; and heat for love. Visible distance behind and before us, is respectively our image of memory and hope.

Who looks upon a river in a meditative hour, and is not reminded of the flux of all things? Throw a stone into the stream, and the circles that propagate themselves are the beautiful type of all influence. Man is conscious of a universal soul within or behind his individual life, wherein, as in a firmament, the natures of Justice, Truth, Love, Freedom, arise and shine. This universal soul, he calls Reason: it is not mine or thine or his, but we are its; we are its property and men. And the blue sky in which the private earth is buried, the sky with its eternal calm, and full of everlasting orbs, is the type of Reason. That which, intellectually considered, we call Reason, considered in rela-[35]tion to nature, we call Spirit. Spirit is the Creator. Spirit hath life in itself. And man in all ages and countries, embodies it in his language, as the FATHER.

It is easily seen that there is nothing lucky or capricious in these analogies, but that they are constant, and pervade nature. These are not the dreams of a few poets, here and there, but man is an analogist, and studies relations in all objects. He is placed in the centre of beings, and a ray of relation passes from every other being to him. And neither can man be understood without these objects, nor these objects without man. All the facts in natural history taken by themselves, have no value, but are barren like a single sex. But marry it to human history, and it is full of life. Whole Floras, all Linnæus' and Buffon's volumes, are but dry catalogues of facts; but the most trivial of these facts, the habit of a plant, the organs, or work, or noise of an insect, applied to the illustration of a fact in intellectual philosophy, or, in any way associated to human nature, affects [36] us in the most lively and agreeable manner. The seed of a plant,—to what affecting analogies in the nature of man, is that little fruit made use of, in all discourse, up to the voice of Paul, who calls the human corpse a seed,—"It is sown a natural body; it is raised a spiritual body." The motion of the earth round its axis, and round the sun, makes the day, and the year. These are certain amounts of brute light and heat. But is there no intent of an analogy between man's life and the seasons? And do the seasons gain no grandeur or pathos from that analogy? The instincts of the ant are very unimportant considered as the ant's; but the moment a ray of relation is seen to extend from it to man, and the little drudge is seen to be a monitor, a little body with a mighty heart, then all its habits, even that said to be recently observed, that it never sleeps, become sublime.

Because of this radical correspondence between visible things and human thoughts, savages, who have only what is necessary, converse [37] in figures. As we go back in history, language becomes more picturesque, until its infancy, when it is all poetry; or, all spiritual facts are represented by natural symbols. The same symbols are found to make the original elements of all languages. It has moreover been observed, that the idioms of all languages approach each other in passages of the greatest eloquence and power. And as this is the first language, so is it the last. This immediate dependence of language upon nature, this conversion of an outward phenomenon into a type of somewhat in human life, never loses its power to affect us. It is this which gives that piquancy to the conversation of a strong-natured farmer or back-woodsman, which all men relish.

Thus is nature an interpreter, by whose means man converses with his fellow men. A man's power to connect his thought with its proper symbol, and so utter it, depends on the simplicity of his character, that is, upon his love of truth and his desire to communicate it without loss. The corruption of man is follow-[38]ed by the corruption of language. When simplicity of character and the sovereignty of ideas is broken up by the prevalence of secondary desires, the desire of riches, the desire of pleasure, the desire of power, the desire of praise,—and duplicity and falsehood take place of simplicity and truth, the power over nature as an interpreter of the will, is in a degree lost; new imagery ceases to be created, and old words are perverted to stand for things which are not; a paper currency is employed when there is no bullion in the vaults. In due time, the fraud is manifest, and words lose all power to stimulate the understanding or the affections. Hundreds of writers may be found in every long-civilized nation, who for a short time believe, and make others believe, that they see and utter truths, who do not of themselves clothe one thought in its natural garment, but who feed unconsciously upon the language created by the primary writers of the country, those, namely, who hold primarily on nature.

[39] But wise men pierce this rotten diction and fasten words again to visible things; so that picturesque language is at once a commanding certificate that he who employs it, is a man in alliance with truth and God. The moment our discourse rises above the ground line of familiar facts, and is inflamed with passion or exalted by thought, it clothes itself in images. A man conversing in earnest, if he watch his intellectual processes, will find that always a material image, more or less luminous, arises in his mind, cotemporaneous with every thought, which furnishes the vestment of the thought. Hence, good writing and brilliant discourse are perpetual allegories. This imagery is spontaneous. It is the blending of experience with the present action of the mind. It is proper creation. It is the working of the Original Cause through the instruments he has already made.

These facts may suggest the advantage which the country-life possesses for a powerful mind, over the artificial and curtailed life of cities. We [40] know more from nature than we can at will communicate. Its light flows into the mind evermore, and we forget its presence. The poet, the orator, bred in the woods, whose senses have been nourished by their fair and appeasing changes, year after year, without design and without heed,—shall not lose their lesson altogether, in the roar of cities or the broil of politics. Long hereafter, amidst agitation and terror in national councils,—in the hour of revolution,—these solemn images shall reappear in their morning lustre, as fit symbols and words of the thoughts which the passing events shall awaken. At the call of a noble sentiment, again the woods wave, the pines murmur, the river rolls and shines, and the cattle low upon the mountains, as he saw and heard them in his infancy. And with these forms, the spells of persuasion, the keys of power are put into his hands.

3. We are thus assisted by natural objects in the expression of particular meanings. But how great a language to convey such pepper-corn informations! Did it need such noble [41] races of creatures, this profusion of forms, this host of orbs in heaven, to furnish man with the dictionary and grammar of his municipal speech? Whilst we use this grand cipher to expedite the affairs of our pot and kettle, we feel that we have not yet put it to its use, neither are able. We are like travellers using the cinders of a volcano to roast their eggs. Whilst we see that it always stands ready to clothe what we would say, we cannot avoid the question, whether the characters are not significant of themselves. Have mountains, and waves, and skies, no significance but what we consciously give them, when we employ them as emblems of our thoughts? The

world is emblematic. Parts of speech are metaphors because the whole of nature is a metaphor of the human mind. The laws of moral nature answer to those of matter as face to face in a glass. "The visible world and the relation of its parts, is the dial plate of the invisible." The axioms of physics translate the laws of ethics. Thus, "the whole is greater than its part;" "reaction is equal to [42] action;" "the smallest weight may be made to lift the greatest, the difference of weight being compensated by time;" and many the like propositions, which have an ethical as well as physical sense. These propositions have a much more extensive and universal sense when applied to human life, than when confined to technical use.

In like manner, the memorable words of history, and the proverbs of nations, consist usually of a natural fact, selected as a picture or parable of a moral truth. Thus; A rolling stone gathers no moss; A bird in the hand is worth two in the bush; A cripple in the right way, will beat a racer in the wrong; Make hay whilst the sun shines; 'T is hard to carry a full cup even; Vinegar is the son of wine; The last ounce broke the camel's back; Long-lived trees make roots first;—and the like. In their primary sense these are trivial facts, but we repeat them for the value of their analogical import. What is true of proverbs, is true of all fables, parables, and allegories.

[43] This relation between the mind and matter is not fancied by some poet, but stands in the will of God, and so is free to be known by all men. It appears to men, or it does not appear. When in fortunate hours we ponder this miracle, the wise man doubts, if, at all other times, he is not blind and deaf;

> ——— "Can these things be,
> And overcome us like a summer's cloud,
> Without our special wonder?"

for the universe becomes transparent, and the light of higher laws than its own, shines through it. It is the standing problem which has exercised the wonder and the study of every fine genius since the world began; from the era of the Egyptians and the Brahmins, to that of Pythagoras, of Plato, of Bacon, of Leibnitz, of Swedenborg. There sits the Sphinx at the road-side, and from age to age, as each prophet comes by, he tries his fortune at reading her riddle. There seems to be a necessity in spirit to manifest itself in material [44] forms; and day and night, river and storm, beast and bird, acid and alkali, preëxist in necessary Ideas in the mind of God, and are what they are by virtue of preceding affections, in the world of spirit. A Fact is the end or last issue of spirit. The visible creation is the terminus or the circumference of the invisible world. "Material objects," said a French philosopher, "are necessarily kinds of *scoriæ* of the substantial thoughts of the Creator, which must always preserve an exact relation to their first origin; in other words, visible nature must have a spiritual and moral side."

This doctrine is abstruse, and though the images of "garment," "scoriæ," "mirror," &c., may stimulate the fancy, we must summon the aid of subtler and more vital expositors to make it plain. "Every scripture is to be interpreted by the same spirit which gave it forth,"—is the fundamental law of criticism. A life in harmony with nature, the love of truth and of virtue, will purge the eyes to understand her text. By degrees we may come to know the [45] primitive sense of the permanent objects of nature, so that the world shall be to us an open book, and every form significant of its hidden life and final cause.

A new interest surprises us, whilst, under the view now suggested, we contemplate the fearful extent and multitude of objects; since "every object rightly seen, unlocks a new faculty of the soul." That which was unconscious truth, becomes, when interpreted and defined in an object, a part of the domain of knowledge,—a new amount to the magazine of power.

[46] ## CHAPTER V.

DISCIPLINE.

IN view of this significance of nature, we arrive at once at a new fact, that nature is a discipline. This use of the world includes the preceding uses, as parts of itself.

Space, time, society, labor, climate, food, locomotion, the animals, the mechanical forces, give us sincerest lessons, day by day, whose meaning is unlimited. They educate both the Understanding and the Reason. Every property of matter is a school for the understanding,—its solidity or resistance, its inertia, its extension, its figure, its divisibility. The understanding adds, divides, combines, measures, and finds everlasting nutriment and room for its activity in this worthy scene. Meantime, Reason transfers all these lessons into its own world of thought, by perceiving the analogy that marries Matter and Mind.

[47] 1. Nature is a discipline of the understanding in intellectual truths. Our dealing with sensible objects is a constant exercise in the necessary lessons of difference, of likeness, of order, of being and seeming, of progressive arrangement; of ascent from particular to general; of combination to one end of manifold forces. Proportioned to the importance of the organ to be formed, is the extreme care with which its tuition is provided,—a care pretermitted in no single case. What tedious training, day after day, year after year, never ending, to form the common sense; what continual reproduction of annoyances, inconveniences, dilemmas; what rejoicing over us of little men; what disputing of prices, what reckonings of interest,—and all to form the Hand of the mind;—to instruct us that "good thoughts are no better than good dreams, unless they be executed!"

The same good office is performed by Property and its filial systems of debt and credit. Debt, grinding debt, whose iron face the widow, the orphan, and the sons of genius fear and [48] hate;—debt, which consumes so much time, which so cripples and disheartens a great spirit with cares that seem so base, is a preceptor whose lessons cannot be foregone, and is needed most by those who suffer from it most. Moreover, property, which has been well compared to snow,—"if it fall level to-day, it will be blown into drifts to-morrow,"—is merely the surface action of internal machinery, like the index on the face of a clock. Whilst now it is the gymnastics of the understanding, it is hiving in the foresight of the spirit, experience in profounder laws.

The whole character and fortune of the individual are affected by the least inequalities in the culture of the understanding; for example, in the perception of differences. Therefore is Space, and therefore Time, that man may know that things are not huddled and lumped, but sundered and individual. A bell and a plough have each their use, and neither can do the office of the other. Water is good to drink, coal to burn, wool to wear; but wool cannot be [49] drunk, nor water spun, nor coal eaten. The wise man shows his wisdom in separation, in gradation, and his scale of creatures and of merits, is as wide as nature. The foolish have no range in their scale, but suppose every man is as every other man. What is not good they call the worst, and what is not hateful, they call the best.

In like manner, what good heed, nature forms in us! She pardons no mistakes. Her yea is yea, and her nay, nay.

The first steps in Agriculture, Astronomy, Zoölogy, (those first steps which the farmer, the hunter, and the sailor take,) teach that nature's dice are always loaded; that in her heaps and rubbish are concealed sure and useful results.

How calmly and genially the mind apprehends one after another the laws of physics! What noble emotions dilate the mortal as he enters into the counsels of the creation, and feels by knowledge the privilege to BE! His insight refines him. The beauty of nature shines in his own breast. Man is greater that he can see [50] this, and the universe less, because Time and Space relations vanish as laws are known.

Here again we are impressed and even daunted by the immense Universe to be explored. 'What we know, is a point to what we do not know.' Open any recent journal of science, and weigh the problems suggested concerning Light, Heat, Electricity, Magnetism, Physiology, Geology, and judge whether the interest of natural science is likely to be soon exhausted.

Passing by many particulars of the discipline of nature we must not omit to specify two.

The exercise of the Will or the lesson of power is taught in every event. From the child's successive possession of his several senses up to the hour when he saith, "thy will be done!" he is learning the secret, that he can reduce under his will, not only particular events, but great classes, nay the whole series of events, and so conform all facts to his character. Nature is thoroughly mediate. It is made to serve. It receives the dominion of man as meekly as the ass on which the Saviour rode. It offers all its [51] kingdoms to man as the raw material which he may mould into what is useful. Man is never weary of working it up. He forges the subtile and delicate air into wise and melodious words, and gives them wing as angels of persuasion and command. More and more, with every thought, does his kingdom stretch over things, until the world becomes, at last, only a realized will,—the double of the man.

2. Sensible objects conform to the premonitions of Reason and reflect the con-

science. All things are moral; and in their boundless changes have an unceasing reference to spiritual nature. Therefore is nature glorious with form, color, and motion,
that every globe in the remotest heaven; every chemical change from the rudest crystal up to the laws of life; every change of vegetation from the first principle of growth
in the eye of a leaf, to the tropical forest and antediluvian coal-mine; every animal
function from the sponge up to Hercules, shall hint or thunder to man the laws of
right and wrong, and echo the Ten Commandments. Therefore [52] is nature always
the ally of Religion: lends all her pomp and riches to the religious sentiment. Prophet
and priest, David, Isaiah, Jesus, have drawn deeply from this source.

This ethical character so penetrates the bone and marrow of nature, as to seem the
end for which it was made. Whatever private purpose is answered by any member or
part, this is its public and universal function, and is never omitted. Nothing in nature
is exhausted in its first use. When a thing has served an end to the uttermost, it is
wholly new for an ulterior service. In God, every end is converted into a new means.
Thus the use of Commodity, regarded by itself, is mean and squalid. But it is to the
mind an education in the great doctrine of Use, namely, that a thing is good only so
far as it serves; that a conspiring of parts and efforts to the production of an end, is
essential to any being. The first and gross manifestation of this truth, is our inevitable
and hated training in values and wants, in corn and meat.

[53] It has already been illustrated, in treating of the significance of material
things, that every natural process is but a version of a moral sentence. The moral law
lies at the centre of nature and radiates to the circumference. It is the pith and
marrow of every substance, every relation, and every process. All things with which we
deal, preach to us. What is a farm but a mute gospel! The chaff and the wheat,
weeds and plants, blight, rain, insects, sun,—it is a sacred emblem from the first
furrow of spring to the last stack which the snow of winter overtakes in the fields. But
the sailor, the shepherd, the miner, the merchant, in their several resorts, have each
an experience precisely parallel and leading to the same conclusions. Because all organizations are radically alike. Nor can it be doubted that this moral sentiment which
thus scents the air, and grows in the grain, and impregnates the waters of the world,
is caught by man and sinks into his soul. The moral influence of nature upon every
individual is that amount of truth which it illustrates to him. [54] Who can estimate
this? Who can guess how much firmness the sea-beaten rock has taught the fisher-
man? how much tranquillity has been reflected to man from the azure sky, over whose
unspotted deeps the winds forevermore drive flocks of stormy clouds, and leave no
wrinkle or stain? how much industry and providence and affection we have caught
from the pantomime of brutes? What a searching preacher of self-command is the
varying phenomenon of Health!

Herein is especially apprehended the Unity of Nature,—the Unity in Variety,—
which meets us everywhere. All the endless variety of things make a unique, an identical impression. Xenophanes complained in his old age, that, look where he would,
all things hastened back to Unity. He was weary of seeing the same entity in the

tedious variety of forms. The fable of Proteus has a cordial truth. Every particular in nature, a leaf, a drop, a crystal, a moment of time is related to the whole, and partakes of the perfection of the whole. Each particle is a mi-[55]crocosm, and faithfully renders the likeness of the world.

Not only resemblances exist in things whose analogy is obvious, as when we detect the type of the human hand in the flipper of the fossil saurus, but also in objects wherein there is great superficial unlikeness. Thus architecture is called 'frozen music,' by De Stael and Goethe. 'A Gothic church,' said Coleridge, 'is a petrified religion.' Michael Angelo maintained, that, to an architect, a knowledge of anatomy is essential. In Haydn's oratorios, the notes present to the imagination not only motions, as, of the snake, the stag, and the elephant, but colors also; as the green grass. The granite is differenced in its laws only by the more or less of heat, from the river that wears it away. The river, as it flows, resembles the air that flows over it; the air resembles the light which traverses it with more subtle currents; the light resembles the heat which rides with it through Space. Each creature is only a modification of the other; the likeness in them is more than the difference, and [56] their radical law is one and the same. Hence it is, that a rule of one art, or a law of one organization, holds true throughout nature. So intimate is this Unity, that, it is easily seen, it lies under the undermost garment of nature, and betrays its source in universal Spirit. For, it pervades Thought also. Every universal truth which we express in words, implies or supposes every other truth. *Omne verum vero consonat.* It is like a great circle on a sphere, comprising all possible circles; which, however, may be drawn, and comprise it, in like manner. Every such truth is the absolute Ens seen from one side. But it has innumerable sides.

The same central Unity is still more conspicuous in actions. Words are finite organs of the infinite mind. They cannot cover the dimensions of what is in truth. They break, chop, and impoverish it. An action is the perfection and publication of thought. A right action seems to fill the eye, and to be related to all nature. "The wise man, in doing one thing, does all; or, in the one thing he does rightly, he sees the likeness of all which is done rightly."

[57] Words and actions are not the attributes of mute and brute nature. They introduce us to that singular form which predominates over all other forms. This is the human. All other organizations appear to be degradations of the human form. When this organization appears among so many that surround it, the spirit prefers it to all others. It says, 'From such as this, have I drawn joy and knowledge. In such as this, have I found and beheld myself. I will speak to it. It can speak again. It can yield me thought already formed and alive.' In fact, the eye,—the mind,—is always accompanied by these forms, male and female; and these are incomparably the richest informations of the power and order that lie at the heart of things. Unfortunately, every one of them bears the marks as of some injury; is marred and superficially defective. Nevertheless, far different from the deaf and dumb nature around them, these

all rest like fountain-pipes on the unfathomed sea of thought and virtue whereto they alone, of all organizations, are the entrances.

[58] It were a pleasant inquiry to follow into detail their ministry to our education, but where would it stop? We are associated in adolescent and adult life with some friends, whó, like skies and waters, are coextensive with our idea; who, answering each to a certain affection of the soul, satisfy our desire on that side; whom we lack power to put at such focal distance from us, that we can mend or even analyze them. We cannot chuse but love them. When much intercourse with a friend has supplied us with a standard of excellence, and has increased our respect for the resources of God who thus sends a real person to outgo our ideal; when he has, moreover, become an object of thought, and, whilst his character retains all its unconscious effect, is converted in the mind into solid and sweet wisdom,—it is a sign to us that his office is closing, and he is commonly withdrawn from our sight in a short time.

[59]   CHAPTER VI.

IDEALISM.

THUS is the unspeakable but intelligible and practicable meaning of the world conveyed to man, the immortal pupil, in every object of sense. To this one end of Discipline, all parts of nature conspire.

A noble doubt perpetually suggests itself, whether this end be not the Final Cause of the Universe; and whether nature outwardly exists. It is a sufficient account of that Appearance we call the World, that God will teach a human mind, and so makes it the receiver of a certain number of congruent sensations, which we call sun and moon, man and woman, house and trade. In my utter impotence to test the authenticity of the report of my senses, to know whether the impressions they make on me correspond with outlying objects, what difference does it make, whether Orion is up there in heaven, or some [60] god paints the image in the firmament of the soul? The relations of parts and the end of the whole remaining the same, what is the difference, whether land and sea interact, and worlds revolve and intermingle without number or end,—deep yawning under deep, and galaxy balancing galaxy, throughout absolute space, or, whether, without relations of time and space, the same appearances are inscribed in the constant faith of man. Whether nature enjoy a substantial existence without, or is only in the apocalypse of the mind, it is alike useful and alike venerable to me. Be it what it may, it is ideal to me, so long as I cannot try the accuracy of my senses.

The frivolous make themselves merry with the Ideal theory, as if its consequences were burlesque; as if it affected the stability of nature. It surely does not. God never jests with us, and will not compromise the end of nature, by permitting any inconsequence in its procession. Any distrust of the permanence of laws, would paralyze the faculties of man. Their perma-[61]nence is sacredly respected, and his faith therein is perfect. The wheels and springs of man are all set to the hypothesis of the permanence of nature. We are not built like a ship to be tossed, but like a house to stand. It is a natural consequence of this structure, that, so long as the active powers predominate over the reflective, we resist with indignation any hint that nature is more short-lived or mutable than spirit. The broker, the wheelwright, the carpenter, the tollman, are much displeased at the intimation.

But whilst we acquiesce entirely in the permanence of natural laws, the question of the absolute existence of nature, still remains open. It is the uniform effect of culture on the human mind, not to shake our faith in the stability of particular phenomena, as of heat, water, azote; but to lead us to regard nature as a phenomenon, not a substance; to attribute necessary existence to spirit; to esteem nature as an accident and an effect.

To the senses and the unrenewed understanding, belongs a sort of instinctive belief in the [62] absolute existence of nature. In their view, man and nature are indissolubly joined. Things are ultimates, and they never look beyond their sphere. The presence of Reason mars this faith. The first effort of thought tends to relax this despotism of the senses, which binds us to nature as if we were a part of it, and shows us nature aloof, and, as it were, afloat. Until this higher agency intervened, the animal eye sees, with wonderful accuracy, sharp outlines and colored surfaces. When the eye of Reason opens, to outline and surface are at once added, grace and expression. These proceed from imagination and affection, and abate somewhat of the angular distinctness of objects. If the Reason be stimulated to more earnest vision, outlines and surfaces become transparent, and are no longer seen; causes and spirits are seen through them. The best, the happiest moments of life, are these delicious awakenings of the higher powers, and the reverential withdrawing of nature before its God.

[63] Let us proceed to indicate the effects of culture. 1. Our first institution in the Ideal philosophy is a hint from nature herself.

Nature is made to conspire with spirit to emancipate us. Certain mechanical changes, a small alteration in our local position apprizes us of a dualism. We are strangely affected by seeing the shore from a moving ship, from a balloon, or through the tints of an unusual sky. The least change in our point of view, gives the whole world a pictorial air. A man who seldom rides, needs only to get into a coach and traverse his own town, to turn the street into a puppet-show. The men, the women,—talking, running, bartering, fighting,—the earnest mechanic, the lounger, the beggar, the boys, the dogs, are unrealized at once, or, at least, wholly detached from all relation to the observer, and seen as apparent, not substantial beings. What new thoughts are suggested by seeing a face of country quite familiar, in the rapid movement of the rail-road car! Nay, the most wonted objects, (make a very slight change in the point of vis-[64]ion,) please us most. In a camera obscura, the butcher's cart, and the figure of one of our own family amuse us. So a portrait of a well-known face gratifies us. Turn the eyes upside down, by looking at the landscape through your legs, and how agreeable is the picture, though you have seen it any time these twenty years!

In these cases, by mechanical means, is suggested the difference between the observer and the spectacle,—between man and nature. Hence arises a pleasure mixed with awe; I may say, a low degree of the sublime is felt from the fact, probably, that man is hereby apprized, that, whilst the world is a spectacle, something in himself is stable.

2. In a higher manner, the poet communicates the same pleasure. By a few strokes he delineates, as on air, the sun, the mountain, the camp, the city, the hero, the maiden, not different from what we know them, but only lifted from the ground and afloat before the eye. He unfixes the land and the sea, makes them revolve around the axis of his primary thought, and dis-[65]poses them anew. Possessed himself by a heroic passion, he uses matter as symbols of it. The sensual man conforms thoughts to things; the poet conforms things to his thoughts. The one esteems nature as rooted and fast; the other, as fluid, and impresses his being thereon. To him, the refractory world is ductile and flexible; he invests dust and stones with humanity, and makes them the words of the Reason. The imagination may be defined to be, the use which the Reason makes of the material world. Shakspeare possesses the power of subordinating nature for the purposes of expression, beyond all poets. His imperial muse tosses the creation like a bauble from hand to hand, to embody any capricious shade of thought that is uppermost in his mind. The remotest spaces of nature are visited, and the farthest sundered things are brought together, by a subtile spiritual connexion. We are made aware that magnitude of material things is merely relative, and all objects shrink and expand to serve the passion of the poet. Thus, in his [66] sonnets, the lays of birds, the scents and dyes of flowers, he finds to be the *shadow* of his beloved; time, which keeps her from him, is his *chest*; the suspicion she has awakened, is her *ornament*;

> The ornament of beauty is Suspect,
> A crow which flies in heaven's sweetest air.

His passion is not the fruit of chance; it swells, as he speaks, to a city, or a state.

> No, it was builded far from accident;
> It suffers not in smiling pomp, nor falls
> Under the brow of thralling discontent;
> It fears not policy, that heretic,
> That works on leases of short numbered hours,
> But all alone stands hugely politic.

In the strength of his constancy, the Pyramids seem to him recent and transitory. And the freshness of youth and love dazzles him with its resemblance to morning.

> Take those lips away
> Which so sweetly were forsworn;
> And those eyes,—the break of day,
> Lights that do mislead the morn.

[67] The wild beauty of this hyperbole, I may say, in passing, it would not be easy to match in literature.

This transfiguration which all material objects undergo through the passion of the poet,—this power which he exerts, at any moment, to magnify the small, to micrify the great,—might be illustrated by a thousand examples from his Plays. I have before me the Tempest, and will cite only these few lines.

> ARIEL. The strong based promontory
> Have I made shake, and by the spurs plucked up
> The pine and cedar.

Prospero calls for music to sooth the frantic Alonzo, and his companions;

> A solemn air, and the best comforter
> To an unsettled fancy, cure thy brains
> Now useless, boiled within thy skull.

Again;

> The charm dissolves apace
> And, as the morning steals upon the night,
> Melting the darkness, so their rising senses
> Begin to chase the ignorant fumes that mantle
> Their clearer reason.
[68] >   Their understanding
> Begins to swell: and the approaching tide
> Will shortly fill the reasonable shores
> That now lie foul and muddy.

The perception of real affinities between events, (that is to say, of *ideal* affinities, for those only are real,) enables the poet thus to make free with the most imposing forms and phenomena of the world, and to assert the predominance of the soul.

3. Whilst thus the poet delights us by animating nature like a creator, with his own thoughts, he differs from the philosopher only herein, that the one proposes Beauty as his main end; the other Truth. But, the philosopher, not less than the poet, postpones the apparent order and relations of things to the empire of thought. "The problem of philosophy," according to Plato, "is, for all that exists conditionally, to find a ground unconditioned and absolute." It proceeds on the faith that a law determines all phenomena, which being known, the phenomena can be predicted. That law, when in the [69] mind, is an idea. Its beauty is infinite. The true philosopher and the true poet are one, and a beauty, which is truth, and a truth, which is beauty, is the aim of both. Is not the charm of one of Plato's or Aristotle's definitions, strictly like that of the Antigone of Sophocles? It is, in both cases, that a spiritual life has been imparted to nature; that the solid seeming block of matter has been pervaded and dissolved by a thought; that this feeble human being has penetrated the vast masses of nature with an informing soul, and recognised itself in their harmony, that is, seized their law. In physics, when this is attained, the memory disburthens itself of

its cumbrous catalogues of particulars, and carries centuries of observation in a single formula.

Thus even in physics, the material is ever degraded before the spiritual. The astronomer, the geometer, rely on their irrefragable analysis, and disdain the results of observation. The sublime remark of Euler on his law of arches, "This will be found contrary to all experience, [70] yet is true;" had already transferred nature into the mind, and left matter like an outcast corpse.

4. Intellectual science has been observed to beget invariably a doubt of the existence of matter. Turgot said, "He that has never doubted the existence of matter, may be assured he has no aptitude for metaphysical inquiries." It fastens the attention upon immortal necessary uncreated natures, that is, upon Ideas; and in their beautiful and majestic presence, we feel that our outward being is a dream and a shade. Whilst we wait in this Olympus of gods, we think of nature as an appendix to the soul. We ascend into their region, and know that these are the thoughts of the Supreme Being. "These are they who were set up from everlasting, from the beginning, or ever the earth was. When he prepared the heavens, they were there; when he established the clouds above, when he strengthened the fountains of the deep. Then they were by him, as one brought up with him. Of them took he counsel."

[71] Their influence is proportionate. As objects of science, they are accessible to few men. Yet all men are capable of being raised by piety or by passion, into their region. And no man touches these divine natures, without becoming, in some degree, himself divine. Like a new soul, they renew the body. We become physically nimble and lightsome; we tread on air; life is no longer irksome, and we think it will never be so. No man fears age or misfortune or death, in their serene company, for he is transported out of the district of change. Whilst we behold unveiled the nature of Justice and Truth, we learn the difference between the absolute and the conditional or relative. We apprehend the absolute. As it were, for the first time, *we exist*. We become immortal, for we learn that time and space are relations of matter; that, with a perception of truth, or a virtuous will, they have no affinity.

5. Finally, religion and ethics, which may be fitly called,—the practice of ideas, or the introduction of ideas into life,—have an analo-[72]gous effect with all lower culture, in degrading nature and suggesting its dependence on spirit. Ethics and religion differ herein; that the one is the system of human duties commencing from man; the other, from God. Religion includes the personality of God; Ethics does not. They are one to our present design. They both put nature under foot. The first and last lesson of religion is, "The things that are seen, are temporal; the things that are unseen are eternal." It puts an affront upon nature. It does that for the unschooled, which philosophy does for Berkeley and Viasa. The uniform language that may be heard in the churches of the most ignorant sects, is,—'Contemn the unsubstantial shows of the world; they are vanities, dreams, shadows, unrealities; seek the realities of religion.' The devotee flouts nature. Some theosophists have arrived at a certain hostility and indignation towards matter, as the Manichean and Plotinus. They distrusted in them-

selves any looking back to these flesh-pots of Egypt. Plotinus was ashamed of his body. In [73] short, they might all better say of matter, what Michael Angelo said of external beauty, "it is the frail and weary weed, in which God dresses the soul, which he has called into time."

It appears that motion, poetry, physical and intellectual science, and religion, all tend to affect our convictions of the reality of the external world. But I own there is something ungrateful in expanding too curiously the particulars of the general proposition, that all culture tends to imbue us with idealism. I have no hostility to nature, but a child's love to it. I expand and live in the warm day like corn and melons. Let us speak her fair. I do not wish to fling stones at my beautiful mother, nor soil my gentle nest. I only wish to indicate the true position of nature in regard to man, wherein to establish man, all right education tends; as the ground which to attain is the object of human life, that is, of man's connexion with nature. Culture inverts the vulgar views of nature, and brings the mind to call that apparent, which it uses to call real, and that real, which [74] it uses to call visionary. Children, it is true, believe in the external world. The belief that it appears only, is an afterthought, but with culture, this faith will as surely arise on the mind as did the first.

The advantage of the ideal theory over the popular faith, is this, that it presents the world in precisely that view which is most desirable to the mind. It is, in fact, the view which Reason, both speculative and practical, that is, philosophy and virtue, take. For, seen in the light of thought, the world always is phenomenal; and virtue subordinates it to the mind. Idealism sees the world in God. It beholds the whole circle of persons and things, of actions and events, of country and religion, not as painfully accumulated, atom after atom, act after act, in an aged creeping Past, but as one vast picture, which God paints on the instant eternity, for the contemplation of the soul. Therefore the soul holds itself off from a too trivial and microscopic study of the universal tablet. It respects the end too much, to immerse itself in [75] the means. It sees something more important in Christianity, than the scandals of ecclesiastical history or the niceties of criticism; and, very incurious concerning persons or miracles, and not at all disturbed by chasms of historical evidence, it accepts from God the phenomenon, as it finds it, as the pure and awful form of religion in the world. It is not hot and passionate at the appearance of what it calls its own good or bad fortune, at the union or opposition of other persons. No man is its enemy. It accepts whatsoever befals, as part of its lesson. It is a watcher more than a doer, and it is a doer, only that it may the better watch.

[76]   CHAPTER VII.

SPIRIT.

It is essential to a true theory of nature and of man, that it should contain somewhat progressive. Uses that are exhausted or that may be, and facts that end in the state-

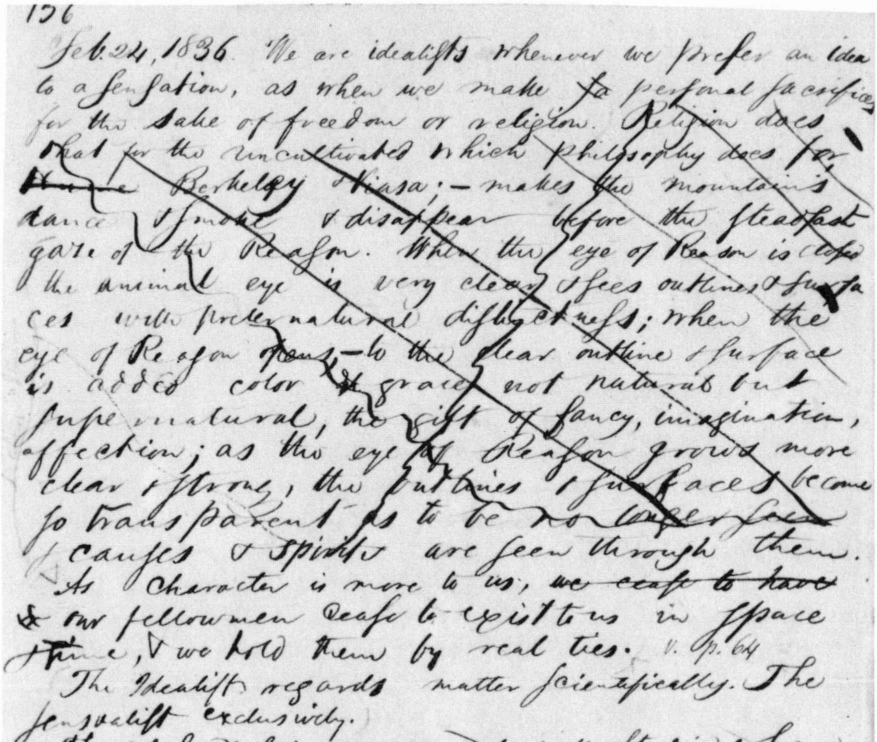
136

Feb. 24, 1836. We are idealists whenever we prefer an idea to a sensation, as when we make ~~a~~ personal sacrifice for the sake of freedom or religion. Religion does that for the uncultivated which philosophy does for ~~Hume~~ Berkeley & Viasa;—makes the mountains dance & smoke & disappear before the steadfast gaze of the Reason. When the eye of Reason is closed the animal eye is very clear & sees outlines & surfaces with preternatural distinctness; when the eye of Reason opens—to the clear outline & surface is added color & grace not natural but supernatural, the gift of fancy, imagination, affection; as the eye of Reason grows more clear & strong, the outlines & surfaces become so transparent as to be ~~no longer seen~~ & causes & spirits are seen through them. As Character is more to us, ~~we cease to have~~ our fellowmen cease to exist to us in space & time, & we hold them by real ties. v. p. 64

The Idealist regards matter scientifically. The sensualist exclusively.

The physical sciences are only well studied when they are explored for ideas. The moment the law is attained i.e. the Idea, the memory disburthens herself of her Centuries of observation, her

The book is always dear which has made us for moments idealists. ~~He who~~ That which can dissipate this block of earth into shining ether is genius.

I have no ~~hostility~~ hatred to the round earth & its gray mountains. I see well enough the sand hill opposite my window. I see with as much pleasure as another a field of corn or a rich pasture, whilst I dispute their absolute

(*The Houghton Library, Harvard University*)

PLATE III

At Concord, February 24, 1836, Emerson sets down ideas used later in Chapter VI of *Nature*, "Idealism" (Journal B, p. 136, in *JMN*, V, 123–124; in the present text, see pp. 24, 27, 28; 62–63).

ment, cannot be all that is true of this brave lodging wherein man is harbored, and wherein all his faculties find appropriate and endless exercise. And all the uses of nature admit of being summed in one, which yields the activity of man an infinite scope. Through all its kingdoms, to the suburbs and outskirts of things, it is faithful to the cause whence it had its origin. It always speaks of Spirit. It suggests the absolute. It is a perpetual effect. It is a great shadow pointing always to the sun behind us.

The aspect of nature is devout. Like the figure of Jesus, she stands with bended head, and hands folded upon the breast. The happiest [77] man is he who learns from nature the lesson of worship.

Of that ineffable essence which we call Spirit, he that thinks most, will say least. We can foresee God in the coarse and, as it were, distant phenomena of matter; but when we try to define and describe himself, both language and thought desert us, and we are as helpless as fools and savages. That essence refuses to be recorded in propositions, but when man has worshipped him intellectually, the noblest ministry of nature is to stand as the apparition of God. It is the great organ through which the universal spirit speaks to the individual, and strives to lead back the individual to it.

When we consider Spirit, we see that the views already presented do not include the whole circumference of man. We must add some related thoughts.

Three problems are put by nature to the mind; What is matter? Whence is it? and Whereto? The first of these questions only, the ideal theory answers. Idealism saith: mat-[78]ter is a phenomenon, not a substance. Idealism acquaints us with the total disparity between the evidence of our own being, and the evidence of the world's being. The one is perfect; the other, incapable of any assurance; the mind is a part of the nature of things; the world is a divine dream, from which we may presently awake to the glories and certainties of day. Idealism is a hypothesis to account for nature by other principles than those of carpentry and chemistry. Yet, if it only deny the existence of matter, it does not satisfy the demands of the spirit. It leaves God out of me. It leaves me in the splendid labyrinth of my perceptions, to wander without end. Then the heart resists it, because it baulks the affections in denying substantive being to men and women. Nature is so pervaded with human life, that there is something of humanity in all, and in every particular. But this theory makes nature foreign to me, and does not account for that consanguinity which we acknowledge to it.

[79] Let it stand then, in the present state of our knowledge, merely as a useful introductory hypothesis, serving to apprize us of the eternal distinction between the soul and the world.

But when, following the invisible steps of thought, we come to inquire, Whence is matter? and Whereto? many truths arise to us out of the recesses of consciousness. We learn that the highest is present to the soul of man, that the dread universal essence, which is not wisdom, or love, or beauty, or power, but all in one, and each entirely, is that for which all things exist, and that by which they are; that spirit creates; that behind nature, throughout nature, spirit is present; that spirit is one and not compound; that spirit does not act upon us from without, that is, in space and time, but spiritually, or through ourselves. Therefore, that spirit, that is, the Supreme Being, does not build up nature around us, but puts it forth through us, as the life of the tree puts forth new branches and leaves through the pores of the old. As a plant upon the earth, so a man rests [80] upon the bosom of God; he is nourished by unfailing fountains, and draws, at his need, inexhaustible power. Who can set bounds to the possibilities of man? Once inspire the infinite, by being admitted to behold the absolute natures of justice and truth, and we learn that man has access to the entire mind of the Creator, is himself the creator in the finite. This view, which admonishes me where the sources of wisdom and power lie, and points to virtue as to

"The golden key
Which opes the palace of eternity,"

carries upon its face the highest certificate of truth, because it animates me to create my own world through the purification of my soul.

The world proceeds from the same spirit as the body of man. It is a remoter and inferior incarnation of God, a projection of God in the unconscious. But it differs from the body in one important respect. It is not, like that, now subjected to the human will. Its serene order is inviolable by us. It is therefore, to us, the present expositor of the divine mind. It is a [81] fixed point whereby we may measure our departure. As we degenerate, the contrast between us and our house is more evident. We are as much strangers in nature, as we are aliens from God. We do not understand the notes of birds. The fox and the deer run away from us; the bear and tiger rend us. We do not know the uses of more than a few plants, as corn and the apple, the potato and the vine. Is not the landscape, every glimpse of which hath a grandeur, a face of him? Yet this may show us what discord is between man and nature, for you cannot freely admire a noble landscape, if laborers are digging in the field hard by. The poet finds something ridiculous in his delight, until he is out of the sight of men.

[82]   CHAPTER VIII.

PROSPECTS.

IN inquiries respecting the laws of the world and the frame of things, the highest reason is always the truest. That which seems faintly possible—it is so refined, is often faint and dim because it is deepest seated in the mind among the eternal verities. Empirical science is apt to cloud the sight, and, by the very knowledge of functions and processes, to bereave the student of the manly contemplation of the whole. The savant becomes unpoetic. But the best read naturalist who lends an entire and devout attention to truth, will see that there remains much to learn of his relation to the world, and that it is not to be learned by any addition or subtraction or other comparison of known quantities, but is arrived at by untaught sallies of the spirit, by a continual self-recovery, and by entire humility. He will perceive that there are far [83] more excellent qualities in the student than preciseness and infallibility; that a guess is often more fruitful than an indisputable affirmation, and that a dream may let us deeper into the secret of nature than a hundred concerted experiments.

For, the problems to be solved are precisely those which the physiologist and the naturalist omit to state. It is not so pertinent to man to know all the individuals of the animal kingdom, as it is to know whence and whereto is this tyrannizing unity in his constitution, which evermore separates and classifies things, endeavouring to reduce the most diverse to one form. When I behold a rich landscape, it is less to my purpose to recite correctly the order and superposition of the strata, than to know why all thought of multitude is lost in a tranquil sense of unity. I cannot greatly honor minuteness in details, so long as there is no hint to explain the relation between things and thoughts; no ray upon the *metaphysics* of conchology, of botany, of the arts, to show the relation of the forms of [84] flowers, shells, animals, architecture, to the mind, and build science upon ideas. In a cabinet of natural history, we become sensible of a certain occult recognition and sympathy in regard to the most bizarre forms of beast, fish, and insect. The American who has been confined, in his own country, to the sight of buildings designed after foreign models, is surprised on entering York Minster or St. Peter's at Rome, by the feeling that these structures are imitations also,—faint copies of an invisible archetype. Nor has science sufficient humanity, so long as the naturalist overlooks that wonderful congruity which subsists between man and the world; of which he is lord, not because he is the most subtile inhabitant, but because he is its head and heart, and finds something of himself in every great and small thing, in every mountain stratum, in every new law of color, fact of astronomy, or atmospheric influence which observation or analysis lays open. A perception of this mystery inspires the muse of George Herbert, the beautiful psalmist of the [85] seventeenth century. The following lines are part of his little poem on Man.

> "Man is all symmetry,
> Full of proportions, one limb to another,
> And to all the world besides.
> Each part may call the farthest, brother;
> For head with foot hath private amity,
> And both with moons and tides.

> "Nothing hath got so far
> But man hath caught and kept it as his prey;
> His eyes dismount the highest star;
> He is in little all the sphere.
> Herbs gladly cure our flesh, because that they
> Find their acquaintance there.

"For us, the winds do blow,
The earth doth rest, heaven move, and fountains flow;
   Nothing we see, but means our good,
   As our delight, or as our treasure;
The whole is either our cupboard of food,
   Or cabinet of pleasure.

"The stars have us to bed:
Night draws the curtain; which the sun withdraws.
   Music and light attend our head.
   All things unto our flesh are kind,
In their descent and being; to our mind,
   In their ascent and cause.

"More servants wait on man
Than he'll take notice of. In every path,
   He treads down that which doth befriend him
   When sickness makes him pale and wan.
Oh mighty love! Man is one world, and hath
   Another to attend him."

[86]

The perception of this class of truths makes the eternal attraction which draws men to science, but the end is lost sight of in attention to the means. In view of this half-sight of science, we accept the sentence of Plato, that, "poetry comes nearer to vital truth than history." Every surmise and vaticination of the mind is entitled to a certain respect, and we learn to prefer imperfect theories, and sentences, which contain glimpses of truth, to digested systems which have no one valuable suggestion. A wise writer will feel that the ends of study and composition are best answered by announcing undiscovered regions of thought, and so [87] communicating, through hope, new activity to the torpid spirit.

I shall therefore conclude this essay with some traditions of man and nature, which a certain poet sang to me; and which, as they have always been in the world, and perhaps reappear to every bard, may be both history and prophecy.

'The foundations of man are not in matter, but in spirit. But the element of spirit is eternity. To it, therefore, the longest series of events, the oldest chronologies are young and recent. In the cycle of the universal man, from whom the known individuals proceed, centuries are points, and all history is but the epoch of one degradation.

'We distrust and deny inwardly our sympathy with nature. We own and disown our relation to it, by turns. We are, like Nebuchadnezzar, dethroned, bereft of reason, and eating grass like an ox. But who can set limits to the remedial force of spirit?

[88] 'A man is a god in ruins. When men are innocent, life shall be longer, and shall pass into the immortal, as gently as we awake from dreams. Now, the world would be insane and rabid, if these disorganizations should last for hundreds of years. It is kept in check by death and infancy. Infancy is the perpetual Messiah, which comes into the arms of fallen men, and pleads with them to return to paradise.

'Man is the dwarf of himself. Once he was permeated and dissolved by spirit. He filled nature with his overflowing currents. Out from him sprang the sun and moon; from man, the sun; from woman, the moon. The laws of his mind, the periods of his actions externized themselves into day and night, into the year and the seasons. But, having made for himself this huge shell, his waters retired; he no longer fills the veins and veinlets; he is shrunk to a drop. He sees, that the structure still fits him, but fits him colossally. Say, rather, once it fitted him, now it corresponds to him from far and on high. [89] He adores timidly his own work. Now is man the follower of the sun, and woman the follower of the moon. Yet sometimes he starts in his slumber, and wonders at himself and his house, and muses strangely at the resemblance betwixt him and it. He perceives that if his law is still paramount, if still he have elemental power, "if his word is sterling yet in nature," it is not conscious power, it is not inferior but superior to his will. It is Instinct.' Thus my Orphic poet sang.

At present, man applies to nature but half his force. He works on the world with his understanding alone. He lives in it, and masters it by a penny-wisdom; and he that works most in it, is but a half-man, and whilst his arms are strong and his digestion good, his mind is imbruted and he is a selfish savage. His relation to nature, his power over it, is through the understanding; as by manure; the economic use of fire, wind, water, and the mariner's needle; steam, coal, chemical agriculture; the repairs of the human body by the dentist and the sur-[90]geon. This is such a resumption of power, as if a banished king should buy his territories inch by inch, instead of vaulting at once into his throne. Meantime, in the thick darkness, there are not wanting gleams of a better light,—occasional examples of the action of man upon nature with his entire force,—with reason as well as understanding. Such examples are; the traditions of miracles in the earliest antiquity of all nations; the history of Jesus Christ; the achievement of a principle, as in religious and political revolutions, and in the abolition of the Slave-trade; the miracles of enthusiasm, as those reported of Swedenborg, Hohenlohe, and the Shakers; many obscure and yet contested facts, now arranged under the name of Animal Magnetism; prayer; eloquence; self-healing; and the wisdom of children. These are examples of Reason's momentary grasp of the sceptre; the exertions of a power which exists not in time or space, but an instantaneous in-streaming causing power. The difference between the actual and the ideal force of man is happi-[91]ly figured by the schoolmen, in saying, that the knowledge of man is an evening knowledge, *vespertina cognitio*, but that of God is a morning knowledge, *matutina cognitio*.

The problem of restoring to the world original and eternal beauty, is solved by the redemption of the soul. The ruin or the blank, that we see when we look at nature, is in our own eye. The axis of vision is not coincident with the axis of things, and so they appear not transparent but opake. The reason why the world lacks unity, and lies broken and in heaps, is, because man is disunited with himself. He cannot be a naturalist, until he satisfies all the demands of the spirit. Love is as much its demand, as perception. Indeed, neither can be perfect without the other. In the uttermost meaning of the words, thought is devout, and devotion is thought. Deep calls unto deep. But in actual life, the marriage is not celebrated. There are in. ocent men who worship God after the tradition of their fathers, but their sense of duty has not yet extended to the use of all their [92] faculties. And there are patient naturalists, but they freeze their subject under the wintry light of understanding. Is not prayer also a study of truth,—a sally of the soul into the unfound infinite? No man ever prayed heartily, without learning something. But when a faithful thinker, resolute to detach every object from personal relations, and see it in the light of thought, shall, at the same time, kindle science with the fire of the holiest affections, then will God go forth anew into the creation.

It will not need, when the mind is prepared for study, to search for objects. The invariable mark of wisdom is to see the miraculous in the common. What is a day? What is a year? What is summer? What is woman? What is a child? What is sleep? To our blindness, these things seem unaffecting. We make fables to hide the baldness of the fact and conform it, as we say, to the higher law of the mind. But when the fact is seen under the light of an idea, the gaudy fable fades and shrivels. We behold the real higher law. To the wise, therefore, a [93] fact is true poetry, and the most beautiful of fables. These wonders are brought to our own door. You also are a man. Man and woman, and their social life, poverty, labor, sleep, fear, fortune, are known to you. Learn that none of these things is superficial, but that each phenomenon hath its roots in the faculties and affections of the mind. Whilst the abstract question occupies your intellect, nature brings it in the concrete to be solved by your hands. It were a wise inquiry for the closet, to compare, point by point, especially at remarkable crises in life, our daily history, with the rise and progress of ideas in the mind.

So shall we come to look at the world with new eyes. It shall answer the endless inquiry of the intellect,—What is truth? and of the affections,—What is good? by yielding itself passive to the educated Will. Then shall come to pass what my poet said; 'Nature is not fixed but fluid. Spirit alters, moulds, makes it. The immobility or bruteness of nature, is the absence of spirit; to pure spirit, it is fluid, it is volatile, [94] it is obedient. Every spirit builds itself a house; and beyond its house, a world; and beyond its world, a heaven. Know then, that the world exists for you. For you is the phenomenon perfect. What we are, that only can we see. All that Adam had, all that Cæsar could, you have and can do. Adam called his house, heaven and earth; Cæsar called his house, Rome; you perhaps call yours, a cobler's trade; a hundred acres of ploughed land; or a scholar's garret. Yet line for line and point for point, your dominion is as great as theirs, though without fine names. Build, therefore, your own world. As fast as you conform your life to the pure idea in your mind, that will unfold its great proportions. A correspondent revolution in things will attend the influx of the spirit. So fast will disagreeable appearances, swine, spiders, snakes, pests, mad-houses, prisons, enemies, vanish; they are temporary and shall be no more seen. The sordor and filths of nature, the sun shall dry up, and the wind exhale. As when the summer comes from the south, the snow-banks melt, and [95] the face of the earth becomes green before it, so shall the advancing spirit create its ornaments along

It is essential to a true theory of Nature & man that it
should contain somewhat prospective, should ascribe free
dom to the will, or benevolent designs to the Deity
And the effect of the ideal theory truly seen is this;
Nature is not stable but fluid. Spirit alters, moulds,
makes it. The immobility or bruteness of nature
is the absence of spirit; to pure spirit it is fluid,
it is volatile, it is obedient. Believe that the
world exists for you. For you is the phenomenon perfect
& what we are, that only we see. All that Adam
had, All that Caesar could, you have & can do.
Adam called it the earth, Caesar called it life Rome,
you perhaps call it a cobbler's trade, yet line for
line & point for point, you have the whole circle
As fast as your spirit quits its earth, disagreeable
appearances, prisons, spiders, snakes, pests, madhouses,
vanish. they are temporary & shall be no more seen
The sordor & filths of nature, the sun shall dry
up & the wind exhale. As before
the Summer, the snow banks melt and the
face of the earth becomes green & shall
the Spirit shall create its ornaments
along its path & carry with it the beauty it
visits & the song which enchants it. creates in
telligent faces & warm hearts and sweet discourse
& heroic acts around its way until evil is no more seen
This kingdom of man over nature which
shall not come with observation. a domin
ion such as now is beyond his dream of God
he shall enter without more wonder than
the blind man feels who is gradually
restored to perfect sight.

(The Houghton Library, Harvard University)

PLATE IV

At Concord, June 24, 1836, Emerson drafts the conclusion of Chapter
VIII of *Nature*, "Prospects" (Journal B, p. 215, in *JMN*, V, 182–183;
in the present text, see pp. 35–36; 43–44, item 18; 65.

its path, and carry with it the beauty it visits, and the song which enchants it; it shall draw beautiful faces, and warm hearts, and wise discourse, and heroic acts, around its way, until evil is no more seen. The kingdom of man over nature, which cometh not with observation,—a dominion such as now is beyond his dream of God,—he shall enter without more wonder than the blind man feels who is gradually restored to perfect sight.'

EMERGENCE OF NATURE

The story of any created work is never completely told, even by its author, and the story of Emerson's first book can of course be no exception. But in Emerson's own manuscripts enough of the written record survives to show a great deal about one writer's way of shaping and ordering the material of his creation. *Nature* as it was published in 1836 is obviously not the book its author had thought of writing in 1832, when he listed nine possible topics or chapters that a book of his might some-day treat. By reference to certain passages of Emerson's journal, to his letters, and to some of his public lectures written during the intervening years we can trace to a surprising degree the emergence of a general subject, a point of view concerning it, and the substance and form both of component parts and of the book as a whole. Such passages are grouped here under two headings: "Emerson Plans His First Book, 1832–1836," and "Journal and Lecture Passages Used in *Nature*." They are only a sampling of the riches to be found in the Emerson papers as modern scholarly editions have made them available for study.

EMERSON PLANS HIS FIRST BOOK, 1832-1836

Numbered entries under this heading bring together excerpts from Emerson's journals, lectures, and letters, 1832–1836, referring either directly or obliquely to the book that became *Nature*; no manuscript of the book itself has survived. Also included are other representative passages that illustrate Emerson's changing responses during these years to nature and the study of natural history. The abbreviations used are listed in the Preface, p. vi above.

1. January 6, 1832 (*JMN*, III, 315–316):
   Shall I not write a book on topics such as follow
   Chap. 1 That the mind is its own place
   Chap. 2. That exact justice is done
   Chap. 3. That good motives are at the bottom of many bad actions.
         e.g. 'Business before friends'
   Chap. 4. That the Soul is immortal
   Chap. 5. On prayers
   Chap. 6 That the best is the true.

Chap. 7 That the Mind discerns all things.

Chap. 8. That the Mind seeks itself in all things

Chap. 9 That truth is its own warrant.

2. At Paris, July 13, 1833 (*JMN*, IV, 198–200):

I carried my ticket . . . to the Cabinet of Natural History in the Garden of Plants. How much finer things are in composition than alone. . . . Ah said I this is philanthropy, wisdom, taste—to form a Cabinet of natural history. . . . Here we are impressed with the inexhaustible riches of nature. The Universe is a more amazing puzzle than ever as you glance along this bewildering series of animated forms,—the hazy butterflies, the carved shells, the birds, beasts, fishes, insects, snakes,—& the upheaving principle of life everywhere incipient in the very rock aping organized forms. Not a form so grotesque, so savage, nor so beautiful but is an expression of some property inherent in man the observer,—an occult relation between the very scorpions and man. I feel the centipede in me—cayman, carp, eagle, & fox. I am moved by strange sympathies, I say continually "I will be a naturalist."

3. At sea off the coast of Ireland, September 6, 1833 (*JMN*, IV, 237):

I like my book about nature & wish I knew where & how I ought to live. God will show me. I am glad to be on my way home. . . .

4. Emerson lectures in Boston on "The Uses of Natural History," November 5, 1833 (*EL*, I, 23):

I have spoken of some of the advantages which may flow from the culture of natural science: health; useful knowledge; delight; and the improvement of the mind and character. I should not do the subject the imperfect justice in my power if I did not add a fifth. It is in my judgment the greatest office of natural science (and one which as yet is only begun to be discharged) to explain man to himself. The knowledge of the laws of nature,—how many wild errors—political, philosophical, theological, has it not already corrected! The knowledge of all the facts of all the laws of nature will give man his true place in the system of being. But more than the correction of specific errors by the disclosure of particular facts, there yet remain questions of the highest interest which are unsolved and on which a far more profound knowledge of Nature will throw light.

5. Emerson lectures in Boston on "The Relation of Man to the Globe," January 6, 1834 (*EL*, I, 48–49):

Now what is the conclusion from these hasty and to some it may appear miscellaneous sketches of the relations of man to the objects around him? I have spoken of the preparation made for man in the slow and secular changes and melioration of the surface of the planet. We have seen that as soon as he could live upon it, he was created; that the air was mixed to suit his lungs; that the temperature ranges between extremes tolerable to him; that the texture of the earth is fit; that the mineral treasures are conveniently bestowed for his use; then, that a most nicely adjusted proportion is established betwixt his powers and the forces with which he has to deal,—provided for in the excellent construction of his frame; then, that such an arrangement of the gifts of nature is made, as to invite man out to activity and commerce; then, that he forms mutually serviceable relations with his fellow creatures the brutes; then, that he improves the face of the planet itself; then, that not only a relation of use but a relation of beauty subsists between himself and nature, which leads him to Science; and, finally, that once embarked on that pursuit, all things stimulate and instruct him,—the dewdrop is a lecture, the rainbow a professor, the white Alps a specimen, the hurricane an experiment, the mine a book, and the planet in its orbit only a ship to transport the astronomer and his telescopes through the navigable heavens to more convenient stations of observation.

In the view of all these facts I conclude that other creatures reside in particular places . . . , but the residence of man is the world. It was given him to possess it. I conclude further, that the snail is not more accurately adjusted to his shell than man to the globe he inhabits; that not only a perfect symmetry is discoverable in his limbs and senses between the head and the foot, between the hand and the eye, the heart and the lungs,—but an equal symmetry and proportion is discoverable between him and the air, the mountains, the tides, the moon, and the sun. I am not impressed by solitary marks of designing wisdom; I am thrilled with delight by the choral harmony of the whole. Design! It is all design. It is all beauty. It is all astonishment.

6. At Newton, May 6, 1834 (*JMN*, IV, 290–291):
Well, my friend, are you not yet convinced that you should study plants & animals? To be sure the reasons are not very mighty; but words. To it again. Say then that I will study Natural history to provide me a resource when business, friends, & my country fail me, that I may never lose my temper nor be without soothing uplifting occupation. It will yet cheer me in solitude or I think in madness, that the mellow voice of the robin is not a stranger to me, that the flowers are reflections to me of earlier, happier, & yet thoughtful hours[.]

Or again say that I am ever haunted by the conviction that I have an interest in all that goes on around me[,] that I would overhear the powers what they say.—No knowledge can be spared, or any advantage we can give ourselves. And this is the knowledge of the laws by which I live. But finally say frankly, that all the reasons seem to me to fall short of my faith upon the subject, therefore—boldly press the cause as its own evidence; say that you love nature, & would know her mysteries, & that you believe in your power by patient contemplation & docile experiment to learn them.

7. At Newton, "For the Lecture on Nat[ural]. His[tory]." (given at Concord, January 1, 1835), written August 15, 1834 (*JMN*, IV, 311):

Natural history by itself has no value; it is like a single sex. But marry it to human history, & it is poetry. Whole Floras, all Linnaeus' & Buffon's volumes contain not one line of poetry, but the meanest natural fact, the habit of a plant, the organs, or work, or noise of an insect applied to the interpretation [of] or even associated [with] a fact in human nature is beauty, is poetry, is truth at once. [Compare "Language," p. 16 above.]

8. At Concord, November 15, 1834 (*JMN*, IV, 335):

Hail to the quiet fields of my fathers! Not wholly unattended by supernatural friendship & favor let me come hither. Bless my purposes as they are simple & virtuous. . . . Henceforth I design not to utter any speech, poem, or book that is not entirely & peculiarly my work.

9. At Concord, March 28, 1835 (*JMN*, V, 25):

If life were long enough among my thousand & one works should be a book of Nature whereof 'Howitt's Seasons' should be not so much the model as the parody. It should contain the Natural history of the woods around my shifting camp for every month in the year. It should tie their astronomy, botany, physiology, meteorology, picturesque, & poetry together. No bird, no bug, no bud should be forgotten on his day & hour.

10. At Concord, May 14, 1835 (*JMN*, V, 40):

When I write a book on spiritual things I think I will advertise the reader that I am a very wicked man, & that consistency is nowise to be expected of me.

When will you mend Montaigne? When will you take the hint of nature? Where are your Essays? Can you not express your one conviction that moral laws hold? Have you not thoughts & illustrations that are your own; the parable of geometry & matter; the reason why the atmosphere is transparent; the power of Composition in nature & in man's thoughts; the Uses & uselessness of travelling; the law of Compensation; the transcendant excellence of truth in character, in rhetoric, in things; the sublimity of Self-reliance; and the rewards of perseverance in the best opinion? Have you not a testimony to give for Shakspear, for Milton? one sentence of real praise of Jesus, is worth a century of legendary Christianity. Can you not write as though you wrote to yourself & drop the token assured that a wise hand will pick it up?

11. Letter to Frederic Henry Hedge, Concord, June 25, 1835 (*L*, I, 447):

And in the winter I must give 8 or 10 lectures before the Diffusion Society. Moreover I please myself with a purpose of publishing by & by a book of Essays chiefly upon Natural Ethics with the aim of bringing a pebble or two to the edification of the new temple whilst so many wise hands are demolishing the old.

12. At Concord, October 10–12, 1835 (*JMN*, V, 92–93):

A man to thrive in literature must trust himself. The voice of society some-times & the writings of great geniuses always, are so noble & prolific that it seems justifiable to follow & imitate. But it is better to be an independent shoemaker than to be an actor and play a king. . . . Shun manufacture or the introducing an artificial arrangement in your thoughts, it will surely crack & come to nothing[,] but let alone tinkering & wait for the natural arrangement of your treasures; that shall be chemical affinity, & is a new & permanent sub-stance added to the world, to be recognized as genuine by every knowing per-son at sight. . . .

A meek self reliance I believe to be the law & constitution of good writing. A man is to treat the world like children who must hear & obey the spirit in which he speaks, but which is not his. If he thinks he is to sing to the tune of the times, is to be the decorous sayer of smooth things, to lull the ear of society, & to speak of religion as the great traditional things to be either mutely avoided or kept at a distance by civil bows he may make a very good workman for the booksellers but he must lay aside all hope to wield or so much as to touch the bright thunderbolts of truth which it is given to the true scholar to launch & whose light flashes through ages without diminution.

13. At Concord, January 22–23, 1836, Emerson begins formulating what became the Introduction to *Nature* (*JMN*, V, 117; see Plate I):

Set men upon thinking & you have been to them a god. All history is poetry; the globe of facts whereon they trample is bullion to the scientific eye. Mean-est life a thread of empyrean light. Scholar converts for them the dishonored facts which they know, into trees of life; their daily routine into a garden of God by suggesting the principle which classifies the facts. We build the sepul-chres of our fathers: can we never behold the Universe as new and feel that we have a stake as much as our predecessors[?]

14. Letter to Frederic Henry Hedge, Concord, March 14, 1836 (L, II, 6–7):

If I think of books that should interest you I am almost ashamed to find how little I have read this winter. To write a very little takes a great deal of time So that if one indulges in that species of dissipation he will have very little to show for his solid days. And there are not many greater misfortunes to peace of mind than to have keen susceptibility to the beautiful in composition and just to lack that additional wit which suffices to create it. So shall a man weary himself and spend good oil in vain attempts to carve Apollos which all turn out scarecrows. My versification of this ancient lament is

Happy Bard or Dunce! but hard
Is it to be half a bard.

A man feels like one who has lost his way in the Universe when he discovers that he has aims which he has no faculties to satisfy.

15. At Concord, March 27, 1836, Emerson formulates the organization of Chapters II–V ("Commodity," "Beauty," "Language," and "Discipline") of *Nature* (*JMN*, V, 146–147):

The moment an idea is introduced among facts the God takes possession. Until then, facts conquer us. The Beast rules Man.

Thus through Nature is there a striving upward. Commodity points toward a greater good. Beauty is nought until the spiritual element. Language refers to that which is to be said . . . .

Finally; Nature is a discipline, & points to the pupil & exists for the pupil. Her being is subordinate; his is superior. Man underlies Ideas. Nature receives them as her god.

16. At Concord, May 31, 1836, Emerson sets down an outline for Chapter III ("Beauty") of *Nature* (*JMN*, V, 166):

Yesterday in the wood it seemed to me that the three aspects of Natural Beauty might take this order. 1. The beauty of the world as a daily delight & luxury—rainbows, moonlight, & perspective; 2. The beauty of the world as it is [—] the drapery of Virtuous actions, Leonidas, Columbus, & Vane, & always the Unconscious Man; 3. The beauty of the World as it becomes an object of the intellect and so the foundation of Art or the voluntary creation of Beauty[.]

17. At Concord, June 22–23, 1836, Emerson drafts what became the final paragraph of Chapter VIII ("Prospects") of *Nature* (*JMN*, V, 180):

The kingdom of man over nature shall not come with observation[.]

To all these wonders, to a dominion such as now is beyond his dream of God, he shall return without more wonder than the blind man feels who is gradually restored to perfect sight.

The sordor & filths of nature the sun shall exhale & the wind dry up.

18. At Concord, June 24, 1836, Emerson revises his draft of the final paragraph of Chapter VIII of *Nature* (*JMN*, V, 182–183):

It is essential to a true theory of nature & man, that it should contain somewhat progressive, should ascribe freedom to the will, or benevolent designs to the Deity. And the effect of the ideal theory truly seen is this; Nature is not stable but fluid. Spirit alters, moulds, makes it. The immobility or bruteness of nature is the absence of spirit; to pure spirit it is fluid, it is volatile, it is obedient. Believe that the world exists for you. For you is the phenomenon perfect & what we are, that only we see. All that Adam had, all that Caesar could, you have & can do. Adam called it the earth, Caesar called life Rome; you perhaps call it a cobler's trade [cf. item 12 above], yet line for line & point for point, you have the whole circle. As fast as your spirit quits its earth, disagreeable appearances, prisons, spiders, snakes, pests, madhouses, vanish; they are temporary & shall be no more seen. The sordor & filths of nature, the sun shall dry up & the wind exhale. As before the Summer, the snowbanks melt and the face of the earth becomes green so the spirit shall create its ornaments along its path & carry with it the beauty it visits & the song which enchants it; create intelligent faces & warm hearts and sweet discourse [&] heroic acts around its way until evil is no more seen. This kingdom of man over nature which shall not come with observation, a dominion such as now is beyond his dream of God[,] he shall enter without more wonder than the blind man feels who is gradually restored to perfect sight.

19. Letter to William Emerson, Concord, June 28, 1836 (*L*, II, 26):
My little book is nearly done. Its title is "Nature." Its contents will not exceed in bulk S[ampson]. Reed's Growth of the Mind [*Observations on the Growth of the Mind*, Boston, 1826: 44 pages]. My design is to follow it by & by with another essay, "Spirit"; and the two shall make a decent volume.

20. Letter to William Emerson, Concord, July 7, 1836 (*L*, II, 28):
Yesterday in town I asked the booksellers what it would cost to print my "Nature"—It would cost a little more than a hundred dollars to make a handsome little book. From the first Edition I shall expect no profit and if it attain to a second the success should be profit enow.

21. Letter to Frederic Henry Hedge, Concord, July 20, 1836 (*L*, II, 30):
Did I tell you I had a Chapter which I call "Nature" in solid prose, & which I shall print I think presently, & send you. Then I wish to write another chapter called "Spirit"[.]

22. Letter to William Emerson, Concord, August 8, 1836 (*L*, II, 32):
Mr Alcott has spent a day here lately, the world-builder. An accomplished lady is staying with Lidian [Mrs. Emerson] now[,] Miss Margaret Fuller. . . . The book of Nature still lies on the table. There is, as always, one crack in it not easy to be soldered or welded, but if this week I should be left alone after the probate affair [concerning the estate of Charles Emerson, who had died on May 9, 1836] I may finish it.

23. At Concord, August 27, 1836 (*JMN*, V, 190–191):
Today came to me the first proof-sheet of "Nature" to be corrected, like a new coat, full of vexations; with the first sentences of the chapters perched like mottoes aloft in small type! The peace of the author cannot be wounded by such trifles, if he sees that the sentences are still good. A good sentence can

never be put out of countenance by any blunder of compositors. It is good in text or note, in poetry or prose, as title or corollary. But a bad sentence shows all his flaws instantly by such dislocation. So that a certain sublime serenity is generated in the soul of the Poet by the annoyances of the press. He sees that the spirit may infuse a subtle logic into the parts of the piece which shall defy all accidents to break their connexion.

24. At Concord, *circa* September 9, 1836, when *Nature* was advertised for sale, Emerson lists 44 persons to whom he had presented or was sending copies of *Nature* (*JMN*, V, 263–264).

25. Letter to Thomas Carlyle, Concord, September 17, 1836 (*CEC*, p. 149):
I send you a little book I have just now published, as an entering wedge, I hope, for something more worthy and significant. This is only a naming of topics on which I would gladly speak and gladlier hear.

26. Letter to William Emerson, Concord, October 23, 1836 (*L*, II, 42):
I thank you for your interest in "Nature" & "Spirit." The little book meets with quite as much attention as I could have anticipated. 500 copies were gone when I inquired a fortnight since; which for a book purely literary or philosophical is a good deliverance. Do you want any copies of it? I will send you some if Mr Loring will give me an opportunity for if I remember truly, I gave one to my sister [i.e., Mrs. William Emerson], none to my brother. [Emerson's recollection is confirmed by his journal entry, item 24 above.]

27. At Concord, November 28, 1836 (*JMN*, V, 257–258):
Notes for the correction or enlargement of "Nature."
John Eliot would be a noble figure to add to the group on p. 26 [i.e., Leonidas, Winkelreid, Columbus, Vane, and Lord Russell: see p. 13 above]. . . .
To the same connexion belongs I think the paragraph upon Eyes in p. 111 of this Journal [*JMN*, V, 101–102].

See the notice of Humboldt J[ournal] 1833[–1834,] p 96 [*JMN*, IV, 331]— for Chap. on Language.

See p 126 J[ournal]. 1833[–1834] [*JMN*, IV, 359–360: on Emerson's response to "Nature in the woods."]

28. At Concord, May 8, 1837 (*JMN*, V, 325–326):
It ought to have been more distinctly stated in "Nature" than it is that life is our inexhaustible treasure of language for thought. Years are well spent in the country in country labors, in towns, in the insight into trades & manufactures, in intimate intercourse with many men & women, in science, in art, to the one end of mastering in all their facts a language by which to illustrate & speak out our emotions & perceptions. I learn immediately from any speaker

how much he has really learned, through the poverty or the splendor of his speech.

My garden is my dictionary. [Compare "The American Scholar," 1837: W, I, 98.]

JOURNAL AND LECTURE PASSAGES USED IN NATURE

The following table lists passages in *Nature* that grew out of previous formulations of the same material in corresponding passages of Emerson's journals (*JMN*) and early lectures (*EL*). (Page references to *JMN* and *EL* cite the standard editions listed on p. vi above; page references to the text of *Nature* are from the present volume.) It should be noted that Emerson customarily indexed his journals to aid him in bringing together, for lectures and essays, his scattered observations on recurrent topics. Citations given here include the dates of journal passages and the dates of initial delivery of lectures (as determined by the editors of *EL*), thus suggesting the growth of Emerson's ideas over the years. Some parts of *Nature* obviously have a relatively long foreground, as the table readily indicates; other passages *not* appearing in the table were presumably drafted especially for the book—in some instances, to tie together sentences or paragraphs taken from previous journal entries or lectures.

Earlier formulations of material used in Chapter IV of *Nature*, the significant chapter on "Language," are printed here in full to bring out their central importance in Emerson's emerging conception of the book he wanted to write. These key passages, arranged in chronological order, illustrate the growth of pivotal ideas as he gradually worked them out in journal entries and in successive lectures on both scientific and literary subjects. Although journal and lecture materials used in other chapters of *Nature* are not printed here in full, being designated by terminal phrasing only, comparison of the texts in *JMN* and *EL* with the versions appearing in *Nature* itself will reveal significant changes in emphasis and tone as well as in actual wording.

The following symbols appear in passages quoted from *JMN*:

⟨ ⟩	Cancellation
↑ ↓	Insertion
/ /	Variant
[ ]	Editorial insertion
[ ]	Emerson's square brackets

PAGE

INTRODUCTION

5   "Our age . . . history of theirs?" *JMN*, V, 117, January 22–23, 1836: "We ⟨stand⟩ . . . our predecessors[?]" (See Plate I and p. 42 above, item 13.)

5   "the most abstract . . . the most practical." *JMN*, V, 175, June 16, 1836: "The more abstract, the more practical."

5   "*Art* . . . a picture." *JMN*, V, 141, March [?], 1836: "Art . . . with Nature."

CHAPTER I. NATURE

7   "To go . . . great they are!" *JMN*, IV, 266–267, March 2, 1834: "It is very seldom . . . great they are!"

7   "If the stars . . . admonishing smile." *JMN*, V, 73, July 1, 1835: "If the stars . . . admonishing smile."

7   "Nature never . . . of his childhood." "Language of Nature," *JMN*, V, 29–30, April 12–13, 1835: "No man ever . . . his childhood."

7   "Miller owns . . . no title." *JMN*, V, 113, January 16, 1836: "Mr Meriam . . . no property in it."

7   "The sun illuminates . . . heart of the child." *JMN*, IV, 292, May 16, 1834: "The sun illuminates . . . the right place[.]"

7–8 "In the presence . . . glad with me." *JMN*, V, 24–25, March 26, 1835: "The wild delight . . . glad with me."

8   "Nature is . . . mourning piece." *JMN*, V, 17, March 17, 1835: "But nature is . . . ↑mourning↓ piece."

8   "Crossing . . . perfect exhilaration." *JMN*, IV, 355, December 8, 1834: "I rejoice . . . my demeanour."

8   "Almost I fear . . . glad I am." *JMN*, V, 25, March 26, 1835: "Almost I fear . . . glad I am."

8   "In the woods too . . . thousand years." (1) *JMN*, IV, 92, October 21, 1833: "When a man . . . loss of wisdom." (2) "The Uses of Natural History," *EL*, I, 21, November 5, 1833: "I apprehend . . . loss of wisdom." (3) *JMN*, V, 119, February 8, 1836: "That to the lover . . . thousand years."

8   "In the woods, we . . . immortal beauty." *JMN*, V, 18, March 19, 1835: "As I walked . . . beauty & power."

8   "In the tranquil . . . his own nature." *JMN*, V, 189, August 12, 1836: "I went to Walden . . . my own nature."

8   "The greatest delight . . . the vegetable." (1) *JMN*, IV, 406 and (as revised) 199–200, July 13, 1833: "Not a form . . . and man." (2) "The

Uses of Natural History," *EL*, I, 10, November 5, 1833: "not a form . . . and man."

8   "I am not alone . . . doing right." *JMN*, V, 179, June 22, 1836: "↑Yesterday I walked . . . doing right."

CHAPTER II. COMMODITY

10   "They all admit . . . Discipline." *JMN*, V, 146–147, March 27, 1836: "Thus through Nature . . . a discipline. . . ." (See p. 43 above, item 15.)

10   "he realizes the fable . . . of his boat." *JMN*, V, 120, March 3, 1836: "↑Steam realizes . . . in the boiler.↓"

10   "The private poor . . . path for him." *JMN*, V, 145–146, March 22, 1836: "I admire specially . . . path for me."

CHAPTER III. BEAUTY

11   "The ancient Greeks . . . κόσμος, beauty." (1) "The Naturalist," *EL*, I, 83, May 7, 1834: "the early Greeks . . . κόσμος or Beauty. . . ." (2) "Michel Angelo Buonaroti," *EL*, I, 100, January 29, 1835: "The ancient Greeks . . . κόσμος or *Beauty*. . . ." Cf. also *JMN*, V, 133, August 13, 1836: "We think when . . . Κοσμος! Beauty."

11   "This seems partly . . . the eye itself. . . . And as the eye . . . first of painters." *JMN*, V, 172, June 10, 1836: "The pilgrim goes . . . Ear the singer."

11   "There is no . . . make beautiful." *JMN*, IV, 376, December 26, 1834: "There is no . . . make beautiful."

11   "Even the corpse . . . own beauty." *JMN*, V, 140, March 14, 1836: "The wise man . . . its own beauty. . . .'"

11   "endless imitations . . . as the palm." *JMN*, V, 185, July 2, 1836: "Will any say . . . should be beautiful."

11   "For better consideration . . . threefold manner." *JMN*, V, 166, May 31, 1836: "Yesterday in the wood . . . creation of Beauty[.]" (See p. 43 above, item 16).

11   "We are never . . . far enough." (1) *JMN*, IV, 255, January 3, 1834: " 'You never . . . see far.' " (2) *JMN*, V, 45, May 29, 1835: "C[harles]. C[hauncy]. E[merson]. affirms . . . far enough.' " (3) *JMN*, VI, 198, undated entry under "My Proverbs.": "You are never . . . C.C.E."

11–12   "I have seen . . . philosophy and dreams." (1) *JMN*, V, 13, January 15, 1835: "Saw the morn . . . is my Germany." (2) "Michel Angelo

Buonaroti," *EL*, I, 100, February 5, 1835: "the great spectacle of morn and evening. . . ."

12   "Not less excellent . . . mute music." *JMN*, IV, 379–380, December 28, 1834: "But ah . . . mute music."

12   "Go out . . . necessary journey." (1) *JMN*, IV, 288, May 3, 1834: "The moon . . . examined separately." (2) Cf. *JMN*, V, 189, August 12, 1836: "I said once . . . becomes tinsel."

12   "The beauty . . . windows of diligence." *JMN*, V, 96–97, October 15, 1835: "The beauty . . . windows of diligence[.]"

12   "Beauty is . . . upon virtue." (1) *JMN*, III, 147, undated entry of 1828: "Sentiment quotes [from Plutarch, "Of Love"] . . . of Virtue." (2) *JMN*, VI, 199, undated entry under "BEAUTY": " 'Beauty . . . of virtue.' "

13   "Every rational . . . visible sphere." (1) *JMN*, VI, 17, undated entry of 1826: " 'The winds & waves . . . ablest navigators.' " (2) *JMN*, V, 108, November 14, 1835: "each rational . . . inharmonious things." (3) "Modern Aspects of Letters," *EL*, I, 384–385, January 14, 1836: "Every rational . . . citizens of the world." (4) *JMN*, V, 166, May 31, 1836: "The beauty . . . Unconscious Man. . . ." (See p. 43 above, item 16.)

14   "All men . . . nell' uno.' " (1) *JMN*, VI, 200, undated entries under "BEAUTY": " 'The old definition . . . Coleridge, Table Talk, vol 2 p 11." "The love of beauty is taste: the creation of beauty is art. R. W. E." (2) *JMN*, VI, 204, 214, undated entries under "TASTE" and "ART": "Taste is the love of beauty. R W E"; "The love of beauty is Taste; the creation of beauty is Art. R. W. E." (3) "Michel Angelo Buonaroti," *EL*, I, 101–102, February 5, 1835: "What is Beauty? . . . creation of Beauty is Art." (4) "English Literature: Introductory," *EL*, I, 229, November 5, 1835: "Every object . . . his admiration." (5) *JMN*, V, 129–130, undated entry (between entries of February 28 and March 5, 1836; translates passage of Goethe previously drawn upon for #3): " 'The Nature of the Beautiful . . . Creative power[.]' " (6) *JMN*, V, 136–137, March 11, 1836: "Every natural . . . of the Whole."

14   "Nothing is . . . beautiful in the whole." (1) *JMN*, V, 26, March 28, 1835: "Nothing is . . . in the Whole." (2) *JMN*, VI, 201, undated entry under "BEAUTY": "Nothing is . . . in the whole. R. W. E."

14   "Thus is art . . . alembic of man." *JMN*, V, 141, March 14, 1836: "Art is a mixture . . . human mind with Nature."

14   "Beauty, in its . . . satisfactory good." (1) Cf. "Michel Angelo Buonaroti," *EL*, I, 102, February 5, 1835: "He labored . . . faithfully delineated."

(2) Cf. "Michel Angelo Buonaroti," *EL*, I, 110: "He was conscious . . . of Goodness."

CHAPTER IV. LANGUAGE

15   "A third use . . . that of Language."

(1) *JMN*, IV, 95, November 2, 1833:

> Nature is a language & every new fact that we learn is a new word; but rightly seen, taken all together it is not ‹only› ↑merely↓ a language ‹but a scripture which contains the whole truth.› but the language put together into a most significant & universal book. I wish to learn the language not that I may know a new set of nouns & verbs but that I may read the great book which is written in that tongue.

(2) "The Uses of Natural History," *EL*, I, 26, November 5, 1833:

> Nature is a language and every new fact we learn is a new word; but it is not a language taken to pieces and dead in the dictionary, but the language put together into a most significant and universal sense. I wish to learn this language—not that I may know a new grammar but that I may read the great book which is written in that tongue.

15   "The use of natural history . . . type of all influence."

(1) *JMN*, V, 64, July 24–26, 1835:

> All the memorable words of the world are these figurative expressions. Light & heat have passed into all speech for knowledge & love. The river is nothing but as it typifies the flux of time. Many of these signs seem very arbitrary & historical. I should gladly know what gave such universal acceptance to Cupid's arrow for the passion of love; & more meanly the horn for the shame of cuckoldom.

(2) *JMN*, V, 66–68, July 27–29, 1835, copied from a manuscript transla-tion—presumably Elizabeth Peabody's—of "G. Oegger's True Messiah [*Le Vraie Messie* (Paris, 1829)] or O[ld]. & N[ew]. Testaments examined acc[ording to]. the principles of the language of nature":

> "By the creation we only have been enabled to perceive a portion of the ↑infinite↓ riches ‹burie› eternally buried in the Div[ine]. ‹mind›Es-sense. . . . Every thing that we see, touch, smell . . . has flowed forth by a supreme reason from that world where all is spirit & life. No fibre in the animal, no blade of grass in the vegetable, no form of crystallization in inanimate matter, is without its clear & well deter-mined correspondence in the moral & metaphysical world. . . .
>
> "And indeed but for all these emblems of life which creation offers, there would be no appreciable moral idea or moral sentiment, no pos-sible means . . . for God to communicate a thought, an affection to

his creature any more than for one feeling creature to communicate it to another. . . .

"Do but take a dictionary of morals & examine the terms in it: you will see that all of them from the first to the last are derived from corporeal & animal life. &c. & but for those emblems furnished by nature herself the moral & metaphysical world would have remained entirely buried in the eternal abyss. . . .

"The passage from the language of nature to languages of convention was made by such insensible degrees that they who made it never thought of tracing the latter back to their source. They knew not the road they had travelled but the distance appeared striking when they became attentive to it. Primitively men could not name objects they must show them; not corporeally it is true but substantially & by the force of thought as those objects exist in God & as we still perceive them in dreams in which there is evidently something more than imagination   [See S[ampson]. Reed's oration on Genius.]"

(3) "English Literature: Introductory," *EL*, I, 220–221, November 5, 1835:

But the objects without him are more than commodities. Whilst they minister to the senses sensual gratification, they minister to the mind as vehicles and symbols of thought. All language is a naming of invisible and spiritual things from visible things. The use of natural history is to give us aid in supernatural history. The use of the outer creation is to give us language for the beings and changes of the inward creation. Every word which is used to express a moral or intellectual fact, if traced to its root, is found to be borrowed from some corporeal or animal fact. *Right* originally means *straight*; *wrong* means *twisted*. Spirit primarily means *wind*. Transgression, the *crossing a line*. Supercilious, the *raising of the eyebrow*. Light and heat in all languages are used as metaphors for wisdom and love. We say the heart to express emotion; the head to denote thought: and "thought" and "emotion" are in their turn mere words borrowed from sense, that have become appropriated to spiritual nature. Most of this process is now hidden from us in the remote time when our language was framed, but the same tendency we may observe now in children and in new words. Children and savages use only nouns or names of things, and continually convert them into verbs, and then apply them to some analogous mental act. Every truth we can learn concerning our Ideas, we find some symbol for, in outward nature, before we can express it in words. "And but for these emblems furnished by Nature herself, the moral and metaphysical world would have remained entirely buried in the eternal abyss." [Emerson's note: "Oeggr" (*sic*).]

But this origin of all words that convey a spiritual meaning is only a small part of the fact. It is not words only that are emblematic: it is things which are emblematic. Every fact in outward nature answers to some state of the mind and that state of the mind can only be described by presenting that natural fact as a picture. A fierce man is a lion; a brave man is a rock; a learned man is a torch. Light and Darkness are not in words but in fact our best expression for knowledge and ignorance. Who looks upon a river in a meditative hour, and is not reminded of the flux of all things? Throw a stone into the stream, and the circles that propagate themselves, are the beautiful type of all influence.

(4) "Shakspear [first lecture]," EL, I, 289, December 10, 1835:

The power of the Poet depends on the fact that the material world is a symbol or expression of the human mind and part for part. Every natural fact is a symbol of some spiritual fact. Light and darkness are our familiar expression for knowledge and ignorance and heat for love. Who looks upon a river in a meditative hour and is not reminded of the flux of all things? Throw a stone into the stream and the circles that propagate themselves are the beautiful type of all influence.

15 "This universal soul . . . property and men." "Of the Nature of the Mind," JMN, V, 271–272, June, 1835:

Reason is the superior principle. Its attributes are Eternity & Intuition. We belong to it, not it to us.

15 "And the blue sky . . . type of Reason." JMN, V, 172–173, June 10, 1836:

The moral influence of nature is that amount of truth which it illustrates to the mind. Who can estimate this? The visible sky ⟨seems to be the true type of⟩ in which the ball of earth is buried with its eternal calm & ⟨the⟩ filled with lights seems to be .the true type of the Eternal Reason into which we are born & the truths which revolve therein.

16 "And man in all ages . . . other being to him."

(1) "The Naturalist," EL, I, 71, May 7, 1834:

But it is the wonderful charm of external nature that man stands in a central connexion with it all; not at the head, but in the midst: and not an individual in the kingdom of organized life but sends out a ray of relation to him.

(2) "English Literature: Introductory," EL, I, 221, November 5, 1835:

It certainly will not be alleged that there is anything fanciful in this analogy between man and nature. . . .

(3) "Shakspear [first lecture]," *EL*, I, 290, December 10, 1835:
The more attention is bestowed on this subject the more clearly it is seen that there is nothing lucky or capricious in these analogies but that they are constant and pervade nature.

(4) *JMN*, V, 138, March 21, 1836:
Man is an analogist.

(5) *JMN*, V, 146, March 27, 1836:
Man is an analogist. He cannot help seeing every thing under its relations to all other things & to himself. The most conspicuous example of this habit of his mind is his naming the Deity Father.

16   "All the facts . . . become sublime."
(1) *JMN*, IV, 311, August 15, 1834:
Natural history by itself has no value; it is like a single sex. But marry it to human history, & it is poetry. ‹at once.› Whole Floras, all Linnaeus' & Buffon's volumes contain not one line of poetry, but the meanest natural fact, the habit of a plant, the ‹noise› ↑organs,↓ or work, ↑or noise↓ of an insect applied to ↑the interpretation [of] or even associated   [with] a fact in human nature is beauty, is poetry, is truth at once.

(2) "English Literature: Introductory," *EL*, I, 221, November 5, 1835:
All the facts in Natural History taken by themselves have no value, but are barren and unfruitful like a single sex. But marry it to human history and it is full of life. Whole Floras, all Linnaeus' and Buffon's volumes are but dry catalogues of facts; but the most trivial natural property, the habit of a plant, the organs or work or noise of an insect applied to the illustration of a fact in intellectual philosophy or even associated to human nature affects us in the most lively and agreeable manner.

(3) "Shakspear [first lecture]," *EL*, I, 289–290, December 10, 1835:
All the facts in natural history taken by themselves have no value but are barren like a single sex but marry it to human history and it is full of life. Whole Floras, all Linnaeus' and Buffon's volumes are but dry catalogues of facts but the most trivial of these facts, the habit of a plant, the organs, the work, or noise of an insect applied to the illustration of a fact in intellectual philosophy or in any way associated to human nature affects us in the most lively and agreeable manner. The seed of a plant;—to what affecting analogies in the nature of man is that little fruit made use of through all conversation up to the voice of Paul who calls the human corpse a seed. "It is sown a natural body; it is raised a spiritual body." The motion of the earth round its axis

and round the sun makes the day and the year. These are certain amounts of brute light and heat. But is there no intent of an analogy between man's life and the seasons? and do the seasons gain no grandeur or pathos from that analogy? The instincts of the ant are very unimportant considered as the ant's but the moment a ray of relation is seen to extend from it to man, and the mite is seen to be a monitor, a little body with a mighty heart, then all its habits even that recently observed that it never sleeps become sublime.

16   "Because of this . . . elements of all languages." "English Literature: Introductory," *EL*, I, 221, November 5, 1835:

It certainly will not be alleged that there is anything fanciful in this analogy between man and nature, when it is remembered that savages converse by these figures. In the writers in the morning of each nation such as Homer, Froissart, and Chaucer every word is a picture. As we go back in history, language becomes more picturesque, until its infancy, when it is all poetry; or, all spiritual facts are represented by natural symbols. The eldest remains of the ancient nations are poems and fables.

16   "This immediate dependence . . . all men relish."

(1) "The Naturalist," *EL*, I, 71, May 7, 1834:

The imagery in discourse which delights all men is that which is drawn from observation of natural processes. It is this which gives that piquancy to the conversation of a strong-minded farmer or backwoodsman which all men relish.

(2) "English Literature: Introductory," *EL*, I, 222, November 5, 1835:

The imagery in discourse which delights all men is that which is drawn from observation of natural processes. It is this which gives that piquancy to the conversation of a strong natured farmer or backwoodsman which all men relish.

17   "The moment our discourse . . . perpetual allegories."

(1) *JMN*, V, 63, July 24–26, 1835:

Good writing & brilliant conversation are perpetual allegories.

(2) *JMN*, V, 78, August 2, 1835:

And I suppose that any man who will watch his ⟨pr⟩ intellectual process will find ⟨an image⟩ a material image cotemporaneous with ⟨his⟩ ↑every↓ thought & furnishing the garment of the thought.

(3) "English Literature: Introductory," *EL*, I, 221, November 5, 1835:

And even now, in our artificial state of society, the moment our discourse rises above the ordinary tone of facts, and is inflamed with passion, or exalted by thought, it immediately clothes itself in images. Indeed if any man will watch himself in conversation, I believe he will find he has always a material image more or less luminous arising in his mind contemporaneous with every thought, [which] furnishes the garment of the thought.

(4) "Shakspear [first lecture]," *EL*, I, 290, December 10, 1835:
The moment our discourse rises above the region of familiar facts and is inflamed with passion or exalted by thought, it clothes itself in images. A man conversing in earnest, if he watch his intellectual process will find that always a material image more or less luminous arises in his mind cotemporaneous with every thought which furnishes the garment of the thought. Hence good writing and brilliant discourse are perpetual allegories.

18   "Parts of speech . . . fables, parables, and allegories."
(1) *JMN*, II, 104, March 18 [?], 1823:
"Vinegar is the Son of Wine."

(2) *JMN*, III, 124, March 28, 1828:
"A cripple in the right way will beat a racer in the wrong." (From Bacon, *The Advancement of Learning*.)

(3) *JMN*, III, 192, July 24, 1830:
. . . as a cripple in the right way will beat a racer in the wrong.

(4) *JMN*, VI, 138–141, undated entries under *"Proverbs"*:
Vinegar is the Son of Wine[.]
. . . .
The rolling stone gathers no moss[.]
. . . .
The last ounce broke the camel's back.
. . . .
A world in the hand is worth two in the bush.
. . . .
' 'Tis hard to carry a full cup even.' *Leighton*
. . . .
'A cripple in the right way will beat a racer in the wrong'
. . . .
"Durable trees make roots first"

(5) *JMN*, III, 255, May 20, 1831:
Not a mathematical axiom but is a moral rule, as [Mme] De Stael has wisely noted. [*Germany*, 1813, III, 151: "Almost all the axioms of physics correspond with the maxims of morals."]

(6) *JMN*, IV, 33, July 15–August 10, 1832:
   Swedenborg "considered the visible world & ↑the relation of↓ its parts as the dial plate of the invisible one." quoted in N[ew]. J[erusalem]. M[agazine]. for July 1832 p. 437[,] [Vol. V, "Emanuel Swedenborg."]

(7) *JMN*, VI, 219, undated entries under "NATURE":
   "The axioms of geometry translate the laws of ethics."

   Most proverbs are significant merely by giving an indefinite extension as a truth in human life, to a trivial natural fact; as 'The rolling stone gathers no moss.' [R.W.E.]

. . . .

   "The visible world is the dial plate of the invisible" Swedenborg.

(8) "The Uses of Natural History," *EL*, I, 24–25, November 5, 1833:
   We not only speak in continual metaphors of the morn, the noon and the evening of life, of dark and bright thoughts, of sweet and bitter moments, of the healthy mind and the fading memory; but all our most literal and direct modes of speech—as right and wrong, form and substance, honest and dishonest etc., are, when hunted up to their original signification, found to be metaphors also. And this, because the whole of Nature is a metaphor or image of the human Mind. The laws of moral nature answer to those of matter as face to face in a glass. "The visible world," it has been well said, "and the relations of its parts is the dial plate of the invisible one." In the language of the poet,

> For all that meets the bodily sense I deem
> Symbolical, one mighty alphabet
> For infant minds. [Coleridge, "The Destiny of Nations"]

It is a most curious fact that the axioms of geometry and of mechanics only translate the laws of ethics. Thus, A straight line is the shortest distance between two points; The whole is greater than its part; The smallest weight may be made to lift the greatest, the difference of force being compensated by time; Reaction is equal to action; and a thousand the like propositions which have an ethical as well as a material sense. They are true not only in geometry but in life; they have a much more extensive and universal signification as applied to human nature than when confined to technical use. And every common proverb is only one of these facts in nature used as a picture or parable of a more extensive truth; as when we say, "A bird in the hand is worth two in the bush." "A rolling stone gathers no moss." " 'Tis hard to carry a full cup even." "Whilst the grass grows the steed starves."—In themselves these are insignificant facts but we repeat them because they are symbolical of moral truths.

(9) *JMN*, IV, 254–255, January 2, 1834:
    It occurs that a selection of natural laws might be easily made from botany, hydraulics, natural philosophy, &c. which should at once express also an ethical sense. Thus, 'Water confined in pipes will always rise as high as its source'. 'A hair line of water is a balance for the ocean if its fount be as high'. "Durable trees make roots first," C[harles]. reads. A cripple in the right road beats a racer in the wrong ↑road↓. "Fractures well cured make us more strong." Action & reaction are equal. Concentrated nourishment is unhealthy; there must be mixture of excrement.

(10) "Shakspear [first lecture]," *EL*, I, 290, December 10, 1835:
    This omnipresent analogy of the visible to the invisible world itself opens so wide a field of inquiry that I can at present only indicate its borders. But the laws of moral nature answer to those of matter as face to face in a glass. The axioms of physics translate the laws of ethics: the whole is greater than a part; reaction is equal to action; the smallest weight may be made to lift the greatest, the difference of weight being compensated by time; and the like, which have an ethical as well as physical sense. Observe too these propositions have a much more extensive and universal sense when applied to human life than when confined to technical use. In like manner the memorable words of history and the proverbs of nations consist usually of a natural fact selected as a picture or parable of moral truth. Thus, "A rolling stone gathers no moss;" "A bird in the hand is worth two in the bush;" "A cripple in the right way will beat a racer in the wrong;" " 'Tis hard to carry a full cup even;" "Vinegar is the son of wine;" "The last ounce broke the camel's back;" "Long lived trees make roots first;" and the like. In their primary sense these are trivial facts but we repeat them for the value of their analogical import.

18   "This relation . . . not blind and deaf. . . ."
(1) *JMN*, V, 103, October 28, 1835:
    Plotinus says of the intuitive knowledge that "it is not lawful to inquire whence it sprang as if it were a thing subject to place & motion for it neither approached hither nor again departs from hence, to some other place, but it either appears to us, or it does not appear." [Quoted by Coleridge, *Biographia Literaria*.] Every man in his moment of reflection sees & records this vision & therefore feels the insufferable impertinence of contradiction from the unthinking as if had uttered a

⟨mere⟩ ↑⟨bare⟩↓ private opinion or caprice & not made himself a ⟨mere⟩ ↑bare↓ pipe for better wisdom to flow through.

(2) "English Literature: Introductory," *EL*, I, 226, November 5, 1835:
It is in the nature not of any particular man but of universal man to *think*; though the action of reflexion is very rare. The relation between thought and the world, of which I have spoken, is not fancied by some poet, but stands in the will of God, and so is free to be known by all men. It appears to men, or it does not appear. But there it is. He who perceives it, and every man, whilst he perceives it, is a poet, is a philosopher. To perceive it, is to take one's stand in the absolute, and consider the passage of things and events purely as a spectacle and not as action in which we partake. This the poet, this the philosopher, this the historian does. The habit of men is to rest in the objects immediately around them, to go along with the tide, and take their impulse from external things. The Thinker takes them aside and makes them see what they did as *in dumb show*.

(3) "Shakspear [first lecture]," *EL*, I, 290, December 10, 1835:
The more attention is bestowed on this subject the more clearly it is seen that there is nothing lucky or capricious in these analogies but that they are constant and pervade nature. This relation between thought and the world is not fancied by some poet but stands in the will of God. It appears to men or it does not appear but there it is. All men sometimes perceive it.

18   "for the universe . . . shines through it."
(1) *JMN*, IV, 96, November 2, 1833:
To an instructed eye the universe is transparent. The light of higher laws than its own shines through it.

(2) *JMN*, VI, 219, an undated entry under "NATURE":
The Universe is transparent; the light of higher laws than its own, shines through it. [R.W.E.]

18   "It is the standing problem . . . reading her riddle."
(1) *JMN*, V, 76, August 1, 1835:
There sits the Sphinx from age to age, in the road Charles [Emerson] says[,] & every wise man ⟨in turn⟩ ↑that comes by↓ has a crack at her.

(2) "English Literature: Introductory," *EL*, I, 224, November 5, 1835:
It is the standing problem which has exercised the wonder and the study of every fine genius since the world began, from the Egyptians and the Brahmins, through Pythagoras, to Plato, to Bacon, to Leibnitz and Swedenborg. There sits the Sphinx at the roadside and from age

to age as each prophet comes by, he tries his fortune at reading her riddle.

18   "A Fact . . . moral side."

(1) *JMN*, V, 66, July 27–29, 1835, copied from a manuscript translation of Oegger's "The True Messiah":

"People suppose that when God produced our visible world the choice that he made of forms & colours for animals, plants, & minerals was entirely arbitrary on his part. This is false. Man may sometimes act from whim; God never can. The visible creation then cannot must not (if we may use such expressions) be anything but the exterior circumference of the invisible & metaphysical world, & material objects are necessarily kinds of scoriae of the substantial thoughts of the Creator; scoriae which must always preserve an exact relation to their first origin; in other words visible nature must have a spiritual & moral side."

(2) *JMN*, V, 176, June 16, 1836:

. . . This also shows how transparent all things are & show God through every part & angle. . . .

. . . Hence doubtless that secret value we attach to facts that interest us ⟨well⟩ much beyond their seeming importance. We think it frivolous to record them, but a wise man records them & they agree with ·the experience & feelings of others. ↑They no doubt are points in this curve of the great circle[.]↓

(3) *JMN*, V, 177, June 17, 1836:

A fact is only a fulcrum of the spirit. It is the terminus of a past thought but only a means now to new sallies of the imagination & new progress of wisdom. . . .

A fact we said was the terminus of spirit. A man, I, am the remote circumference, the skirt, the thin suburb or frontier post of God but go inward & I find the ocean; I lose my individuality in its waves. God is Unity, but always works in variety. I go inward until I find Unity universal, that Is before the World was; I come outward to this body a point of variety.

(4) *JMN*, V, 178, June 22, 1836:

Mr [A. Bronson] Alcott has been here with his Olympian dreams. He is a world-builder. Ever more he toils to solve the problem, Whence is the World? . . . Particulars,—particular thoughts, sentences, facts even, cannot interest him except as for a moment they take their place as a ray from his orb. The Whole,—Nature proceeding from himself, is what he studies. . . . He made here some majestic utterances but so inspired me that even I forgot the words often. The grass[,] the ⟨animals⟩ earth seemed to him "the refuse of spirit."

18–19   " 'Every scripture . . . gave it forth.' "
(1) *JMN*, IV, 31, July 15–August 10, 1832:
George Fox born 1624 son of a weaver was put out to a shoemaker & for him tended sheep. In   he began his wanderings dressed always in leather clothing for strength's sake & suffering much from hunger, thirst, want of lodging, imprisonment, & abuse. He taught 'that the Ss [Sacred Scriptures] could not be understood but by the same spirit that gave them forth.'

(2) "George Fox," *EL*, I, 170, February 26, 1835:
After this he was inwardly made sensible of Christ's sufferings; then, that not all called Christians were Christians; that to be bred at Oxford or Cambridge was not enough to make a minister of Christ; that believers needed no man to teach them but the anointing in man teacheth them; that the Scriptures cannot be understood but by the same spirit that gave them forth. . . .

(3) "On the Best Mode of Inspiring a Correct Taste in English Literature," *EL*, I, 210–211, August 20, 1835:
I see nothing to hinder us from accepting the general conviction of men that we cannot make scholars. They must be born.
Admitting this fact, which being expressed in other words is a canon of philosophy, that a truth or a book of truths can be received only by the same spirit that gave it forth, . . . I know few more agreeable offices . . . than to introduce a good mind to the writings of a kindred intelligence. It must be our main object to consummate this marriage between the mind of the scholar and the mind of the author. Literature resembles religion in many respects and their fortunes have been commonly related. It must be possessed by the man or it is naught.

19   "A new interest . . . magazine of power." *JMN*, V, 189, August 12, 1836:
⟨Every⟩ The reason of the variety & infinity of objects is given in the doctrine that external objects are mere signs of internal essences. Therefore "every object rightly seen unlocks a new faculty of the Soul." [Coleridge, *Aids to Reflection*.] That is to say, it becomes a part of the domain of Consciousness; before it was unconscious truth; now is available Knowledge.

CHAPTER V. DISCIPLINE

19   "Nature is a discipline . . . they be executed!' " (1) *JMN*, III, 299, October 27, 1831, citing Coleridge on method as "progressive arrangement"

(*The Friend* or "Preliminary Treatise on Method"). (2) "Of the Nature of the Mind," *JMN*, V, 272, June, 1835: "The Understanding is the executive faculty, ↑the hand of the mind↓." (3) *JMN*, V, 114, January 22, 1836: "A man is a method; a progressive arrangement. . . ." (4) *JMN*, V, 136, March 9, 1836: "How important is . . . good thoughts . . . they be executed." (Cf. Bacon, "Of Great Place": "For good thoughts . . . are little better than good dreams, except they be put in act. . . .")

19 "Debt, grinding debt . . . suffer from it most." *JMN*, V, 176, June 16, 1836: "Debt makes a large part of our education."

20 "The whole character . . . laws are known." (1) *JMN*, V, 124–125, February 24, 1836: "For the education . . . laws are known." (2) *JMN*, V, 134–135, March 5, 1836: "Gradation; that is . . . call the best."

20 "The exercise of . . . to his character." *JMN*, V, 174, June 14, 1836: "Power is one . . . must he learn[.]"

20 "It is made . . . what is useful." *JMN*, V, 125, February 24–27, 1836: "Nature ‹bec› from . . . becomes a spectacle."

21 "Nothing in nature . . . its first use." (1) *JMN*, V, 184, June 29, 1836: "Nature is yet far from being exhausted." (2) *JMN*, V, 185, July 2, 1836: "Will any say . . . single natural process?"

21 "It has already . . . moral sentence." (1) *JMN*, III, 255, May 20, 1831: "Not a mathematical axiom but is a moral rule, as De Stael has wisely noted [*Germany*: "Almost all the axioms of physics correspond with the maxims of morals."]." (2) *JMN*, IV, 326: "All around us . . . are hid . . . sublimest laws. De Stael saw them."

21 "What is a farm . . . in the fields." *JMN*, V, 177, June 17, 1836: "What is a farm . . . to the last."

21 "The moral influence . . . estimate this?" *JMN*, V, 172, June 10, 1836: "The moral influence . . . estimate this?"

21–22 "Herein is especially . . . innumerable sides." (1) *JMN*, IV, 40, September 14, 1832: " 'Architecture reminds me of frozen music' De Stael [*Corinne*]." (2) *JMN*, IV, 75, June 10, 1833: "Architecture[,] said the lady[,] is frozen music." (3) *JMN*, IV, 337, November 16–18, 1834: "And Mme. De Stael's . . . 'Architecture . . . music,' borrowed from Goethe's '. . . dumb music,' borrowed from Vitruvius, . . . 'the Architect must . . . understand . . . Music'." (4) *JMN*, IV, 367–368, December 21 or 22, 1834: "Vitruvius . . . Music; and M. Angelo said . . . that he who did not understand . . . anatomy . . . could know nothing of that subject." (5) *JMN*, VI, 191, undated entry under "TRUTH": " 'Omne verum vero consonat.' " Translated in *JMN*, IV, 376, December 27, 1834: "We say every truth supposes or implies every other truth." (6) *JMN*, V, 36, May 10 or 12, 1835: "[Coleridge said,] A Gothic Church was a petrified religion." (7) *JMN*, V, 136, 137, March 11, 1836: "All is in Each. . . . expression of this."

22 "The same central Unity . . . is done rightly.' " (1) *JMN*, IV, 75, June 10, 1833 (paraphrasing Carlyle's translation of Goethe's *Wilhelm Meister*): "And Iarno says . . . that he . . . who does the best ⟨does⟩ in each one thing he does, does all. For he sees the connexion between all good things." (2) *JMN*, V, 128, between entries for February 28 and March 5, 1836 (translated by Emerson from Goethe, *Werke*): ". . . and the highest . . . done rightly[.]" (3) *JMN*, V, 137, March 11, 1836: "More sublimely . . . is done rightly.' "

23 "We are associated . . . a short time." *JMN*, V, 174, June 14, 1836: "Have you been associated . . . withdrawn from your sight." (The probable reference is to Emerson's brother Charles, who had died on May 9, 1836.)

CHAPTER VI. IDEALISM

24 "When the eye of Reason . . . before its God." *JMN*, V, 123, February 24, 1836: "Religion does . . . seen through them."

24–25 "We are strangely . . . these twenty years!" (1) *JMN*, IV, 277, April 15, 1834: "The least change . . . takes place at once.—" (2) *JMN*, IV, 323, September 17, 1834: "⟨T⟩Make a very . . . woodhouse & barnyard. See p. 33[.]" (3) *JMN*, V, 26, March 28, 1835: "A wonderful sight . . . pictorial appearance." (4) "English Literature: Introductory," *EL*, I, 226–227, November 5, 1835: "Even a small . . . these twenty years!"

25 ". . . the poet communicates . . . in his mind." (1) "English Literature: Introductory," *EL*, I, 224, November 5, 1835: "Especially is it . . . explain his meaning." (2) *JMN*, VI, 227, undated entries under "Imagination": " '. . . the power of feigning things according to nature.' *Hazlitt*." ". . . the use which Reason makes of Nature for purposes of expression. R. W. E." (3) "Shakspear [first lecture]," *EL*, I, 292, December 10, 1835: "Shakspear possesses . . . in his mind."

25–26 "Take those lips away . . . lie foul and muddy." "Shakspear [first lecture]," *EL*, I, 292–293, December 10, 1835: "What can exceed . . . lie foul and muddy."

26   " 'The problem . . . Plato . . . unconditioned and absolute.' " *JMN*, VI, 202, undated entry under "PHILOSOPHY": " 'The problem . . . Plato . . . to a system.' " (Quoted from Coleridge, *The Friend*.)

27   "Thus even in physics . . . before the spiritual." *JMN*, V, 183, June 24–28, 1836: "Then it occurs . . . of Spirit evermore."

27   "The sublime remark . . . yet is true. . . ." (1) *JMN*, IV, 327, October 27, 1834: "Euler's truth against all experience." (From Coleridge, *Aids to Reflection*.) (2) *JMN*, IV, 332, November 1, 1834: "Euler having . . . doubting its truth.' "

27   "Finally, religion and ethics . . . ideas into life. . . ." *JMN*, V, 146, March 27, 1836: "Ethics again . . . ↑to live↓ Ideas[.]"

27   "The first and last . . . unseen are eternal." *JMN*, V, 125, February 24–27, 1836: "The first . . . unseen, eternal."

27   "It does that . . . Berkeley and Viasa." *JMN*, V, 123, February 24, 1836: "Religion does that . . . Berkel⟨y⟩ey & Viasa. . . ."

27–28   " 'Contemn the insubstantial . . . his body." (1) *JMN*, III, 251, April 25, 1831: "Plotinus . . . in corpore . . . σωματι ειη—Porphyry. Vita Plot[inus]." (2) "Shakspear [first lecture]," *EL*, I, 299, December 10, 1835: "Porphyry relates . . . Plotinus . . . had a body. . . ." (3) *JMN*, V, 145, March 21, 1836: "Under strong . . . contemn the body."

28   "In short, they . . . called into time." (1) "Michel Angelo Buonaroti," *EL*, I, 110, February 5, 1835: "He [Michelangelo, in Sonnet LI] spoke . . . called into Time.' " (2) *JMN*, V, 178, June 17–20, 1835: "Matter is . . . called into time.' "

28   "I have no hostility . . . connexion with nature." (1) *JMN*, V, 123–124, February 24, 1836: "I have no ⟨hostility⟩ . . . of viewing them." (2) *JMN*, V, 146, March 22, 1836: "It is a small . . . sovereignty of Ideas[.]"

28   "Children, it is . . . did the first." *JMN*, V, 172, June 10, 1836: "Certainly children . . . did the first faith[.]"

28   "Idealism sees . . . world in God." *JMN*, V, 149, April 2, 1836: "In these Uses . . . viewed in God."

28   "It sees something . . . the better watch." *JMN*, V, 135, March 5, 1836: "I have no curiosity . . . canst yet impart."

CHAPTER VII. SPIRIT

28 "It is essential . . . somewhat progressive." *JMN*, V, 182, June 24–28, 1836: "It is essential . . . to the Deity."

30 "It always speaks . . . sun behind us." *JMN*, V, 171, June 7, 1836: "The Use of Nature . . . an unseen Sun."

30 "The aspect of Nature . . . lesson of worship." (1) *JMN*, V, 149, April 2, 1836: "This which looks . . . use of Nature is worship." (2) *JMN*, V, 154, May 16–18, 1836: "He [Charles Emerson] thought Christianity . . . not the crucifixion."

31 "Therefore, that spirit . . . pores of the old." *JMN*, V, 187, July 30, 1836: "The self of self . . . surface in my body[.]"

31 "The world proceeds . . . sight of men." (1) *JMN*, V, 184, June 29, 1836: "Nature is the projection . . . in the field." (2) *JMN*, V, 82, August 5, 1835: "The birds fly . . . man & nature."

CHAPTER VIII. PROSPECTS

32 "In a cabinet . . . beast, fish, and insect." (1) *JMN*, IV, 405–406, July 13, 1833: "Cabinet . . . be a naturalist.'" (2) *JMN*, IV, 198–200, July 13, 1833: "I carried my ticket . . . be a naturalist.'" (3) "The Uses of Natural History," *EL*, I, 8–10, November 5, 1833: "The Cabinet . . . be a naturalist."

32 "The American . . . invisible archetype." *JMN*, IV, 75, June 10, 1833: "Architecture,—shall I . . . the little Imp."

32 "Nor has science . . . sufficient humanity. . . ." (1) Cf. *JMN*, V, 168–169, June 4 [?], 1836: "Here are two . . . studied humanly." (2) "Humanity of Science," *EL*, II, 22–40, December 22, 1836, follows the outline given in (1) and incorporates phrases from it; the first two paragraphs of "Prospects" anticipate the lecture.

32–33 "A perception . . . poem on Man . . . to attend him.'" (1) *JMN*, III, 255, May 20, 1831, quotes lines 17–18 of Herbert's "Man." (2) *JMN*, VI, 103, undated entry, quotes lines 13–18, 22, 47–48.

33 "In view of . . . truth than history.'" (1) *JMN*, III, 314, December 20, 1831, two quotations copied from *The Edinburgh Review:* "'Action comes less near to vital truth than description' Plato Republic B[ook]. V"; "'Poetry is something more philosophical & excellent than history.' Aristotle Poet[ics]. c. 10." (2) *JMN*, VI, 173, undated entries under "POETRY" repeat the quotations, in reverse order. (3) *JMN*, IV, 261, February 3,

1834: ". . . as Plato would say, more true than history." (4) *JMN*, IV, 329, October 29, 1834: "For said not Aristotle Action is less near to vital truth than description?"

33   " 'We distrust . . . like an ox." *JMN*, V, 179, June 22, 1836: "We distrust . . . like an ox."

33   " 'A man is a god . . . return to paradise." *JMN*, V, 181, June 22, 1836: "A man is a god . . . return to paradise."

33–34   " 'Man is the dwarf . . . in-streaming causing power." *JMN*, V, 179–180, June 22, 1836: "↑Man is the dwarf . . . in-streaming causing power."

34   "The difference between . . . *matutina cognitio*." (1) *JMN*, VI, 179, undated entry under "GOD": "The schoolmen said . . . Matutina Cognitio. [*John*] Norris." (2) *JMN*, V, 141, March 14–16, 1836: "For Lect[ure]. I . . . Matutina & Vespertina Cognitio[.]"

34–35   "He cannot be a naturalist . . . light of the understanding." "The Naturalist," *EL*, I, 79, May 7, 1834: "This instinct is . . . in the dissection."

35   "Is not prayer . . . without learning something." *JMN*, V, 182, June 24, 1836: "Is it not plain . . . without learning something."

35   "What is a day? . . . What is sleep?" *JMN*, V, 183, June 24, 1836: "Insist upon . . . say to ME?"

35   "We make fables . . . beautiful of fables." *JMN*, V, 175, June 16, 1836: "We fable . . . beautiful of fables."

35   "It were a wise . . . ideas in the mind." *JMN*, V, 175, June 14, 1836: "It were a wise . . . Ideas in us[.]"

35–37   " 'Nature is not fixed . . . to perfect sight.' " (1) *JMN*, V, 180, June 22, 1836: "↑The kingdom of man . . . wind dry up." (2) *JMN*, V, 182–183, June 24, 1836: "It is essential . . . to perfect sight."

HISTORY OF THE TEXT

The 1836 edition of *Nature* has often been described in Carlyle's phrase as a "little azure-coloured" volume; critics of *Nature* from Thomas Wentworth Higginson through Oliver Wendell Holmes to Edward Emerson have repeatedly stated that the anonymous first edition was restricted to 500 copies, many of which supposedly "remained long unsold, so that a second edition was not called for until 1849," as Edward Emerson wrote in the Centenary Edition of his father's works (W, I, 400). But on both counts the record needs correction. *Nature* first appeared not only in an "azure" binding but also in deep blue, dull blue, light brown, dark brown, and green. As for its initial sale, we have Emerson's own testimony that "500 copies were gone" within a month of its publication; "for a book purely literary or philosophical," in his words, this was "a good deliverance" (item 26, p. 45 above).

There is evidence that Emerson had brought out his first book at his own risk and expense, as he did his later works, probably giving its nominal publisher, James Munroe and Company, a commission of 30% to oversee details of printing, binding, and sales (cf. L, III, 307–308, 350–351). In July of 1836, when he inquired in Boston about printing his manuscript as it then stood, he was furnished an estimate of approximately $100 (item 20, p. 44 above); the actual cost of the longer final version is not noted in the Emerson papers. The book appeared on September 9 or 10, 1836, with Munroe's imprint; the Cambridge Press of Metcalf, Torry, & Ballou had done the printing, which had caused Emerson some vexation (item 23, p. 44 above), and B. Bradley the binding. If the printing order was like that for the Essays of 1841, there was a run of 1500 copies; the printing was probably from type metal rather than from stereotype plates, with around 1000 copies bound initially and the remainder left in sheets to be bound as needed. Emerson's accounts with Munroe, in the Harvard College Library, record charges for binding 496 copies between the end of March 1837 and the close of 1842; as for sales, none are listed after 1844, when 23 copies were reported on hand as the year began. The inference is that the first edition remained in sheets for some eight years, from 1836 until 1844. With the standing type long ago dispersed, no more copies could be printed except in a new edition.

Meanwhile in England, where Emerson's fame was spreading, Nature and other early writings were being pirated by several publishers; Emerson not only received none of the profits but he was denied the opportunity to correct or revise the English texts. Before the second American edition appeared in 1849 there were six unauthorized English printings of Nature, beginning in 1841.[1] By 1844, according to a

[1] The following editions or issues of Nature appeared in America and abroad between 1836 and 1849:

Nature. Boston: James Munroe and Company, 1836.

"The Religious Philosophy of Nature," in D. G. Goyder, ed., The Biblical Assistant, and Book of Practical Piety. London: W. Newbery; Manchester, Liverpool, Glasgow, and Boston, 1841.

Nature: An Essay. And Orations. London: William Smith, 1844. (Published in December 1843.)

Nature, An Essay; And Lectures on the Times. London: Henry G. Clarke & Co., 1844.

Nature: An Essay. To Which is Added, Orations, Lectures, Addresses. London: Aylott and Jones, 1845.

Essays, Lectures & Orations. London: Wm. S. Orr and Co., 1848.

Essays, Orations and Lectures. London: William Tegg & Co., 1848.

Nature; Addresses and Lectures. Boston & Cambridge: James Munroe and Co., 1849.

Nature (New Edition). Boston & Cambridge: James Munroe & Company, 1849.

bookseller's report relayed to Emerson by Theodore Parker, "between 5000 & 6000" copies of Emerson's writings, *Nature* included, "had already been sold" in Great Britain (*L*, III, 287, note 30). Later in the same year Emerson wrote to the London publisher John Chapman, who had proposed an authorized collection of his fugitive works, that he was unwilling "to have them reprinted without a careful revision & correction by myself: which . . . I may undertake. But I doubt —Old pieces are not sufficiently attractive to me to seem worth the labor" (*L*, III, 274). In May of 1845, taking note of a particular English piracy, that by William Smith, Emerson acknowledged to Chapman that he "must take some thought for the collecting & the correcting of these things," hoping "soon to send . . . some reasonable word concerning it" (*L*, III, 288), but other commitments evidently received higher priority.

Finally, in May of 1849, Emerson was able to report with some satisfaction, in a letter to his brother William, "I am just reprinting my first little book of 'Nature' with various 'Orations, lectures,' &c. that have not been collected here before, into a volume of the size of the Essays, and it gives me a chance to make many important corrections" (*L*, IV, 149). Revision and proofreading lasted into the summer, and in early September *Nature* reappeared with Munroe's imprint as had the first edition thirteen years before. This time it formed part of a volume entitled *Nature; Addresses, and Lectures,* although some copies were bound separately in a so-called new and revised edition and a few of these, according to Munroe, were bound and cut down in size "to match the Essays." The printing was done from type; and the unbound sheets, after the failure of the Munroe firm, were taken over by Phillips, Sampson, and Company of Boston and used by that house for *Nature: Addresses, and Lectures* in 1850. There is record of an 1855 printing by Phillips, Sampson, but this may be merely the copyright date for that firm's 1856 edition with new plates of *Miscellanies; embracing Nature, Addresses, and Lectures.* There is only one significant substantive change in this 1856 edition, and that apparently a compositor's error corrected in 1870: "part or parcel" for "part or particle" (p. 8); otherwise, a few misprints from the 1849 edition are removed but a few new misprints introduced. From the 1856 plates, which were taken over by Ticknor and Fields of Boston after the deaths of Phillips and Sampson, a constant flow of reprintings continued through the 1860's and 1870's until 1877; statements of Emerson's account in the Ticknor and Fields Cost Book (Harvard College Library) indicate frequent reprinting and binding, 280 copies being the usual run within a year.

In 1869 Emerson made some minor corrections for the two-volume edition of *The Prose Works,* including *Nature,* published in 1870 by Fields, Osgood and Co. of Boston; other changes were evidently introduced by the copy editors and printers. Archaic spellings which had persisted through the earlier editions of *Nature* were now standardized and punctuation was also revised. After 1869 there was only one more edition to include *Nature* in which Emerson himself had a hand: the so-called Little Classics edition of 1876, published by James R. Osgood & Co. of Boston, successor to Fields, Osgood; the revisions are actually very limited and confined largely to accidentals, so that the 1849 text of *Nature* was left almost intact. After Emerson's death in 1882 his friend and literary executor James Elliot Cabot supervised the Riverside Edition (1883–1887) and his son Edward prepared the Centenary Edition (1903–1904), but none of their occasional changes in the text of *Nature* has Emerson's authority.

For textual study of *Nature*, then, the most significant versions are the first edition of 1836, which is reprinted here, and the second American edition of 1849, with the substantive revisions reported below. These changes, it will be observed, do not incorporate the notes for "correction or enlargement" of *Nature* that Emerson had entered in his journal shortly after the first edition had appeared (item 27, p. 45 above). His revisions included correction or alteration of both wording and punctuation; the table that follows records only changes in wording.

SUBSTANTIVE REVISIONS IN *NATURE* (1849)

(Page references are to the text as it appears in the present volume.)

Page and line	*1836 reading*	*1849 reading*
Title-page	"Nature is but an image or imitation of wisdom, the last thing of the soul; nature being a thing which doth only do, but not know." PLOTINUS.	A subtle chain of countless rings The next unto the farthest brings; The eye reads omens where it goes, And speaks all languages the rose; And, striving to be man, the worm Mounts through all the spires of form.
5.21	approximation	approach
5.27	sleep, dreams	sleep, madness, dreams
7.6	vulgar things	what he touches
7.11	preachers	envoys
7.13–14	are always	are
7.16	extort all	extort
7.18	reflected all	reflected
7.28	land-deeds	warranty-deeds
7.28	give them	give
8.9	Almost I fear to think how glad I am.	I am glad to the brink of fear.
8.14	befal	befall
8.18	part or particle	part or particle [1856: part or parcel]
10.25	are but	are

Page and line	1836 reading	1849 reading
11.17	hath	has
11.18	beside	besides
11.34	satisfies the soul purely by	satisfies by
11.35	have seen	see
12.16	with observing the	with the
12.23	make	makes
12.41	will, and never separate.	will.
13.7	an ancient historian	Sallust
13.24–25	to use the simple narrative of his biographer	his biographer says
13.33	whole geography	geography
13.42	other in man	other
14.3	and certainly will	and will
14.9	Therefore the	The
14.28–29	Extend this element to the uttermost, and I call it an ultimate end.	This element I call an ultimate end.
14.34	must therefore stand	must stand
15.3	A THIRD use which Nature subserves to man is that of Language.	LANGUAGE is a third use which Nature subserves to man.
15.6	particular facts.	particular spiritual facts.
15.7	spirits	spirit
15.9	is to give	to give
15.12	*Right* originally	*Right*
15.15	are, in their turn,	are
15.19	they continually convert	they convert
16.10	are but dry	are dry
16.35	Thus is nature an interpreter, by whose means man converses with his fellow men	[Omitted]
16.36	so utter	so to utter
16.40–41	the desire of riches, the desire of pleasure, the desire of power, the desire of praise,	the desire of riches, of pleasure, of power, and of praise,

Page and line	1836 reading	1849 reading
17.7	upon the	on the
17.14	that always a	that a
18.13	whilst	while
19.9–10	new amount to	new weapon in
19.13	of this	of the
19.19–20	everlasting nutriment	nutriment
20.1	is merely the	is the
20.4	is affected	are affected
20.40	More and more, with every thought, does his kingdom stretch over things, until	One after another, his victorious thought comes up with and reduces all things, until
21.7	nature always	nature ever
21.16	the great doctrine	the doctrine
21.20–21	illustrated, in treating of the significance of material things, that	illustrated, that
21.21	is but a	is a
21.28	conclusions.	conclusion:
21.30	and grows	grows
21.40–41	a unique, an identical	an identical
22.1–2	Every particular in nature, a leaf	A leaf
22.8	Goethe.	Goethe. Vitruvius thought an architect should be a musician.
22.11	grass.	grass. The law of harmonic sounds reappears in the harmonic colors.
22.17	Hence it is, that a rule	A rule
22.25	The same	The
22.31	mute and brute	brute
22.31–33	They introduce us to that singular form which predominates over all other forms. This is the human. All other organizations appear to be degradations of the human form.	They introduce us to the human form, of which all other organizations appear to be degradations.

Page and line	1836 reading	1849 reading
22.34	this organization	this
23.8	chuse	choose
24.25	best, the happiest moments	best moments
25.20	to embody any capricious shade	and uses it to embody any caprice
25.22	subtile	subtle
25.22–23	connexion	connection
25.23	is merely	is
25.38	And the	The
26.4–5	exerts, at any moment, to magnify the small, to micrify the great,—	exerts to dwarf the great, to magnify the small,—
26.27	delights us by animating nature like a creator, with	animates nature with
27.3	is ever	is
27.12	beautiful and majestic presence	presence
27.12	our outward being	the outward circumstance
28.2	all better say	all say
28.13	connexion	connection
28.34	befals	befalls
30.16	the great organ	the organ
30.30	baulks	balks
31.1	that spirit is one	one
31.2	that spirit does	it does
31.8	Once inspire the infinite, by being	Once inhale the upper air, being
32.10	endeavouring	endeavoring
32.18–19	most bizarre forms	most unwieldy and eccentric forms
33.19	the eternal attraction	the attraction
35.19	hath	has
37.2	and warm	warm
37.2	and wise	wise

2. VARIED RESPONSES TO *NATURE*, 1836–1978

CONTEMPORARY COMMENTS, 1836-1841

1836

"a gem throughout"

by Amos Bronson Alcott

[77; August 2, 1836] Mr. Waldo Emerson . . . [78] is now writing a book of a high intellectual character which he calls *Nature*. In beauty and finish of style he is unrivalled among American writers. There is also more philosophic depth than in any other writer. He is superior to Channing. I left with him "Psyche" for criticism.

[78; September 11, 1836] I have just finished reading *Nature*, by R. W. Emerson. It is a beautiful work. Mr. E. attempts to show the meaning of Nature to the minds of men. It is the production of a spiritualist, subordinating the visible and outward to the inward and invisible. Nature becomes a transparent emblem of the soul. Psyche animates and fills the earth and external things.

The book is small, scarce running to 100 pages, 12mo., but it is a gem throughout. I deem it the harbinger of an order of works given to the elucidation and establishment of the Spiritual. Mr. E. adverts, indirectly, to my "Psyche," now in his hands, in the work.

From *The Journals of Bronson Alcott*, selected and edited by Odell Shepard (Boston: Little, Brown and Company, 1938), pp. 77–78. Reprinted with the permission of the publisher.

1836

"a singular book"

by Orestes A. Brownson

This is a singular book. It is the creation of a mind that lives and moves in the Beautiful, and has the power of assimilating to itself whatever it sees, hears or touches. We cannot analyze it; whoever would form an idea of it must read it.

We welcome it however as an index to the spirit which is silently at work among us, as a proof that mind is about to receive a new and a more glorious manifestation; that higher problems and holier speculations than those which have hitherto engrossed us, are to engage our attention; and that the inquiries, what is perfect in Art, and what is true in Philosophy, are to surpass in interest those which concern the best place to locate a city, construct a rail road, or become suddenly rich. We prophesy that it is the forerunner of a new class of books, the harbinger of a new Literature as much superior to whatever has been, as our political insti[t]utions are superior to those of the Old World.

This book is æsthetical rather than philosophical. It inquires what is the Beautiful rather than what is the True. Yet it touches some of the gravest problems in metaphysical science, and may perhaps be called philosophy in its poetical aspect. It uniformly subordinates nature to spirit, the understanding to the reason, and mere hand-actions to ideas, and believes that ideas are one day to disenthrall the world from the dominion of semi-shadows, and make it the abode of peace and love, a meet Temple in which to enshrine the Spirit of universal and everlasting Beauty.

The author is a genuine lover of nature, and in a few instances he carries his regard for woods and fields so far as to be in danger of forgetting his socialities, and that all nature combined is infinitely inferior to the mind that contemplates it, and invests it with all its charms. And what seems singular to us is, that with all this love for nature, with this passion for solitary woods and varied landscapes, he seems seriously to doubt the existence of the external world except as [a] picture which God stamps on the mind. He all but worships what his senses seem to present him, and yet is not certain that all that which his senses place out of him, is not after all the mere subjective laws of his own being, existing only to the eye, not of a necessary, but of an irresistible Faith.

From the weekly *Boston Reformer*, September 10, 1836, p. 2, cols. 1–2[?]; courtesy of Professor Joel Myerson and *The Concord Saunterer*. See Joel Myerson, "Brownson Reviews Emerson's *Nature*," *The Concord Saunterer*, XIII (Spring, 1978), 5–6.

Some great minds have, we know[,] had this doubt. This was the case with the acute and amiable Bishop Berkeley, the audacious Fichte and several others we could mention. Taking their stand-point in the creative power of the human soul, and observing the landscape to change in its coloring as the hues of their own souls change, they have thought the landscape was nothing but themselves projected, and made an object of contemplation. The notion is easily accounted for, but we confess that we should think so accute [sic] a philosopher as our author would easily discover its fallacy.

The Reason is undoubtedly our only light, our only criterion of certainty; but we think the Reason vouches for the truth of the senses as decidedly and as immediately as it does for its own conceptions. He who denies the testimony of his senses, seems to us to have no ground for believing the apperceptions of consciousness; and to deny those is to set oneself afloat upon the ocean of universal scepticism. The whole difficulty seems to us to be in not duly understanding the report of the senses. The senses are the windows of the soul through which it looks out upon a world existing as really and as substantially as itself; but what the external world is, or what it is the senses report it to be, we do not at first understand. The result of all culture, we think will not be as our author thinks, to lead to Idealism, but to make us understand what it is we say, when we say, there is an external world.

The author calls the external world phenomenal, that is, an Appearance; but he needs not to be told that the appearance really exists, though it exists as an appearance, as that which appears, as the Absolute. Man is phenom[e]nal in the same sense as is the universe, but man exists. The author calls him "the apparition of God." The apparition exists as certainly as God exists, though it exists as an apparition, not as absolute being. God is absolute being.—Whatever is absolute is God; but God is not the universe, God is not man; man and the universe exist as manifestations of God. His existence is absolute, theirs is relative, but real.

But we are plunging too deeply into metaphysics for our readers and perhaps for ourselves.—In conclusion, we are happy to say that however the author may deviate from what we call sound philosophy, on his road, he always comes to the truth at last. In this little book he has done an important service to his fellow men.—He has clothed nature with a poetic garb, and interpenetrated her with the living spirit of Beauty and Goodness, showed us how we ought to look upon the world round and about us, set us an example of a calm, morally independent, and devout spirit discoursing on the highest and holiest topics which can occupy the human soul, and produced a book which must ever be admired as a perfect specimen of Art. We thank him for what he has done and commend his book—his poem we might say—to every lover of the True, the Beautiful and the Good.

1837

"it certainly will be called remarkable"

by Samuel Osgood

[385]
> ————————————For I have learned
> To look on Nature, not as in the hour
> Of thoughtless youth; but hearing oftentimes
> The still, sad music of humanity,
> Not harsh, nor grating, though of ample power
> To chasten and subdue. And I have felt
> A presence, that disturbs me with the joy
> Of elevated thoughts: a sense sublime,
> Of something far more deeply interfused,
> Whose dwelling is the light of setting suns,
> And the round ocean and the living air,
> And the blue sky, and in the mind of man.
> A motion and a spirit, that impels
> All thinking things, all objects of all thoughts,
> And rolls through all things.—*Wordsworth's* **Tintern Abbey**.

It would be interesting to study the Poetry, Philosophy and Religion of Mankind, in the different stages of its progress, [386] in order to learn the various views and sentiments with which Nature has been regarded. Such a study would lead us to consider all periods of our race:—the infant period when the heart of man had the freshness of childhood, and . . . he saw Nature clad with the freshness of its new born beauty:—the savage period, when man looked upon Nature, only as a means of supplying his physical wants, or drew from it a language for his passions; . . . the mystic period in human progress, when as in the central oriental world, Nature was regarded as a dreamy shadow, and the indolent soul, absorbed in its own fond visions, scorned the world of matter as being unreal, or shrunk from it as contaminating: then . . . the period in which the material universe engrossed the mind, and the soul was too intent on the finite to rise to the infinite . . . : then comes the period in which Nature is prized, mainly for her physical uses—the age of natural science and material utility. In this latter period, we find our own lot to be cast, and should rejoice to find ourselves emerging from it. We should rejoice at those signs, that are appearing, which promise that Nature shall ere long have her due, and be looked on

From *The Western Messenger*, II (January, 1837), 385-393.

with the right spirit— . . . loved as the emblem of the Divine Beauty, and reverenced as being instinct with the Divine Spirit, and an expression of the Divine Wisdom, Love and Power. When this day comes, man will look on Nature with the same eye, as when in the Eden of primitive innocence and joy, and at the same time, with all the lights which science and varied experience afford.

Christianity teaching the immortality of the soul, and revealing to us God in all things, has been the cause of this happy change. It puts a spiritual aspect on all things—on all Providence and all creation. It forbids our being engrossed with finite things. It also forbids our being lost in the mazes of the Infinite. It teaches us to ascend to the Infinite from the Finite. It does not take us away from Nature, but in Nature shows to us our God.

Now certainly all those books, which throw a religious light on Nature, should be encouraged by all, who wish to redeem the souls of men from the thraldom of the senses: not only those books which exhibit the argument for religion, . . . [387] but those which shew the correspondence of the material world, with our own higher nature, and teach us to look on Nature with the spiritual eye—with something of that same spirit in which God made his creation.

The strong hold, which Coleridge and Wordsworth have taken, of so many minds, . . . shews, that they have but given expression to thoughts and feelings, which before existed and were growing in the minds of their readers. We rejoice at the influence of such poets. We rejoice that a poetry of Nature, truly Christian, is springing up among us. We rejoice, that those to whom it is given to pass within the veil, and to see in Nature a Beauty, that is hid to common eyes, have so made the Beautiful minister to the Good and True. We hail with joy every inspiration of genius, which connects sentiment with religion. Sentiment, we well know, is not the whole of religion. But it is a rightful minister of religion. The Beautiful is the rightful priest of the True. . . .

In our own bustling country, where banks, steam boats and rail roads seem to engross the nation's attention, we are happy to find some spirits, who keep aloof from the vulgar melee, and in calm of soul, live for Nature and for God. No greater exception to the common spirit of our nation, could be pointed out, than the author of a little work, recently published at the East. "Nature" is its title. . . .

The work is a remarkable one, and it certainly will be called remarkable by those, who consider it "mere moonshine," as well as those, who look upon it with reverence, as the effusion of a prophet-like mind. Whatever may be thought of the merits, or of the extravagances of the book, no one, we are sure, can read it, without feeling himself more wide awake to the beauty and meaning of Creation. . . .

[389] The author is not such a dreamer on the beauties of the universe, as to forget its material uses. In the chapter on Commodity, he gives a view of the advantages, which our senses owe to Nature, as broad as if he were looking down on our earth with a mighty telescope, from some distant orb.

Is not the author right in considering Beauty one of the uses—one of the true final causes of Nature? Is not Beauty in itself merely considered one form of utility? Is there not a high utility, even in Beauty of outward form? Surely this simplest aspect of Beauty gives delight, and what gives inmost delight is truly useful. . . .

But a higher element than beauty of form, must be recognized, before we can see the full loveliness of Nature's beauty. . . .

[390] In the chapter on Language, . . . the great law of correspondence, which runs through creation, is pointed out, that great law of analogy, which he, who shall understand truly, will know more of the universe, and be a wiser seer into the regions of undiscovered truth, than an eternity spent in groping round the world, endeavoring, without such light, to classify its scattered phenomena, could make him. . . .

[391] In the last chapter on the uses of Nature—that on Discipline, the world around us is considered as disciplining our understanding and conscience. . . .

Coming to the chapter on Idealism, many will be tempted to shut the book in disgust, and lament, that so sensible a man as the writer has before shewn himself to be, should shew such folly. And we ourselves doubt much the wisdom of the speculation in this chapter, although we would not call him insane, who thinks the material world only ideal, believing as we do, that as Turgot has said, "He, who has never doubted the existence of matter, may be assured, he has no aptitude for metaphysical inquiries." We do not think, that Idealism leads to such dangerous conclusions, as are sometimes apprehended, since it implies no distrust in natural laws. The idealist, who believes matter to be only phenomenal, will conduct in exactly the same way, as the most thorough going materialist. The idealist will be just as cautious about cutting his finger, as the materialist will: for both will believe, that the pain is really felt, whatever they may think as to the finger or the knife being real or only apparent.

We are unable to perceive the bearing of the writer's argument, in proof of Idealism, or to allow the advantage, which he claims for his theory. All his arguments, it seems to us, go to prove merely the superiority of mind over matter. And all the advantage, which he claims for Idealism, is owned by that common spiritual philosophy, which subordinates matter to mind. We own there is much fine thought and good writing in this chapter, little as the sentiments agree with our Eclecticism. . . .

[392] In the chapter on Spirit, the lessons, which Nature teaches, are summed up in a single one:— . . . "It always speaks of Spirit. It suggests the absolute. It is a perpetual effect. It is a great shadow pointing always to the sun behind us. . . . The happiest man is he who learns from nature the lesson of worship."

There are some things in this book, which we do not understand. The Orphic sentences at the end, "which a certain poet sang to the author," are especially dark to our misty vision. But probably the fault lies in ourselves. . . .

The many will call this book dreamy, and perhaps it is so. It may indeed naturally seem, that the author's mind is somewhat onesided, that he has not mingled enough with common humanity, to avoid running into eccentricity, that he has been so careful to keep his own individuality, that he has confounded his idiosyncrasies, with universal truth. All this may be. But it is not for the vulgar many to call such a man a dreamer. If he does dream, the many are more deluded dreamers. His dreams are visions of the eternal realities of the spiritual world: their's [sic] are of the fleeting phantoms of earth. Indeed the real visionary is not to be found, in the mystic's cell, or the philosopher's study, but in the haunts of busy life. . . .

[393] Not so with him, who puts his thoughts on things eternal. He sees the world as it really is. He looks on the temporal in the light of the Eternal. "So he comes to look on the world with new eyes." So he learns the high truths which nature teaches. Let us therefore hear the Orphic poet's saying:

" 'Build, therefore, your own world. . . .' "

1837

"uncertain and obscure"

by Francis Bowen

[371] We find beautiful writing and sound philosophy in this little work; but the effect is injured by occasional vagueness of expression, and by a vein of mysticism, that pervades the writer's whole course of thought. The highest praise that can be accorded to it, is, that it is a *suggestive* book, for no one can read it without tasking his faculties to the utmost, and relapsing into fits of severe meditation. But the effort of perusal is often painful, the thoughts excited are frequently bewildering, and the results to which they lead us, uncertain and obscure. The reader feels as in a disturbed dream, in which shows of surpassing beauty are around him, and he is conversant with disembodied spirits, yet all the time he is harassed by an uneasy sort of consciousness, that the whole combination of phenomena is fantastic and unreal.

In point of taste in composition, some defects proceed from over anxiety to avoid common errors. The writer aims at simplicity and directness, as the ancient philosopher aimed at humility, and showed his pride through the tatters of his cloak. He is in love with the Old Saxon idiom, yet there is a spice of affectation in his mode of using it. He is sometimes coarse and blunt, that he may avoid the imputation of sickly refinement, and writes bathos with malice prepense, because he abhors forced dignity and unnatural elevation.

These are grave charges, but we make them advisedly, for the author knows better than to offend so openly against good taste, and, in many passages of great force and beauty of expression, has shown that he can do better. The following sentences, taken almost at random, will show the nature of the defects alluded to.

"Now many are thought not only unexplained but inexplicable, as language, sleep, dreams, beasts, sex." . . .

"Standing on the bare ground, my head bathed by the blithe air,—and uplifted into infinite space,—all egotism vanishes. I became a transparent eyeball." . . .

"Whilst we use this grand cipher to expedite the affairs of our pot and kettle, we feel that we have not put it to its use, neither are able."

"Therefore is Space, and therefore Time, that men may know [372] that things are not huddled and lumped, but sundered and individual." . . .

From *The Christian Examiner*, XXI (January, 1837), 371–385.

"I expand and live in the warm day, like corn and melons." . . .

The purpose of the book, so far as it may be said to have a purpose, is, to invite us to the observation of nature, and to point out manifestations of spirit in material existences and external events. The uses to which the outward world is subservient are divided into four classes,—Commodity, Beauty, Language, and Discipline. These ends the writer considers as the final cause of every thing that exists, except the soul. To the consideration of each he allots a chapter, and displays, often with eloquence and a copious fund of illustration, the importance of the end, and the aptitude of the means provided for its attainment. In the latter part of the work, he seems disposed to neutralize the effect of the former, by adopting the Berkeleyan system, and denying the outward and real existence of that Nature, which he had just declared to be so subservient to man's spiritual wants. Of the chapters on "Spirit" and "Prospects," with which the work concludes, we prefer not to attempt giving an account, until we can understand their meaning.

From this sketch of the author's plan, it would seem, that he had hardly aimed at originality. What novelty there is in the work, arises not from the choice or distribution of the subject, but from the manner of treatment. The author is not satisfied with that cautious philosophy which traces the indirect influences of outward phenomena and physical laws on the individual mind, and contemplates the benevolence of the Deity in particular instances of the adaptation and subserviency of matter to spirit. He contemplates the Universe from a higher point of view. Where others see only an analogy, he discerns a final cause. The fall of waters, the germination of seeds, the alternate growth and decay of organized forms, were not originally designed to answer the wants of our physical constitution, but to acquaint us with the laws of mind, and to serve our intellectual and moral advancement. The powers of Nature have been forced into the service of man. The pressure of the atmosphere, the expansive force of steam, the gravity of falling bodies, are our ministers, and do our bidding in levelling the earth, in changing a wilderness into a habitable city, and in fashioning raw materials into products available for the gratification of sense and the protection of body. Yet these ends are only of secondary [374] importance to the great purpose for which these forces were created and made subject to human power. Spiritual laws are typified in these natural facts, and are made evident in the whole material constitution of things. Man must study matter, that he may become acquainted with his own soul. . . .

Thus far, whatever we may think of the truth and soberness of the writer's views, he is at least intelligible. But his imagination now takes a higher flight, and the bewildered reader strives in vain through the cloud-capt phraseology to catch a glimpse of more awful truths. Who will be the Œdipus to solve the following enigmas?

"This relation between the mind and matter is not fancied by some poet, but stands in the will of God, and so is free to be known by all men. It appears to men, or it does not appear." . . .

[375] Having thus considered the uses of the material world, its adaptation to man's physical wants, to his love of beauty, and his moral sense, the author turns and aims a back blow at the universe, which he has been leading us to admire and love. The heavens are rolled together like a scroll, the solid earth cracks beneath our feet,

> Wide wilderness and mountain, rock and sea,
> Peopled with busy transitory groups,

[376] are shadows, and exist only in mind. Matter is nothing, spirit is all. Man is alone in the vast inane with his God.

We have no quarrel with Idealism. Philosophers may form what dreams they choose, provided their speculations affect favorably their own faith and practice, and can never, from their very nature, command the belief, or bewilder the understanding of the mass of mankind. But we do protest against the implied assertion of the idealist, that the vulgar entertain opinions less philosophically just than his own. In the pride of opinion, he has overrated his own success, which at the utmost amounts only to this, that he has shown the inconclusiveness of the arguments commonly adduced to prove the outward and independent existence of matter. But he has brought no positive arguments to disprove the existence of any thing exterior to mind. He has not shown, that the common opinion involves any repugnancy or inconsistency in itself. The bridge on which we relied for support may be broken down, but we are not whelmed in the waters beneath. The belief still exists, and its universality is a fact for which the idealist cannot account. This fact puts the burden of proof upon him, and it is a load which he cannot support. . . .

On reviewing what we have already said of this singular work, the criticism appears to be couched in contradictory terms; we can only allege in excuse the fact, that the book is a contradiction in itself. . . .

But enough of the work itself; it belongs to a class, and may be considered as the latest representative of that class.

[377] Within a short period, a new school of philosophy has appeared, the adherents of which have dignified it with the title of Transcendentalism. In its essential features, it is a revival of the Old Platonic school. It rejects the aid of observation, and will not trust to experiment. The Baconian mode of discovery is regarded as obsolete; induction is a slow and tedious process, and the results are uncertain and imperfect. General truths are to be attained without the previous examination of particulars, and by the aid of a higher power than the understanding. "The hand-lamp of logic" is to be broken, for the truths which are *felt* are more satisfactory and certain than those which are *proved*. The sphere of intuition is enlarged, and made to comprehend not only mathematical axioms, but the most abstruse and elevated propositions respecting the being and destiny of man. Pure intelligence usurps the place of humble research. Hidden meanings, glimpses of spiritual and everlasting truth are found, where former observers sought only for natural facts. The observation of sensible phenomena can lead only to the discovery of insulated, partial, and

relative laws; but the consideration of the same phenomena, in a typical point of view, may lead us to infinite and absolute truth,—to a knowledge of the reality of things.

As the object and method of philosophizing are thus altered, it is obvious that language also must be modified, and made to subserve other purposes than those for which it was originally designed. Transcendental philosophy took its rise in Germany, and the language of that country, from the unbounded power which it affords of composition and derivation from native roots, is well adapted to express results that are at once novel and vague. Hence the mysticism and over refinement, which characterize the German school of philosophy, art, and criticism. Our own tongue is more limited and inflexible. It must be enriched by copious importations from the German and Greek, before it can answer the ends of the modern school. And this has been done to such an extent, that could one of the worthies of old English literature rise from his grave, he would hardly be able to recognize his native tongue.

Among other innovations in speech made by writers of the Transcendental school, we may instance the formation of a large class of abstract nouns from adjectives,—a pecularity as consonant with the genius of the German language, as it is foreign to the nature of our own. Thus we now speak of the *Infinite,* [378] the *Beautiful,* the *Unconscious,* the *Just,* and the *True.* A new class of verbs also has been formed from the same or similar roots, such as *individualize, materialize, externize,* &c. For instances of new and awkward compounds, take the following; *instreaming, adolescent, symbolism, unconditioned, theosophists, internecive.*

We deprecate the introduction of a new class of philosophical terms, as it encourages tyros to prate foolishly and flippantly about matters, which they can neither master nor comprehend. Once let a peculiar diction gain footing in philosophy, as it has already done in poetry, and we shall have as great a cloud of pretenders and sciolists in the former, as already exercise our patience in the latter. Nonsense cannot be concealed in plain and sober prose. It stands conspicuous in its jejuneness and sterility. But by ringing the changes on the poetical vocabulary, a *mirage* of meaning is produced, and the mass of readers are cheated into the belief that the author says something. So is there reason to fear that a great portion of modern metaphysics and what is termed *æsthetic* criticism, is made up of "words, words," and very awkward and affected words too. Translate a passage of such writing into English, and it will be found to transcend both reason and common sense. . . .

It would avail but little, perhaps, with some Transcendentalists to assert, that the deepest minds have ever been the clearest, and to quote the example of Locke and Bacon, as of men who could treat the most abstruse subjects in the most familiar and intelligible terms. If in their modesty they did not rank themselves above such names as these, they would probably allege the different nature of their tasks, and attribute the difficulty of communication to daring originality in the choice of ends and means. But it is evident that novelty both of plan and execution, though it may retard progress, ought not to vitiate results. We do not complain of the New School for doing little, but for doing nothing in a satisfactory manner; for boasting of [379] progress, when they cannot show clear evidence of having advanced a step. We cannot believe, that there is a large class of truths, which in their very nature are incomprehensible to the greater part of mankind. Of course, we speak not of the multitude, whose incapacity results from ignorance and the want of experience in thinking. But the Transcendentalists more than insinuate, that the majority of educated and reflecting men are possessed of minds so unlike their own, that they doubt their power of constructing a bridge which may serve for the transmission of ideas to persons so little fitted to receive them. What a frivolous excuse for being unintelligible is this! There is an essential unity in Truth, in the means of research, and in the vehicle of communication. There is but one philosophy, though there are many theories; and but one mode of expressing thought, (namely, by symbols,) though there are many languages. Philosophy is the love of wisdom, and wisdom is the knowledge of things and their relations. To perceive them at all is to perceive them clearly, and the perception cannot fail of being conveyed to others, except through a very school-boy's ignorance of the force of terms. . . .

[380] But we are not left to infer vagueness and incompleteness of thought from obscurity of language. The writers of whom we speak, openly avow their preference of such indistinct modes of reflection, and justify loose and rambling speculations, mystical forms of expression, and the utterance of truths that are but half perceived, on the same principle, it would seem, that influences the gambler, who expects by a number of random casts to obtain at last the desired combination. In this respect, the philosophy of the New School is well summed up by the writer before us in the following assertions[:] "that a guess is often more fruitful than an indisputable affirmation, and that a dream may let us deeper into the secret of nature than a hundred concerted [381] experiments." "Poetry comes nearer to vital truth than history." Why not follow the principle of the gambler entirely, by shaking a number of words in a hat, and then throwing them upon a table, in the hope that, after a number of trials, they may so arrange themselves as to express some novel and important truth? . . .

If it be urged, that vagueness is not inconsistent with reality and truth, we reply, that this assertion does not meet the point, nor resolve the difficulty. In the imperfect conceptions of man, mystery may envelope truth, but it does not constitute that truth, any more than the veil of the temple is in itself the "Holy of Holies." Still less is there any *necessary* connexion between dimness and reality; for truth, considered as the object of Divine contemplation, is light itself, and glimpses of the spiritual world are blinding to man, only because they dazzle with excessive brightness. We live in the twilight of knowledge, and though ignorant of the points of the compass, it argues nothing but blind perverseness, to turn to the darkest part of the horizon for the expected rising of the sun.

We have a graver complaint to make of the spirit in which the disciples of the modern school have conducted their inquiries and answered their opponents. "It might seem incredible," says Mackintosh, "if it were not established by the experience of all ages, that those who differ most from the opinions of their fellow men, are most confident of the truth of their own." Dogmatism and the spirit of innovation go hand in hand. And the reason is obvious, for there is no common ground on which the opponents can stand, and cultivate mutual good will in the partial unity of their interests and pursuits. Both the means and the ends, which other philosophers have proposed to themselves, are rejected by the new sect of hierophants. They are among men, but not of men. From the heights of mystical speculation, they look down with a ludicrous self-complacency and pity on the mass of mankind, on the ignorant and the educated, the learners and the teachers, and should any question the grounds on which such feelings rest, they are forthwith branded with the most opprobrious epithets, which the English or the Transcendental language can supply. It is not going too far to say, that to the bitterness and scorn, with which Coleridge and some of his English adherents have replied [382] to modest doubts and fair arguments, no parallel can be found, save in the scholastic controversies of the Middle Ages.

But the world has grown too old and too proud to be sent to school again by any sect. It boasts of having accomplished something by the labor of ages, of having settled some principles and ascertained some facts; and though it will thankfully accept any addition to its treasury, it will not regard as useless all its former stores, and begin the career of discovery anew. The Transcendentalists have been unwise, therefore, in adopting an offensive tone in the outset, and promulgating new views of things in an overbearing and dictatorial manner. . . .

[383] The distinguishing trait of the Transcendental philosophy, is the appeal which it makes from the authority of reason and argument to that of passion and feeling. We are aware, that the miserable sophistries of skepticism can in no way be so effectually exposed, as by a reference to the original, simple, and unadulterated impressions of mind. In one sense, the heart is wiser than the head; the child is the teacher of the man. A process of reasoning, which leads to a false result, is a mere logical puzzle, and so far from establishing that result, it only demonstrates the weakness of the reasoning faculty, that cannot discover the mistake, which, through the medium of a higher power, we know must exist. The foundations of moral and religious truth are like the axioms on which the mathematician grounds his argument; if, either directly or by necessary inference, conclusions are found to be at variance with these first principles, they are at once rejected as being demonstrably absurd.

But some bounds must be set to the application of views like these. Postulates must not be confounded with axioms. He who mingles controverted propositions with essential truths, in a vain attempt to obtain the evidence of consciousness for each, corrupts, so far as in him lies, the fountain head of argument, and introduces confusion into the very elements of knowledge. The distinction, so much insisted on by the New School, between the Reason and the Understanding, if it mean any thing, must be [384] coincident with that which exists between the mind's active and creating power on the one side, and its passive and recipient faculty on the other. If not so,—if the two faculties agree in being each perceptive of truth,—we ask, what difference in kind can there be between two classes of truths, that separate powers are necessary for their reception? In *kind*, we say; for that a variety in degree should require the exercise of different faculties, is as absurd to suppose, as that a man must have one eye to see a mountain, and another for a molehill. We know that we shall be asked, whether moral truth is recognised by the same exertion of mind that admits the demonstrations of the geometer; and we reply, that the question is not a pertinent one. Our assertion is, that the argument for the existence of a God, or the immateriality of the soul, is tested by the same power of mind that discovered and proved any proposition in Euclid. The motive for supposing the existence of a mental faculty distinct from the Understanding, and which is denominated *par excellence* the Reason, seems to have been, to obtain evidence in favor of intuitive truths, equal or superior to that which is afforded to another class of propositions by demonstration. It is a needless supposition; for demonstration itself proceeds by intuition, the several steps being linked together by the immediate and necessary perception of their agreement with each other.

The aim of the Transcendentalists is high. They profess to look not only beyond facts, but without the aid of facts, to principles. What is this but Plato's doctrine of innate, eternal, and immutable ideas, on the consideration of which all science is founded? Truly, the human mind advances but too often in a circle. The New School has abandoned Bacon, only to go back and wander in the groves of the Academy, and to bewilder themselves with the dreams which first arose in the fervid imagination of the Greeks. Without questioning the desirableness of this end, of considering general truths without any previous examination of particulars, we may well doubt the power of modern philosophers to attain it. Again, they are busy in the inquiry (to adopt their own phraseology,) after the Real and the Absolute, as distinguished from the Apparent. Not to repeat the same doubt as to their success, we may at least request them to beware lest they strip Truth of its relation to Humanity, and thus deprive it of its usefulness. Granted that we are imprisoned in matter, why beat against the bars in a fruitless attempt to escape, when a little labor might convert [385] the prison to a palace, or at least render the confinement more endurable. The frame of mind which longs after the forbidden fruit of knowledge in subjects placed beyond the reach of the human faculties, as it is surely indicative of a noble temperament, may also, under peculiar circumstances, conduce to the happiness of the individual. But if too much indulged, there is danger lest it waste its energies in mystic and unprofitable dreams, and despondency result from frequent failures, till at last, disappointment darkens into despair.

In offering these suggestions, we trust not to have appeared as arguing against a generous confidence in the power of the human intellect, and in the progress and efficacy of truth. There is a wide field still open for the exertion of mind, though we cease to agitate questions which have baffled the acuteness, ingenuity, and skill of the philosophers of all time. But arrogance and self-sufficiency are no less absurd in philosophy, than criminal in morals; and we cannot but think, that these qualities are displayed by men who censure indiscriminately the objects which the wise and good have endeavoured to attain, and the means which they have employed in the pursuit. A fair and catholic spirit will ever incline to eclecticism in its inquiries and systems; while it is the mark of a narrow mind to consider novelty as a mark of truth, or to look upon the difficulties of a question as evincing the importance of its solution. To regard Franklin as a greater name than that of Plato, might be unjust, were not the comparison itself fanciful and improper; but we may safely assert, that there are few, very few, who would not do better to look at the American rather than the Grecian sage, as their model of the philosophical character.

1837

"the Foundation and Ground-plan"

by Thomas Carlyle

[157; February 13, 1837] Your little azure-coloured *Nature* gave me true satisfaction. I read it, and then lent it about to all my acquaintance that had a sense for such things; from whom a similar verdict always came back. You say it is the first chapter of something greater. I call it rather the Foundation and Ground-plan on which you may build whatsoever of great and true has been given you to build. It is the true Apocalypse this when the "open secret" becomes revealed to a man. I rejoice much in the glad serenity of soul with which you look out on this wondrous Dwelling-place of yours and mine,—with an ear for the . . . *"Ewigen Melodien,"* which pipe in the winds round us, and utter themselves forth in all sounds and sights and things: *not* to be written down by gamut-machinery; but which all right writing is a kind of attempt to write down. You will see what the years will bring you. It is not one of your smallest qualities in my mind, that you *can* wait so quietly and let the years do their hest. He that cannot keep himself quiet is of a morbid nature; and the thing he yields us will be like him in that, whatever else it be.

1838

Nature—A Prose Poem

Anonymous

[319] Minds of the highest order of genius draw their thoughts most immediately from the Supreme Mind, which is the fountain of all finite natures. And hence they clothe the truths they see and feel, in those forms of nature which are generally intelligible to all ages of the world. With this poetic instinct, they have a natural tendency to withdraw from the *conventions* of their own day; and strive to forget, as much as possible, the arbitrary associations created by temporary institutions and local pecularities. Since the higher laws of suggestion operate in proportion as the lower laws are made subordinate, suggestions of thought by mere proximity of time and place must be subtracted from the habits of the mind that would cultivate the principle of analogy; and this principle of suggestion, in its turn, must be made to give place to the higher law of cause and effect; and at times even this must be set aside, and Reason, from the top of the being, look into the higher nature of original truth, by Intuition,—no unreal function of our nature:

> Nor less I deem that there are powers,
>   Which, of themselves, our minds impress;
> That we can feed these minds of ours,
>   In a wise passiveness.

But if it is precisely because the most creative minds take the symbols of their thoughts and feelings from the venerable imagery of external nature, or from that condition of society which is most transparent in its simplicity, that, when they utter themselves, they speak to all ages, it is also no less true, that this is the reason why the greatest men, those of the highest order of intellect, often do not appear very great to their contemporaries. Their most precious sayings are naked, if not invisible, to the eyes of the conventional, precisely because they are free of the thousand circumstances and fashions which interest the acting and unthinking many. The greatest minds take no cognizance of the local interests, the party [320] spirit, and the pet subjects of the literary coteries of particular times and places. Their phraseology is pure from the ornament which is the passing fashion of the day. As, however, they do

From *The Democratic Review*, I (February, 1838), 319–321.

not think and speak for their own order only, as they desire to address and receive a response from the great majority of minds—even from those that doubt their own power of going into the holy of holies of thought for themselves—there is needed the office of an intermediate class of minds, which are the natural critics of the human race. For criticism, in its worthiest meaning, is not, as is too often supposed, fault-finding, but interpretation of the oracles of genius. Critics are the priests of literature. How often, like other priests, they abuse their place and privilege, is but too obvious. They receive into their ranks the self-interested, the partisan, the lover of power, besides the stupid and frivolous; and thus the periodical literature of the day is in the rear, rather than in advance of the public mind.

After this preamble, which we trust has suitably impressed the minds of our readers with the dignity of the critical office, we would call all those together who have feared that the spirit of poetry was dead, to rejoice that such a *poem* as "Nature" is written. It grows upon us as we reperuse it. It proves to us, that the only true and perfect mind is the poetic. Other minds are not to be despised, indeed; they are germs of humanity; but the poet alone is the man—meaning by the poet, not the versifier, nor the painter of outward nature merely, but the total soul, grasping truth, and express-ing it melodiously, equally to the eye and heart.

The want of apprehension with which this *poem* has been received, speaks ill for the taste of our literary priesthood. Its title seems to have suggested to many persons the notion of some elementary treatise on physics, as physics; and when it has been found that it treats of the *metaphysics* of nature—in other words, of the highest designs of God, in forming nature and man in relations with each other—it seems to have been laid down with a kind of disgust, as if it were a cheat; and some reviewers have spoken of it with a stupidity that is disgraceful alike to their sense, taste, and feeling.

It has, however, found its readers and lovers, and those not a few; the highest intellectual culture and the simplest instinctive innocence have alike received it, and felt it to be a divine Thought, borne on a stream of 'English undefiled,' such as we had almost despaired could flow in this our world of grist and saw mills, whose utili-tarian din has all but drowned the melodies of nature. The time will come, when it will be more universally seen to be "a gem of purest ray serene," and be dived after, into the dark unfathomed caves of that ocean of frivolity, which the literary produc-tions of the present age spread out to the eyes of despair.

[321] We have said that "Nature" is a poem; but it is written in prose. The author, though "wanting the accomplishment of verse," is a devoted child of the great Mother; and comes forward bravely in the midst of the dust of business and the din of machinery; and naming her venerable name, believes that there is a reverence for it left, in the bottom of every heart, of power to check the innumerable wheels for a short Sabbath, that all may listen to her praises.

In his introduction, he expresses his purpose. He tells us, that we concede too much to the sceptic, when we allow every thing venerable in religion to belong to history. He tells us that were there no past, yet nature would tell us great truths; and, rightly read, would prove the prophecies of revelation to be "a very present God;" and also, that the past itself, involving its prophets, divine lawgivers, and the human life of Him of Nazareth, is comparatively a dead letter to us, if we do not freshen these traditions in our souls, by opening our ears to the living nature which forevermore prepares for, and re-echoes, their sublime teachings.

"The foregoing generations," he says, "beheld God face to face: we, through their eyes. Why should not *we* also enjoy an original relation to the Universe?"

Why should we not indeed? for *we* not only have the Universe, which the fore-going generations had, but *themselves* also. Why are we less wise than they? Why has our wisdom less of the certainty of intuition than theirs? Is it because we have more channels of truth? It may be so. The garden of Eden, before the fall of man, and when God walked in its midst, was found to be a less effective school of virtue, than the workshop of a carpenter, in a miserable town of Judea, of which 'an Israelite without guile' could ask, "*Can* any good come out of Nazareth?" And is not this, by the way, a grave warning to the happily circumstanced of all time to tremble—lest they grow morally passive, just in proportion to their means of an effective activity? With the religion of history must always be combined the religion of experience, in order to a true apprehension of God. The poet of "Nature" is a preacher of the latter. Let us "hear him gladly," for such are rare.

The first Canto of this song respects the outward form of Nature. He sketches it in bold strokes. The stars of Heaven above—the landscape below—the breathing atmosphere around—and the living forms and sounds—are brought up to us, by the loving spirit of the singer; who recognizes in this drapery of the world without, the same Disposer that arranged the elements of his own conscious soul. Thus, in his first recognition of Nature's superficies, he brings us to Theism. There is a God. Our Father is the author of Nature. The brotherly "nod" of companionship assures us of it.

But wherefore is Nature? The next Canto of our Poem answers this question in the most obvious relation. It is an answer that [322] "all men apprehend." Nature's superficies is for the well-being of man's body, and the advantage of his material interests. This part of the book requires no interpretation from the critic. Men are active enough concerning commodity, to understand whatever is addressed to them on this head. At least there is no exception but in the case of the savage of the tropics. *His* mind has not explored his wants even to the extent of his body. He does not comprehend the necessities of the narrowest civilization. But whoever reads Reviews, whoever can understand our diluted English, can understand still better this concentrated and severely correct expression of what every child of civilization experiences every day. There is but one sentence here, that the veriest materialist can mistake. He may not measure all that the poet means when he says, man is thus conveniently waited upon in order "that he may work." He may possibly think that "work" relates to the physical operations of manufacture or agriculture. But what is really meant is no less than this; "man is fed that he may work" with his mind; add to the treasures of thought; elaborate the substantial life of the spiritual world. This is a beautiful doctrine, and worthy to be sung to the harp, with a song of thanksgiving. Undoubtedly Nature, by working for man with all her elements, is adequate to supply him with so much "commodity" that the time may be anticipated when all men will have leisure to be artists, poets, philosophers,—in short, to live through life in the exercise of their proper humanity. God speed to the machinery and application of science to the arts which is to bring this about!

The third Song is of Nature's Beauty, and we only wonder why it was not sung first; for surely the singer found out that Nature was beautiful, before he discovered that it was convenient. Some children, we know, have asked what was the use of flowers, and, like little monkeys, endeavouring to imitate the grown-up, the bearings of whose movements they could not appreciate, have planted their gardens with potatoes and beans, instead of sweet-briar and cupid's-delights. But the poet never made this mistake. In the fullness of his first love for his "beautiful mother," and his "gentle nest," he did not even find out those wants, which the commodity of Nature supplies. . . .

[323] The second passage on Beauty, is one of those which recalls the critic to the office of interpreter, for it is one which the world has called mystical. To say the same thing in worse English, the oracle here tells us, that if we look on Nature with pleasurable emotions only, and without, at the same time, exerting our moral powers, the mind grows effeminate, and thus becomes incapable of perceiving the highest beauty of whose original type the external forms are but the varied reflections or shadows. When man's moral power is in action, the mind spontaneously traces relations between itself and surrounding things, and there forms with Nature one whole, combining the moral delight which human excellence inspires, with that suggested by Nature's forms.

The next passage rises a step higher in the praise of Beauty. It recognizes the cherishing influence of Nature's forms upon the faculties. Nature not only calls out taste, not only glorifies virtue, and is in its turn by virtue glorified, but it awakens the creative impulse—God's image in man. Hence Art, or "Nature in miniature." And the works of Art lead back to Nature again. Thus Beauty circulates, and becomes an aspect of Eternity.

The next chapter, showing that Language is founded on material Nature, is quite didactic. But even here one critic * quotes a sentence, of which he says, he cannot understand "what it means."

This relation between the mind and matter is not fancied by some poet, but stands in the will of God, and so is free to be known by all men. It appears to men, or it does not appear.

* Christian Examiner. [Cf. p. 82 above in the review by Francis Bowen.]

Where lies the obscurity? We have heard some men say that they did not believe that the forms of Nature bore any relation to the being of God, which his children could appreciate; but even these men could not understand the simple proposition of the opposite theory. Men may think that all nations, whose language has yet been discovered, have called youth *the morning of life,* by accident; but it is inconceivable that they should not understand the simple words in which other men say that there is *no accident in the world,* but all things relate to the spirit of God to which man also has relation and access. Perhaps, however, it is the second sentence which [is] unintelligible, "it appears to men, or it does not appear." In other words, *to people with open eyes there are colors; to people with shut eyes, at least, to those born blind, there are no colors.*

But having come to this fact, viz: that "the relation between mind and matter stands in the will of God," our poet grows silent with wonder and worship. The nature of this relation he acknowledges to be the yet unsolved problem. He names some of the principal men who have attempted a solution. Many readers of his book would have been glad, had he paused to tell us, in his brief [324] comprehensive way, what was the solution of Pythagoras, and Plato, Bacon, Leibnitz, and Swedenborg, with remarks of his own upon each.

As to his own solution, some say he is unintelligible, talks darkly. They do not seem to have observed that he says nothing in the way of solution, so that nothing can be darkly said. This is what has disappointed the best lovers of his book. But if he does not give his own solution of the enigma, he does what is next best, he tells us the condition of solving it ourselves.

A life in harmony with nature, the love of truth and virtue, will purge the eyes to understand her text. By degrees we may come to know the primitive sense of the permanent objects of Nature, so that the world shall be to us an open book, and every form significant of the hidden life and final cause.

The chapter on Discipline is still more didactic than the one on Language. The first portion treats of the formation of the Understanding by the ministry of Nature to the senses, and faculty of deduction. The second section is in a higher strain. It treats of the developement of the Reason and Conscience, by means of that relation between matter and mind, which "appears" so clearly to some men, and to all in a degree. . . .

In the last part of this chapter on Discipline, the author makes a bold sally at the cause of the analogy between the external world and the moral nature. He implies that causes (the spiritual seeds of external things) are identical with the principles that constitute our being; and that *virtues* (the creations of our own heaven-aided wills) correspond to God's creations in matter; the former being the natural growth in the moral world, the latter the natural growth in the material world; or to vary the expression once more, Goodness being the projection inward—Beauty the projection outward—of the same all-pervading Spirit.

Our author here leaves the didactic, and "the solemn harp's harmonious sound" comes full upon the ear and the heart from the next Canto of his poem—Idealism. No part of the book has been so mistaken as this. Some readers affect to doubt his Practical Reason, because he acknowledges, that we have no evidence of there being essential outlying beings, to that which we certainly see, by consciousness, by looking inward, *except 'a constant faith' which God gives us of this truth.* But why should 'the noble [325] doubt,' which marks the limit of the understanding, be so alarming, when it is found to be but an introduction of the mind to the *superior certainty* residing in that 'constant faith?' Do we not advance in truth, when we learn to change the childish feeling by which we ascribe reality to the 'shows of things,' for a feeling involving a sense of God, as the only real—immutable—the All in All?

The theory of Idealism has doubtless been carried to absurdity by individuals who but half understood it; and has still more often been represented in a way which was not only useless but injurious to minds entirely dependent on what others say: for, to borrow two good compounds from Coleridge, the *half-Ideas* of many would-be Idealist writers, have passed, perforce, into the *no-Ideas* of many would-be Idealist readers. But Mr. Emerson has sufficiently guarded his Idealism by rigorous and careful expression, to leave little excuse for cavilling at his words or thoughts, except, indeed, by professed materialists and atheists, to whom he gives no ground.

"The frivolous make themselves merry," he says, "with the Ideal theory, as if its consequences were burlesque; as if it affected the stability of nature. It surely does not. God never jests with us, and will not compromise the end of Nature, by permitting any inconsequence in its procession. Any distrust of the permanence of laws, would paralyse the faculties of man. Their permanence is sacredly respected, and his faith therein is perfect. The wheels and springs of man are all set to the hypothesis of the permanence of Nature. We are not built like a ship to be tossed, but like a house to stand."

He proceeds to give the progressive appearances of Nature, as the mind advances, through the ministry of the senses, to "the best and the happiest moments of life, those delicious awakenings of the higher powers,—the withdrawing of Nature before its God." The means by which Nature herself, Poetic genius, Philosophy, both natural and intellectual—and, above all, Religion and Ethics, work, to idealize our thought and being, are then minutely pointed out. No careful thinker can dispute a step of the process. . . .

Many philosophers have stopped at Idealism. But, as Mr. Emerson says, this hypothesis, if it only deny, or question the existence of matter "does not satisfy the demands of the Spirit. It leaves God out of me. It leaves me in the splendid labyrinth of my [326] perceptions, to wander without end. Then the heart resists it, because it baulks the affections, in denying substantive being to men and women."

Mr. Emerson then proceeds to his chapter on Spirit, by which he means to suggest to us the substantial essence of which Idealism is the intellectual form. But this chapter is not full enough, for the purposes of instruction. One passage is indeed of great significance:

But when, following the invisible steps of thought, we come to inquire, Whence is matter? and whereto?—many truths arise out of the depths of consciousness. We learn that the highest is present to the soul of man; that the great universal essence which is not wisdom, or love, or beauty, or power, but all in one and each entirely, is that for which all things exist, and that by which what they are; *that Spirit creates;* that behind Nature, throughout Nature, *Spirit is present,* that Spirit is one and not compound; that Spirit does not act upon us from without, that is, in space [or] time, but spiritually or through ourselves. Therefore, that Spirit, that is the Supreme Being, does not build up Nature around us, but puts it forth through us, as the life of the tree puts forth new branches and leaves through the pores of the old. As a plant upon the bosom of God, he is nourished by unfailing fountains, and draws at his need inexhaustible power. Who can set bounds to the possibilities of Man? Once inspire the infinite, by being admitted to behold the absolute natures of justice and truth, and we learn that man has access to the entire mind of the Creator in the finite. This view, which admonishes me where the sources of wisdom and power lie, and points to virtue as

The golden key
Which opes the palace of Eternity,

carries upon its face, the highest certificate of truth, because it animates me to create my own world through the purification of my soul.

This is not only of refreshing moral *aura,* but it is a passage of the highest imaginative power, (taking the word *imaginative* in that true signification which farthest removes it from *fanciful,*) the mind must become purified indeed which can take this point of view, to look at "the great shadow pointing to the sun behind us." Sitting thus at the footstool of God, it may realise that all that we see is created by the light that shines through ourselves. Not until thus purified, can it realise that those through whose being more light flows, see more than we do; and that others, who admit less light, see less. What assistance in human culture would the application of this test give us! How would our classifications of men and women be changed, did the positive pure enjoyment of Nature become the standard of judgment! But who may apply the standard? Not every mawkish raver about the moon, surely, but only a comprehender of Nature. And has there yet been any one in human form, who could be called a comprehender of Nature, save Him who had its secret, and in whose hands it was plastic, even to the raising of the dead?

Mr. Emerson must not accuse us of ingratitude, in that after he had led his readers to this high point of view, they crave more, and accuse him of stopping short, where the world most desires and needs farther [327] guidance. We want him to write another book, in which he will give us the philosophy of his "orphic strains," whose meaning is felt, but can only be understood by glimpses.

He does, indeed, tell us that "the problem of restoring to the world original and eternal beauty," (in other words, of seeing Nature and Life in their wholeness), "is solved by the redemption of the soul." It is not unnecessary for the philosopher thus to bring his disciples round, through the highest flights of speculation, to the primitive faith of the humblest disciple, who sits, in the spirit of a child, at the feet of Jesus. But we should like to hear Mr. Emerson's philosophy of Redemption. It is very plain that it consists of broad and comprehensive views of human culture; worthy to employ the whole mind of one who seeks reproduction of Christ within himself, by such meditations as the following, which must be our last extract:

Is not Prayer also a study of truth—a sally of the soul into the unfound infinite? No man ever prayed heartily without learning something. But when a faithful thinker, resolute to detach every object from personal relations, and see it in the light of thought, shall, at the same time, kindle science with the fire of the holiest affections, then will God go forth anew into the creation.

1838-1840

"Nature . . . is nearly
thumbed to pieces"

by Thomas Carlyle

[195; September 25, 1838] The New England Pamphlets will be greedily expected. More than one inquires of me, Has that Emerson of yours written nothing else? And I have lent them the little book *Nature*, till it is nearly thumbed to pieces.

[223; April 13, 1839] The people are beginning to quote you here: *tant pis pour eux!* I have found you in two Cambridge books. A certain Mr. Richd M. Mylnes M.P. a beautiful little Tory dilettante poet and politician whom I love much, applied to me for *Nature* (the others he has) that he might write upon it. . . . Emerson is not without a select public, the root of a select public on this side of the water too.

[257; January 6, 1840] Farther I must not omit to say that Richard Monckton Mylnes purposes, thro' the strength of Heaven, to *review* you! In the next N° of the *London and Westminster*, the courageous youth will do this feat, if they let him. Nay, *he* has already done it, the Paper being actually written: he employed me last week in negotiating with the Editor about it; and their answer was, "Send us the Paper, it promises very well." We shall see whether it comes out or not; keeping silence till then. . . . Let us hear now what *he* will say of the American V*ates*.

1839

A Response from America

by John A. Heraud

[344] We have received from Boston the books quoted at the foot of this page, which, we perceive, are connected with a class of thinking that sufficiently interprets why they are sent to us. The spirit of Coleridge, Wordsworth, and Thomas Carlyle, has spread beyond the Atlantic, and we hear the echoes thereof from afar. . . .

We have long well known what influence by the elect of the school, in which we have matriculated, had been acquired over the growing intelligence of a rising country. We have rejoiced that the light of true philosophy had visited the unfettered intellect of a republican land; and while we rejoiced for their sakes, we regretted for our own, that similar principles received but slow acknowledgement under our own free institutions. . . .

[346] On Mr. Alcott's *Conversations with Children*, we shall have something to say when we come to consider the great subject of education and the educator. . . . In the meantime, we shall, in this paper, say something on a little volume, which, from the style, we doubt not to be his, but which we now see for the first time, and which is entitled simply and boldly—

"NATURE,"

with this epigraph:—

Nature is but an image or imitation of wisdom, the last thing of the soul; nature being a thing which doth only do, but not know. PLOTINUS.

This little work consists of eight short chapters, and an introduction altogether as brief. It begins manfully.

Our age is retrospective. It builds the sepulchres of the fathers. It writes biographies, histories, and criticism. The foregoing generations beheld God and Nature face to face; we, through their eyes. Why should not we also enjoy our [sic] original relation to the universe?

From *The Monthly Magazine* (London), II (September, 1839), 344–352. In addition to *Nature*, the article reviews Alcott's *Doctrine and Discipline of Human Culture* (Boston, 1836), Emerson's *Oration delivered before the Phi-Beta-Kappa Society* ("The American Scholar"), 2nd edition (Boston, 1838), and *The Boston Quarterly Review* (edited by Orestes Brownson) for October, 1838.

Why should [not] a man have a poetry and philosophy of insight and not of tradition, and a religion by revelation to us, and not the history of them [theirs]?

Yes—even to this demand the perusal of Coleridge and Wordsworth has excited the American mind: to it, it is a possibility. A direct revelation to these times! Has the old world lost the faith in it, and is it reserved for the new? "The Sun," says Alcott, truly, "shines to day also!"

The universe, according to Alcott, is composed of Nature and the Soul. Strictly speaking, therefore, all that is separate from us, all which philosophy distinguishes as the NOT ME, that is, both Nature and Art, all other men and my own body, must be ranked under this name, Nature.

He begins his contemplation of this Nature with recognising the beauty of the stars, and the reverence that, from their inaccessibility, we feel for them. "All natural objects" says he, "make a kindred impression, when the mind is open to their influence. Neither does the wisest man extort all her secrets, and lose his curiosity by finding out all her perfection. Nature never became a toy to a wise spirit. The flowers, the animals, the mountains, reflected all the wisdom of his best hour, as much as they had delighted the simplicity of his childhood. Yet the delight that we feel in Nature is not owing to Nature. The delight resides in man, or in the harmony of him and Nature. To a man labouring under calamity, the heat of his own fire hath sadness in it. Then there is a kind of contempt of the landscape felt by him who has just lost by death a dear friend. The sky is less grand as it shuts down over less worth in the creation."

We cannot read such passages, without recollecting *Wordsworth's Ode on Immortality* and *Coleridge's Ode on Dejection.*

The analysis of the rest of the Book is indicated in two sentences. "Whoever considers the final cause of the world, will discern a multitude of uses that enter as parts into that result. They all admit of being thrown into one of the following classes; Commodity, Beauty, Language, and Discipline." . . .

[349] From the significance of nature, is inferrible nature as a discipline—for the exercise of the understanding—the will—the reason—the conscience. But in all there is the same central unity. Also to the one end of discipline, all parts of Nature conspire. Is this end the final cause of the universe? and does not [*sic*] nature outwardly exist? . . . [Alcott] would reduce all the apocalypse of the mind, without fear, since the active powers of man predominate so much over the reflective, as to induce him in general to resist with indignation, any hint that nature is more short-lived or mutable than spirit. . . .

[350] Spirit, according to Alcott, does not act upon us from without, that is, in space and time, but spiritually, or through ourselves. Therefore, that spirit, that is, the Supreme Being, does not build up nature around us, but puts it forth through us, as the life of the tree puts forth new branches and leaves through the pores of the old. As a plant upon the earth, so a man rests upon the bosom of God; he is nourished by unfailing fountains, and draws, at his need, inexhaustible power.

The highest reason is the truest—empirical science clouds the the [sic] sight—the savant becomes unpoetic—the best-read naturalist is deficient in that knowledge which teaches the relations between things and thoughts. He has to learn that a guess is often more fruitful than an indisputable affirmation, and that a dream may let us deeper into the secret of nature than a hundred concerted experiments. Poetry, says Plato, comes nearer to vital truth than history.

Meditating which things, Alcott concludes his very excellent essay with some traditions of man and nature which, he says, a certain poet sang to him; and which, as they have always been in the world, and perhaps reappear to every bard, may be both history and prophecy. . . .

[351] Alcott indulges in the liveliest hopes of man's prospects. Understanding and reason are ever reconquering nature, though inch by inch. The problem of restoring to the world original and eternal beauty, he finds is solved by the redemption of the soul. Prayer is a study of truth—a sally of the soul into the unfound infinite. No man ever prayed heartily without learning something. But when a faithful thinker, resolute to detach every object from personal relations, and see in the light of thought, shall, at the same time, kindle science with the fire of the holiest affections, then will God go forth anew into the creation. . . .

So much at present for Mr. Alcott. . . .

[352] The books before us shew that in America philosophy, relatively to a few minds, has travelled on the à priori road; but it was against the grain of public opinion nevertheless. . . . When shall we in England substitute [Coleridge's *Aids to Reflection*] for Locke's *Essay on the Human Understanding?* The progress made in America will react on England—and this notice will not be in vain.

1840
"an Idealistic Pantheism"
by Richard Monckton Milnes

[345] The writings of Mr Carlyle have already received our criticism and commendation, and it may not be unpleasing to our readers to receive some supplementary notice of a mind cognate indeed to his, however inferior in energies and influences, and to us especially significant as the eldest palpable and perspicuous birth of American Philosophy. The utterances of Mr Carlyle are in the streets and schools of experienced and studious Europe, but this voice has come to us over the broad Atlantic, full of the same tender complaint, the same indignant exhortation, the same trust and distrust, faith and incredulity, yet all sufficiently modified by circumstances of personality and place to show that the plant is assimilated to the climate and the soil, although the seed may have been brought from elsewhere.

It is with no disrespect to Mr Emerson that we would say that there is little in such of his works as have reached us (and we have read all that we could find), which would be new to the competent student of European Philosophy; for we must couple this with the assertion that to the general English reader there is much that would appear extravagantly, absurdly original; and we believe that no one, however well read, would feel anything but gratification at reading thoughts already familiar to him, arrayed in language so freshly vigorous, so eloquently true.

Nor is it a matter unworthy of consideration that the Transcendental Philosophy should have been more cordially received and more generally understood in America than in Great Britain. It is certain that among the Anglo-American people, a taste for the higher speculation is large and growing, and that much is there finding its way into the popular heart which for us remains totally extraneous and unperceived. We remember hearing Coleridge, in his latter days, remark, "I am a poor Poet in England, but I am a great Philosopher over the At-[346]lantic." His 'Aids to the Creation' [i.e., *Aids to Reflection*] went through many editions there before the first was ex-

From "American Philosophy—Emerson's Works," *The Westminster Review*, XXXIII (March, 1840), 345–372. In preparing this article Milnes had received not only the encouragement of Carlyle but also information about Emerson supplied by Charles Sumner. See T. Wemyss Reid, *The Life, Letters, and Friendships of Richard Monckton Milnes, First Lord Houghton*, 2 vols. (London, 1890), I, 224–226, 237–240; Reid, I, 241–242, also prints Emerson's letter to Milnes, May 30, 1840, acknowledging receipt of the article and an accompanying note.

hausted at home. The loftier and more suggestive poetry of Wordsworth was there working out its purposes of living good, while it encumbered the shelves of the London bookseller. Mr Carlyle received a liberal share of the profits of the American edition of the 'French Revolution' before the English one had paid its expenses; and the volumes of his collected Essays now in circulation are a portion of the large American impression, commercially transferred to this country.

In these facts, too, imagination would trace a confirmation of the analogy commonly drawn between the present state of the American nation and the childhood of the life of man; for not only do we there recognise the untiring activity, the curiosity, the imitativeness, the wilfulness, the susceptibility that characterize the early stages of sensuous existence, but there are not wanting

> those obstinate questionings
> Of sense and outward things,
> Fallings from us, vanishings,
> Blank misgivings of a creature
> Moving about in worlds not realized.

And perhaps the deeper that we look below the surface of things the more natural may we find this inclination to the Idealist Philosophy in the thoughtful inhabitants of the United States. In ancient and ordered Europe it is no easy matter for a reflective mind so to adjust the outer and the inner life that the whole machine may go on harmoniously without grittiness or stoppage. In England, indeed, the existence of a large class, born independent, and (at least in the theory of the society) set apart for intellectual pursuits, together with the habit of the majority of the men engaged in the active business of life to retire after a certain period of struggle and labour into comparative repose, shades off and softens the lines of distinction between the worlds of action and of thought; while in Germany a whole army of scholars find ample employment and emolument in the genial occupations of public instruction; and statesmen, and ambassadors, and military commanders have had time and inclination to illustrate their names as Poets, Arch[æ]ologists, Historians, or Philosophers. But in the present position of America, the task of reconciling the exercise of the daily duties of social existence with that of the higher faculties and the nobler aspirations is painfully difficult. The work of the present moment there demands the entire man; he must be of the world or out of it: the sole tenure of respectability and regard among his fellow men [347] is his ability to do the thing that is before him; and this condition of itself operates as an exclusion from all search of truth for truth's sake, and, indeed, from all provinces of speculation whatever, except those which happen to be on the banks of some full and rapid tide of theological controversy. Therefore will the American, who, with outraged sensibilities, blasted hopes, and thwarted affections, turns from the external world, accept with earnest gratitude a theory which shall reduce all this self-important pomp and tumult to a poor unreality, which shall turn into mere phantasmagoria all those confusions and conflicts of passions and of interests, and shall invest with the one everlasting kingliness him, the thinker, alone.

Nor in this consideration is the peculiar relation of man to nature in that hemisphere to be forgotten. The growth of things, from the den of the wild beast to the hut of the savage, from the howlings of the hungry animals to the cries of the hungry hunters, does not there naturally and equally advance; but in one sharp transition the primeval forest becomes the village of skilful artizans; the silence of ages is invaded by the machinery elaborated from the ripest intellects of the west; the book latest born of the mature mind of man is read on the fresh-fallen trunk of the eldest child of vegetative nature; the red man and the newspaper have come together. And between these two regions of phenomena stands the American philosopher, resting on each a meditative eye, and rejoicing in a theory which brings them both under his spiritual control, and at once delivers him from the contest of feelings and principles in which he might else have been involved.

Thus, then, as a just reaction from the subjective life of the American acting, we find the objective speculation of the American thinking; thus, out of the difficulty of harmonizing nature and man, comes the desire of the Absolute, into which they both shall merge and be no more separately seen. And when we come to speak personally of Mr Emerson, we shall discover in his mind and its workings many slight indications of these things, many involuntary expressions all tending thitherward, many undesigned proofs that, however original and surprising he may appear, he is nevertheless such a man as this age of the American mind should naturally and healthfully engender.

Mr Emerson is the son of a country clergyman, and having distinguished himself at Cambridge [i.e., Harvard], the oldest and best University of the Union, was *settled* (to use the native phrase) as pastor of an Unitarian congregation in Boston. Whether from dogmatical differences with his co-religionists, or from distaste on his part to perform some ministerial functions, we know not, but some seven years ago he resigned his pulpit, and has since remained without [348] any charge, though generally regarded as a Christian minister. Unitarianism in America seems to have its orthodoxy like any other profession, and probably Dr Channing there exercises the same kind of Popedom as Dr Chalmers occupies in Calvinistic Scotland. Although it would seem that if Unitarianism is destined to so important a mission as to be the sole ultimate antagonist of Romanism in America, (a position asserted for her by many within, and some without her communion,) she must open an ample embrace to philosophical scepticism, and not be too critical of the especial belief and disbelief of those who seek her as a great home and refuge of Christian liberty. It is only under this form that Unitarianism can have any *religious* pretensions whatever. An Unitarian should be capable, without in any degree compromising his profession, of seeing more Godhead in the lowest forms of nature and humanity, than many a Trinitarian can perceive in the person of Christ. And above all things he should be tolerant of the faiths of others, whatever they are; for without this he has only the pains of doubt, and not the good that accompanies its action on the better mind. The value of faith and its operations may perhaps be most truly estimated by those who believe no longer, and while the votary of one superstition is almost necessarily impatient of and unjust to the votary of another, the wise sceptic may look up to all belief from the level of reason, with an earnest yet tearful eye, scanning the proportions and conditions of each in a large spirit of reverential compassion, which contains at once both himself and them. The Unitarians of Boston ought not to have parted with Mr Emerson.

After this separation he retired to a little country-house at Concord, within sight of the spot where the first soldier fell in the War of Independence: and there he has remained, reading, thinking, and writing, in evident observance of the principle enacted by Jean Paul, "never to write on a subject till you have first read yourself full on it, and never to read on a subject till you have thought yourself hungry on it." . . .

[360] The Philosophy of Mr Emerson is an Idealistic Pantheism. It would hardly be fair to pronounce it superficial on merely negative proof, for these writings are in nowise of a controversial character; and the exposition and illustration of his system, as far as it is given, is as earnest and sincere as if the soul of the very man were laid bare before us. But, at the same time, we cannot but regard the confidence with which he proffers his doctrine, the axiomatic character with which he invests his conclusions, and the solemnity with which he urges his hearers to act them out fully and immediately, as evidence that he has not probed the depth of the ground on which he is standing, but that, knowing it to be strong enough to bear himself at that moment, he has believed it capable of supporting the world. All religious philosophy has perhaps a basis of pantheism, but here there is little or no superstructure. The identity of man with nature, the primary duty of "a wise passiveness" to the superincumbent spirit, the "occult relation between man and the vegetable," the creed "I am nothing—I see all—the currents of the Universal Being circulate through me—I am part or particle of God" (*Nature*,—p. 13), have been uttered often before, and in many [361] senses; but here they are all-in-all, and they are propounded as if they lay on the surface of truth and within the grasp of all men, and contained not problems, or parts of problems, in the solution of which the lives of thoughtful men have gone by, leaving the giant contradictions of our moral being just as they were, standing face to face, irreconcileable.

The first look of such a system as Mr Emerson's has assuredly much that is attractive for assertors of the democratic principle in general, and for a people so circumstanced as the Americans in particular. The "vox populi vox Dei," assumes a very special import when the "vox populi" does not merely mean an historical utterance, but an expression of the universal Spirit, which is at once the Thought of God and the Instinct of Man: the sense of the majority is no longer a sum of separate wills and passions, but an absolute and transcending power, only not supernatural because it is the most perfect development of nature. The question of the truth or falsehood of these conclusions lies far too deep for our present employment, but it is plain that such conclusions might be drawn. . . .

1840

"it is clear that he has read
the writings of Swedenborg"

by Jonathan Bayley

[188] This work is, we think, the production of one of our trans-Atlantic [Sweden-borgian] brethren, whose name is unknown to us. We hail its appearance with great gratification as affording the assurance that the pure principles of eternal truth are spontaneously, as it were, exhibiting themselves in the world. The truths of the new dispensation are progressing more rapidly than we think of. The seeds of truth are carried on the wings of every wind, and every clime will become receptive of their influence. Religion is a principle inherent in the whole human race, and it becomes daily more manifest, that there is a close relationship between us and the unseen world, and we may confidently hope, that, as the doctrines of the Lord's New Church [i.e., the Swedenborgians] become more generally known and received into the heart, the human mind will acquire greater powers of perception and thought; daily and hourly it will cast off the shackles and impurities of sin, break away from the seductions of a vain and empty world, and enter more and more fully into association with the kingdom of heaven. Religion, then, will become the fountain of our actions, our hopes, and our desires, and love, the supreme end of our existence. As the humble coral is continually at work rearing up out of the deep, vast continents for the abode of our race, so the eternal principles of truth are ever silently but surely emerging from the great ocean of spiritual life.

In the little work before us, it is plainly to be observed that the beautiful and heart-cheering doctrine of correspondences is the basis on which the writer's peculiar views have been founded. The mode [189] in which the subject generally is treated, is highly calculated to fill the heart with pure and lasting images. It is assuredly wise for all who can, to cherish a love of nature, and occasionally of solitude; not indeed for the purpose of gratifying the lone enthusiasm of our spirits, by the indefinite creations of an ideal world, but to re-conquer our fading sensibilities, and to renew the freshness of virtuous emotion. The truly contemplative and pious mind will often

From *The Intellectual Repository and New Jerusalem Magazine* (London), N.S. I (April, 1840), 188–191.

gladly turn from the noise and fervour of restless occupation, to the deep and quiet solitudes of nature, ascend some mount of Olives, or enter some desert of Bethsaida, where, beneath the pure heavens, and surrounded by nature with her features and form unchanged by human art, will feel himself alone with his maker and his God. The living rock, the shaded brook, and the unviolated spring, will all speak to him in that blessed language of which they are the outward types of the beauty and glory of his heavenly home. . . . .

The . . . chapter which is headed "Language," we could have wished to have given entire, had our space permitted. If the Author is not a member of the New Church, it is clear that he has read the [190] writings of Swedenborg, and that his mind is imbued with their truths.

1841

"beautifully replete
with correspondence"

by David George Goyder

[vi] The section entitled the Religious Philosophy of Nature, is written by an American Unitarian; consequently the divinity of the Lord is not recognised, and Swedenborg is alluded to in the usual language of the transcendentalists. Why, then, it will be asked, has the Editor introduced it? He answers, because the whole subject is so beautifully replete with correspondence. The Editor rejoices to behold these evidences of approximation to a purer state of things, and hails them as harbingers to a more accurate knowledge of the Scripture; he anticipates a period when many of those who are now against us will be for us. The few errors which this section contains will be more than counter-balanced by their unquestionable beauties. The Editor will, however, in a second edition, for which there is every probability [vii] of a demand, take care to remove them, and he feels sorry that so much pure wisdom should be obscured, even by the few dark spots which this section undoubtedly contains.

From the Editor's "Advertisement" to *The Biblical Assistant, and Book of Practical Piety* . . . , edited by the Rev. D. G. Goyder (London, Manchester, Liverpool, Glasgow, and Boston, 1841), pp. v–ix. In this volume Goyder, a Swedenborgian minister of Glasgow, reprinted *Nature* in its entirety.

1841

"that mock sun of
transcendental vanity"

by John Westall

[48] It is with extreme reluctance that we insert the following remarks upon "*Nature*;" not however because we do not agree with the writer's views, but from an unwillingness to censure the course of our brethren in the [Swedenborgian] New Church. But since the work has not only been commended in the "Intellectual Reposi-[49]tory," but republished by Mr. Goyder, in a series of papers especially designed for the use of the young and inexperienced, who are thus exposed to the deadly influence of its infidel and insidious poison, we do not feel at liberty to close the pages of the Magazine to a notice of the sad mistake.—Ed[itor]. . . .

For the tendency of some portions of "Nature," is to confuse the mind upon those points, which the New Church is endeavoring to reduce to order; to weaken man's power of perceiving the True Light; instead of which it places before him that mock sun of transcendental vanity, whose fatuous light shines only to deceive and destroy. . . . To the reader of Swedenborg's writings, "Nature" contains much with which he is already acquainted, and which, if it were in better company, he would be pleased to meet with again; but the pervading spirit of the work, and several of the expressions used, will make him sorry to see it where it is. . . .

[51] Here then we find the glorification of the Lord's Humanity spoken of simply as "an example of the action of man upon nature, with his entire force;" the Word included in the same category with the traditions of antiquity, and the miracles of the Shakers; . . . and that the teachings of Swedenborg are of the same relative value as the philosophical speculations of the Egyptians, Brahmins, &c. And these principles pervade the work. We find nowhere any reference to the Lord, by whom all things were made, "and without whom there was not any thing that was made," as the Creator of the universe; but we find the writer asking in wonderment, "What angels invented these splendid ornaments. . . ." We find the name of the Saviour used without reverence, and in a manner which a mind receptive of the truth that the Lord Jesus Christ "is God over all," would not dare to adopt.

[52] We believe every reference to the Lord Jesus Christ conveys the Unitarian

From *The New Jerusalem Magazine* (Boston), XV, No. CLXX (October, 1841), 48–52.

idea, that He was a man; more perfect than other men it is true, but still a man, not the Divine Man of the Word, but the limited creation of Socinus. This being the fact . . . the conclusion is forced upon us, that to represent such a work as containing "the religious philosophy of nature," taught by the New Church, when it does not even recognize the God whom we worship as the God of nature, and of course cannot lead us up to Him, is calculated to produce evil, is a grievous error, and seems to require that this portion of the "Biblical Assistant" should be recalled and repudiated at the earliest moment. . . .

That "the religious philosophy of nature" will some day be written for the New Church, we have no doubt. But it will be by some one who receives her doctrines, whose spirituality consists in something more than the mere vaporization of self, and whose theology, rejecting the Pantheism sublimated in the alembic of fancy, which now passes under the imposing name of Transcendentalism, will be derived from the Word, as the source of all truth, the pillar and ground of Faith.

"Nature" was not written by a New Churchman, as a writer in the Intellectual Repository supposes, but is commonly understood to be the production of Mr. Ralph Waldo Emerson.

THE LATER NINETEENTH
CENTURY, 1862-1898

1862
"a Nature à la Pompadour"
by Delia M. Colton

[52] Thus, while Carlyle, bold, versatile, shrewd, untrammeled, worked upon the Unitarian element in America, Coleridge, evangelical, polished, yet adventurous, leavened the Congregationalists and other shades of orthodox Christians with the same result. But the first literary outgrowth and original product of the Transcendental movement in America was Emerson's Essay on Nature, which appeared in 1838 [sic], forming a nucleus for the writings of the Dial-ists, and proving a sort of *prolegomena* to the new edition of Hermetic Philosophy. '*Non est philosophus nisi fingit et pinxit*' [One is not a philosopher unless he moulds (feigns?) and paints], said the great pioneer. Here Emerson does both, proving, by inversion, his claim to the title. Whatever may be the negative virtues of this preliminary essay, it undoubtedly possesses the positive one of having given a strong impulse to the study and love of Nature. True, the man who is to grasp its details, sympathies, significations, to hear, in all their grand harmony, its various discordant symphonies and fugues, to see its marvelous associations, needs to be Briarean-armed, Israfel-hearted and Argus-eyed, as perhaps none in our imperfect day and generation can claim to be. But at least this 'Nature' of Emerson's insinuated, dimly and dreamily, in spite of its positive air, an occult relation between man and Nature. It invested rock and sky and air with new and startling attributes. The deep thinker might even draw upon its pages some *pays-de-Cocagne* landscape, flowing indeed with milk and honey, but in Tantalian distance. Nature's true heart is invested with a pericardium so thick that it resists the

From "Ralph Waldo Emerson," *The Continental Monthly*, I (1862), 49–62. For Emerson's comments on the article in a letter to Charles Godfrey Leland, December 23, 1861, see "A Sheaf of Emerson Letters," ed. Kenneth Walter Cameron, *American Literature*, XXIV (January, 1953), 477.

scalpel of the skillful critics, to whom the stethoscope alone betrays the healthful throb of vitality beneath. With portly arguments, Emerson bars the door to the simple but earnest-hearted. That Nature, whose prophet he is, gleams, bright and unloving, down from a cold, unsympathizing heaven.

> Not every one doth it beseem to question
> The far-off, high Arcturus.

And we, the lazzaroni on the piazza, can not even see the sky for the mist of 'mottoes Italianate and Spanish terms' of an effete logic that has risen before it.

Nevertheless, here are the first gleams of a genial appreciation of the *Æsthetik* of Germany, that large-hearted discernment that grasps similitudes from the antipodes of Thought, and writes them upon its sunny equator. And there are appeals to those finer impulses and experiences of every feeling soul that manifest a sense, imperfect yet animated, of that [53] marvelous sympathy that exists between all phases of life, whether in humanity or in external nature. His natural outbursts of feeling are rare, but delicious as *caviare*, with a certain quaver of piquancy. 'Give me health and a day, and I will make the pomp of emperors ridiculous. The dawn is my Assyria; the sunset and moon-rise my Paphos and unimaginable realms of faërie; broad noon shall be my England of the senses and the understanding, and night shall be my Germany of mystic philosophy and dreams.' Only a fantasy, and yet how he bends Nature to suit the curve of his own temperament. And who has not felt the involuntary exhilaration, appalling from its very depth, that possessed him, crossing a bare common, on a bleak October afternoon, sunless and chill, with gray winds sweeping by—'I was glad to the brink of fear.' An intense emotion is imprisoned in these words,—the irresistible intoxication of deep delight, the consciousness of an unbounded faculty for enjoyment, and a lurking but delicious dread of the lavish power of sensation cooped within the senses. . . . Still, Emerson's Nature is rather a Nature à la Pompadour, in powdered hair and jeweled stomacher and high-heeled slippers; not the dear green mother of our dreams, who was wooed by the bending heavens. . . . But Nature had been broached and Society was scandalized. Like the Chancellor in Faust, it mounted its tripod and solemnly proclaimed its verdict upon the inadmissible theory, so inadequately proved[,] of the identity of Nature and Spirit. . . .

The Transcendental movement did not fail to attract severe opposition, not only to its agitators, but toward the whole body of Unitarians, from a portion of which it in a great measure sprang. . . . The consequence of the renewed attack upon this already sorely aggrieved sect was its virtual separation into moderates and extremists: the one holding to its primitive theories, the other inclining graciously to the more comprehensive and fascinating, because more liberal and mystical, tenets of the new faith.

1881

"an idealism rare, subtle, and noble"

by George Willis Cooke

[40] As the result of these studies, while living in the "Old Manse" he wrote a little book on *Nature*, in which he gave expression to his philosophical opinions. It was published in September, 1836. The author's name was not given. The title-page bore these words from Plotinus, "Nature is but an image or imitation of wisdom, the last thing of the soul; nature being a thing which doth only do, but not know." Its leading thought is that contained in its original motto,—

> A subtle chain of countless rings
> The next unto the farthest brings;
> The eye reads omens where it goes,
> And speaks all languages the rose;
> And, striving to be man, the worm
> Mounts through all the spires of form.

It is pure idealism which he teaches throughout this little book of less than one hundred pages,—an idealism rare, subtle, and noble. The universe exists, he says, to the end of discipline; and it may be doubted "whether nature outwardly exists." Nature always speaks of spirit, and exists only for the unfolding of a spiritual being. This is the thought of the book, and it is written to vindicate this philosophy. The soul needs to be developed, and to that end should be all our living. Instead, man applies to nature but half his force, and lives a low commercial life, a life of the senses.

He developed his ideas in *Nature* more systematically than elsewhere; and he has given there a very simple, and yet a consistent, system of philosophy. A glance at what he attempts there to do will open the way to an understanding of all his subsequent teachings. He writes with the greatest enthusiasm of the attractions of nature, and finds the source of that attraction in the harmony which exists between man and the outward world. The first use nature has for man is, that it ministers to the wants of the senses. It answers, however, to a higher want still, the love of beauty. Its [41] beautiful forms delight him, but the heroic actions of men add to it a higher

From *Ralph Waldo Emerson, His Life, Writings, and Philosophy* (Boston: Osgood and Co., 1881), pp. 40–43.

charm. It becomes also a teacher of the intellect, re-forming itself in the harmonious action of the mind. Nature rises higher than beauty, and becomes an instrument of language, the vehicle of thought. The use of the outer creation is to give us language for the beings and changes of the inward creation, and nature becomes an aid in understanding the supernatural. Natural facts give us words as their signs, and in a yet more perfect manner nature is itself emblematic of the spiritual facts on which it rests. "Every natural fact is a symbol of some spiritual fact. Every appearance in nature corresponds to some state of the mind, and that state of the mind can only be described by presenting that natural appearance as its picture." Nature becomes a means of expression for those spiritual truths and experiences which could not otherwise be interpreted. Its laws, also, are moral laws when applicable to man; and so they become to man the language of the divine will.

Because the physical laws become moral laws the moment they are related to human conduct, nature has a much higher purpose than that of beauty or language, in that it is a discipline. At first it is a disciple to the understanding in intellectual truths; it trains reason, and it develops the intellect. Nature is the great moral teacher, its every fact and law a means of ethical culture. All parts of nature conspire to this one end of discipline. . . .

So thoroughly does nature answer to this end of discipline, we begin to question if this is not its only use, [42] and if nature outwardly exists. "It is a sufficient account of that appearance we call the world, that God will teach a human mind, and so makes it the receiver of a certain number of congruent sensations, which we call sun and moon, man and woman, house and trade." It is here we see Emerson's resemblance to Swedenborg, in that he cares for nature only as a symbol and revelation of spiritual realities. Because we are led to doubt the reality of outward nature, we are led on to idealism. The first work of the ideal philosophy is to emancipate us from the dominion of the senses, opening to us a larger life. It teaches us that the laws of the natural world are the ideas of the spiritual. We cease to believe in matter as final; and our attention is fastened "upon immortal necessary uncreated natures, that is, upon ideas; and in their presence we feel that the outward is a dream and a shade." Then nature becomes "an appendix of the soul." So looking upon nature we apprehend the absolute; and, as it were, for the first time we exist. Religion and ethics constantly teach us that nature depends on spirit; that the seen and outward world is temporal, while the unseen and spiritual is eternal. Idealism gives consistency to this teaching, sees the world in God, so that it is at each moment his direct revelation. Then we find that nature always speaks of spirit, suggests the absolute, is a perpetual effect of divine causes, is a great shadow pointing to the sun behind it. The aspect of nature is devout, teaches the lesson of worship, to stand before God with bended head; but when we try to describe him, both language and thought desert us, and then we find that nature is but the apparition of God.

Idealism teaches us that in consciousness is the only source of knowledge; the world is a dream, a shadow, but "the mind is a part of the nature of things." God is directly revealed to the soul of man; and we learn that "the Universal Essence, which is not wisdom or love or beauty or power, but all in one and each entirely, is that for which all things exist, and that by which they are; that spirit creates; that behind nature, [43] throughout nature, spirit is present; one, and not compound, it does not act upon us from without, that is, in space and time, but spiritually, or through ourselves." The world is a remoter and inferior incarnation of God, a projection of God in the unconscious; but it is of the same spirit with the body of man. It is a present and a fixed expositor of the divine mind, and serves always to show man his nearness to, or remoteness from, the truth.

This little book met with but a small sale, five hundred copies being sold only after twelve years; yet it attracted the attention and the warmest enthusiasm of a few persons. In England it met with an even heartier reception than here; one writer praising it in the most cordial terms, attributing its authorship to Alcott, who was better known than Emerson. Francis Bowen devoted an article to it in *The Christian Examiner*, criticising severely the transcendental philosophy. . . .

On the other hand, a writer in *The Democratic Review* was very enthusiastic in his praise. . . .

1882

"the dawn of a great idea"

by Moncure D. Conway

[150] In 1836, when Darwin returned from his voyage on the "Beagle" and sat down to his mighty task, the pattern of what he was to do was seen in the mount at Concord, and published that year in the little book entitled "Nature." A writer in the "Saturday Review," after speaking of "the great men whom America and England have jointly lost"—Emerson and Darwin—remarks that "some of those who have been forward in taking up and advancing the impulse given by Darwin, not only on the general ground where it started, but as a source of energy in the wider application of scientific thought, have once and again openly declared that they owe not a little to Emerson." This just remark may be illustrated by Tyndall's words in 1873: "The first time I ever knew Waldo Emerson was when, years ago, I picked up at a stall a copy of his 'Nature.' I read it with such delight, and I have never ceased to read it; and if any one can be said to have given the impulse to my mind, it is Emerson: whatever I have done the world owes to him."

Dr. Tyndall tells me that in the volume so purchased he wrote, "Purchased by inspiration." And he might have said, "Written by inspiration." The work was [151] inspired by the dawn of a great idea in the writer's mind—Evolution. It has a prelude of six lines—

> A subtle chain of countless rings
> The next unto the farthest brings;
> The eye reads omens where it goes,
> And speaks all languages the rose;
> And striving to be man, the worm
> Mounts through all the spires of form.

In this essay occur such phrases as—"every chemical change, from the rudest crystal up to the laws of life; every change of vegetation, from the first principle of growth in the eye of a leaf to the tropical forest and antediluvian coal-mine; every animal function, from the sponge up to Hercules,"—showing the direction in which his eye is turned. And there are these pregnant sentences:—"Nothing in Nature is

From *Emerson at Home and Abroad* (Boston: James R. Osgood and Company, 1882), pp. 150–153.

exhausted in its first use. When a thing has served an end to the uttermost, it is wholly new for an ulterior service." "Herein is especially apprehended the unity of Nature—the unity in variety—which meets us everywhere. All the endless variety of things make an identical impression." "Each creature is only a modification of the other." "Any distrust of the permanence of laws would paralyse the faculties of man." "If the reason be stimulated to more earnest vision, outlines and services become transparent, and are no longer seen: causes and spirits are seen through them." "The world proceeds from the same spirit as the body of man." "In a cabinet of natural history we become sensible of a certain occult recognition and sympathy in regard to the most unwieldy and eccentric [152] forms of beast, fish, and insect." "Nor has science sufficient humanity so long as the naturalist overlooks that wonderful congruity which subsists between man and the world, of which he is lord, not because he is the most subtile inhabitant, but because he is its head and heart, and finds something of himself in every great and small thing, in every mountain stratum, in every new law of colour, fact of astronomy, or atmospheric influence which observation or analysis lay open."

A careful perusal of the sentences just cited will show that Emerson's mind had fully conceived the idea of relationship between all organic forms, and that of the harmony of each and all with elemental environment. It may now be further noted that the notions of a mechanical creation, and of a creation passed and ended, have disappeared from his thought. God is "the universal spirit," whose "essence refuses to be recorded in propositions." The "universal essence, which is not wisdom, or love, or beauty, or power, but all in one, and each entirely, is that for which all things exist, and that by which they are." "Spirit creates." "That which, intellectually considered, we call reason, considered in relation to nature we call spirit." This spirit now creates through man. "He (man) is placed in the centre of beings, and a ray of relation passes from every other being to him. And neither can man be understood without these objects, nor these objects without man." "Spirit, that is, the Supreme Being, does not build up Nature around us, but puts it forth through us, as the life of the tree puts forth new branches and leaves through the pores of the [153] old." "Who can set bounds to the possibilities of man?" "Man has access to the entire mind of the Creator, is himself the creator in the finite." "The reason why the world lacks unity and lies broken and in heaps, is because man is disunited with himself."

"When a faithful thinker, resolute to detach every object from personal relations, and see it in the light of thought, shall, at the same time, kindle science with the fire of the holiest affections; then will God go forth anew into the creation." "Nature is not fixed, but fluid. Spirit alters, moulds, makes it. The immobility or bruteness of Nature is the absence of spirit; to pure spirit it is fluid, it is volatile, it is obedient." "All good is eternally reproductive. The beauty of Nature reforms itself in the mind, and not for barren contemplation but for new creation."

This, Emerson's first work, ends with these great words:—"The kingdom of man over Nature, which cometh not with observation,—a dominion such as now is beyond his dream of God,—he shall enter without more wonder than the blind man feels who is gradually restored to perfect sight." Forty years later the prophecy rose again when Clifford said: "Those who can read the signs of the times read in them that the kingdom of Man is at hand."

1884

"a strange sort of philosophy
in the language of poetry"

by Oliver Wendell Holmes

[91] In the year 1836 there was published in Boston a little book of less than a hundred very small pages, entitled "Nature." It bore no name on its title-page, but was at once attributed to its real author, Ralph Waldo Emerson.

The Emersonian adept will pardon me for burdening this beautiful Essay with a commentary which is worse than superfluous for him. For it has proved for many . . a very narrow bridge, which it made their heads swim to attempt crossing, and yet they must cross it, or one domain of Emerson's intellect will not be reached.

It differed in some respects from anything he had hitherto written. It talked a strange sort of philosophy in the language of poetry. Beginning simply enough, it took more and more the character of a rhapsody, until, as if lifted off his feet by the deepened and stronger undercurrent of his thought, the writer dropped his personality and repeated the words which "a certain poet sang" to him.

This little book met with a very unemotional reception. Its style was peculiar. . . It was vague, mystic, incomprehensible, to most of those who call themselves common-sense people. Some of its expressions [92] lent themselves easily to travesty and ridicule. But the laugh could not be very loud or very long, since it took twelve years, as Mr. Higginson tells us, to sell five hundred copies. It was a good deal like Keats's

> doubtful tale from fairy-land
> Hard for the non-elect to understand.

The same experience had been gone through by Wordsworth. . . .

No writer is more deeply imbued with the spirit of Wordsworth than Emerson, as we cannot fail to see in turning the pages of "Nature," his first thoroughly characteristic Essay. There is the same thought in the Preface to "The Excursion" that we find in the Introduction to "Nature." . . .

From *Ralph Waldo Emerson* (Boston and New York: Houghton, Mifflin and Company copyright 1884]), pp. 91–107.

[93] "Nature" is a reflective prose poem. It is divided into eight chapters, which might almost as well have been called cantos.

Never before had Mr. Emerson given free utterance to the passion with which the aspects of nature inspired him. He had recently for the first time been at once master of himself and in free communion with all the planetary influences above, beneath, around him. The air of the country intoxicated him. There are sentences in "Nature" which are as exalted as the language of one who is just coming to himself after being etherized. Some of these expressions sounded to a considerable part of his early readers like the vagaries of delirium. Yet underlying these excited outbursts there was a general tone of serenity which reassured the anxious. The gust passed over, the ripples smoothed themselves, and the stars shone again in quiet reflection. . . .

[99] The poet animates Nature with his own thoughts, perceives the affinities between Nature and the soul, with Beauty as his main end. The philosopher pursues Truth, but, "not less than the poet, postpones the apparent order and relation of things to the empire of thought." Religion and ethics agree with all lower culture in degrading Nature and suggesting its dependence on Spirit. "The devotee flouts Nature."—"Plotinus was ashamed of his body."—"Michael Angelo said of external beauty, 'it is the frail and weary weed, in which God dresses the soul, which He has called into time.' " Emerson would not undervalue Nature as looked at through the senses and "the unrenewed understanding." "I have no hostility to Nature," he says, "but a child's love of it. I expand and live in the warm [100] day like corn and melons."—But, "seen in the light of thought, the world always is phenomenal; and virtue subordinates it to the mind. Idealism sees the world in God,"—as one vast picture, which God paints on the instant eternity, for the contemplation of the soul.

The unimaginative reader is likely to find himself off soundings in the . . . chapter . . . *Spirit*. . . .

[101] Man may have access to the entire mind of the Creator, himself become a "creator in the finite."

As we degenerate, the contrast between us and our house is more evident. We are as much strangers in nature as we are aliens from God. We do not understand the notes of birds. The fox and the deer run away from us; the bear and the tiger rend us.

All this has an Old Testament sound as of a lost Paradise. In the next chapter he dreams of Paradise regained.

This next and last chapter is entitled *Prospects*. He begins with a bold claim for the province of intuition as against induction, undervaluing the "half sight of science" as against the "untaught sallies of the spirit," the surmises and vaticinations of the mind,—the "imperfect theories, and sentences which contain glimpses of truth." In a word, he would have us leave the laboratory and its crucibles for the sibyl's cave and its tripod. We can all—or most of us, certainly—recognize something of truth, much of imagination, and more of danger in speculations of this sort. They belong to visionaries and to poets. Emerson feels distinctly enough that he is getting into the realm of [102] poetry. He quotes five beautiful verses from George Herbert's "Poem on Man." Presently he is himself taken off his feet into the air of song, and finishes his Essay with "some traditions of man and nature which a certain poet sang to me." . . . It is a kind of New England Genesis in place of the Old Testament one. We read in the Sermon on the Mount: "Be ye therefore perfect as your Father in Heaven is perfect." The discourse which comes to us from the Trimount oracle commands us, "Build, therefore, your own world. As fast as you conform your life to the pure idea in your mind, that will unfold its great proportions." The seer of Patmos foretells a heavenly Jerusalem, of which he says, "There shall in no wise enter into it anything that defileth." The sage of Concord foresees a new heaven on earth. "A correspondent revolution in things will attend the influx of the spirit. So fast will [103] disagreeable appearances, swine, spiders, snakes, pests, mad-houses, prisons, enemies, vanish; they are temporary and shall be no more seen."

It may be remembered that Calvin, in his Commentary on the New Testament, stopped when he came to the book of the "Revelation." He found it full of difficulties which he did not care to encounter. Yet, considered only as a poem, the vision of St. John is full of noble imagery and wonderful beauty. "Nature" is the Book of Revelation of our Saint Radulphus. It has its obscurities, its extravagances, but as a poem it is noble and inspiring. It was objected to on the score of its pantheistic character, as Wordsworth's "Lines composed near Tintern Abbey" had been long before. But here and there it found devout readers who were captivated by its spiritual elevation and great poetical beauty, among them one who wrote of it in the "Democratic Review" in terms of enthusiastic admiration [pp. 90–97 above].

Mr. Bowen, the Professor of Natural Theology and Moral Philosophy in Harvard University, treated this singular semi-philosophical, semi-poetical little book in a long article in the "Christian Examiner" [pp. 81–88 above]. . . . The acute and learned Professor [104] meant to deal fairly with his subject. But if one has ever seen a sagacious pointer making the acquaintance of a box-tortoise, he will have an idea of the relations between the reviewer and the reviewed as they appear in this article. The professor turns the book over and over,—inspects it from plastron to carapace, so to speak, and looks for openings everywhere, sometimes successfully, sometimes in vain. He finds good writing and sound philosophy, passages of great force and beauty of expression, marred by obscurity, under assumptions and faults of style. He was not, any more than the rest of us, acclimated to the Emersonian atmosphere, and after some not unjust or unkind comments with which many readers will heartily agree, confesses his bewilderment, saying:—

On reviewing what we have already said of this singular work, the criticism seems to be couched in contradictory terms; we can only allege in excuse the fact that the book is a contradiction in itself.

. . . [105] The first edition of "Nature" had prefixed to it the following words from Plotinus: "Nature is but an image or imitation of wisdom, the last thing of the soul; Nature being a thing which doth only do, but not know." This is omitted in after editions, and in its place we read:—

> A subtle chain of countless rings
> The next unto the farthest brings;
> The eye reads omens where it goes,
> And speaks all languages the rose;
> And striving to be man, the worm
> Mounts through all the spires of form.

The copy of "Nature" from which I take these lines, his own, of course, . . . was printed in the year 1849, ten years before the publication of Darwin's "Origin of Species," twenty years and more before the publication of [106] "The Descent of Man." But the "Vestiges of Creation," published in 1844, had already popularized the resuscitated theories of Lamarck. It seems as if Emerson had a warning from the poetic instinct which, when it does not precede the movement of the scientific intellect, is the first to catch the hint of its discoveries. There is nothing more audacious in the poet's conception of the worm looking up towards humanity, than the naturalist's theory that the progenitor of the human race was an acephalous mollusk. "I will not be sworn," says Benedick, "but love may transform me to an oyster." For "love" read science.

Unity in variety, "*il piu nell uno*," symbolism of Nature and its teachings, genera- tion of phenomena,—appearances,—from spirit, to which they correspond and which they obey; evolution of the best and elimination of the worst as the law of being; all this and much more may be found in the poetic utterances of this slender Essay. It fell like an aerolite, unasked for, unaccounted for, unexpected, almost unwelcome,—a stumbling-block to be got out of the well-trodden highway of New England scholastic intelligence. But here and there it found a reader to whom it was, to borrow, with slight changes, its own quotation,—

> The golden key
> Which opes the palace of eternity,

[107] inasmuch as it carried upon its face the highest certificate of truth, because it animated them to create a new world for themselves through the purification of their own souls.

1897

"a sort of Yankee Shelley"

by John Jay Chapman

[31] In 1836, at the age of thirty-three, Emerson published the little pamphlet called Nature, which was an attempt to state his creed. Although still young, he was not without experience of life. He had been assistant minister to the Rev. Dr. Ware from 1829 to 1832, when he resigned his ministry on account of his views regarding the Lord's Supper. He had married and lost his first wife in the same interval. He had been abroad and had visited Carlyle in 1833. He had returned and settled in Concord, and had taken up the profession of lecturing, upon which he in part supported himself ever after. It is unnecessary to review these early lectures. . . . Suffice it that through them Emerson had become so well known that although Nature was published anonymously, he was recognized as the author. Many people had heard of him at the time he resigned his charge, and the story went abroad that the young minister of the Second Church had gone mad. The lectures had not discredited the story, and Nature seemed to corroborate it. Such was the impression which the book made upon Boston in 1836. As we read it to-day, we are struck by its extraordinary beauty of language. It is a supersensuous, lyrical, and sincere rhapsody, written evidently by a man of genius. It reveals a nature compelling respect,—a Shelley, and yet a sort of Yankee Shelley, who is mad only when the wind is nor'-nor' west; a mature nature which must have been nourished for years upon its own thoughts, to speak this new language so eloquently, to stand so calmly on its feet. The deliverance of his thought is so perfect that this work adapts itself to our mood and has the [32] quality of poetry. This fluency Emerson soon lost; it is the quality missing in his poetry. It is the efflorescence of youth. The pamphlet called Nature showed the clouds of speculation in which Emerson had been walking. With what lightning they were charged was soon seen.

From "Emerson, Sixty Years Later," *The Atlantic Monthly,* LXXIX (January–February, 1897), 27–41, 222–240; subsequently collected in Chapman's *Emerson and Other Essays* (1898).

1898

Emerson's Philosophy of Nature

by William T. Harris

[339] The eminent physicist, Tyndall, has told us that he considers Emerson a profoundly religious influence. Emerson accepted all new discoveries in science without dismay, and without loss of reverence or of faith in the supremacy of the divine in the world. This certainly is a trait that belongs to a religious nature.

There is another aspect of science, that of its relation to poetry or poetic art, that interests us when we take up Emerson's poetry. It has been supposed by some that the age of poetry is now past, and no longer possible, because of the advent of modern natural science and the invention of labor-saving machines. "The Muses have fled and Nature is forever disenchanted." If this were true, the spiritual uses of Nature would have become obsolete. Nature could not be used as a symbol of mind and a means of expression of spiritual nature. An iron age of empty show and pretence would indeed be upon us; for no poetic tropes or metaphors could be found [340] with which we could express invisible nature by visible images. If such were used, they must needs be feigned,—a sham performance imitating consciously the Greek view of Nature, which was a genuine one. An age of hollowness and insincerity, profoundly sceptical of the very existence of spiritual things, is bound to appear when men lose their insight into the correspondence between the material and spiritual, and cease to regard nature as the type whose archetype is mind. Accordingly in this epoch of prose science and machinery an unusual interest attaches to the work of its poets. The original poet of this time is the one that makes incursions into the realm of nature, with the aid of the newest scientific theories, and is able to discover spiritual correspondences in prose realities, whether they be cosmic laws or mere machines.

It is in this important field that Emerson may be regarded as the poet of the future. He sees in their poetic aspect the generalizations of astronomy, geology, and biology, —the theories of nebular consolidation and the evolution of life. The essential characteristic of poetry is to be found in metaphor and personification rather than in the forms of rhythm and rhyme. Hebrew poetry, for example, . . . has no rhythm or

From *The Genius and Character of Emerson*, edited by Frank B. Sanborn (Boston and New York: Houghton, Mifflin and Company, 1898), pp. 339–364.

rhyme, but only parallelism and correspondence, for its external dress. Much of the so-called poetry lacks metaphor and personification, although it possesses the jingle of rhyme and its metres are perfect. [341] Such writing lacks the poetic vision that sees the invisible and spiritual in the visible and material. Hence the attempt to use modern discoveries in natural science for poetic matter has for the most part failed, by reason of the lack of a deeper insight which discerned their spiritual significance.

Emerson's poetry abounds in metaphors taken from the modern theories of nature. His spiritual vision pierces through the prose hull to the vital kernel. . . .

[345] In Emerson's first published work we find an attempt to make an inventory of the various aspects of the world in time and space. His most important principle reached is this:—

It is a sufficient account of that appearance we call the world, that God will teach a human mind, and so makes it the receiver of a certain number of congruent [346] sensations, which we call the sun and moon, man and woman, house and trade.

Considering the universe as composed of nature and soul, he defines the former: "Strictly speaking, all that is separate from us, all which philosophy distinguishes as the NOT ME, that is, both nature and art, all other men and my own body, must be ranked under this name, NATURE." Four uses include the purposes served by objects of nature. These are commodity, beauty, language, discipline. . . .

[348] Coming to the fourth use of Nature, discipline, he finds this to include all the others. "Nature . . . offers all its kingdoms to man as the raw material which he may mould into what is useful." "One after another his victorious thought comes up with and reduces all things until the world becomes at last only a realized will,—the double of man."

Moreover, everything has a moral aspect. "All things with which we deal preach to us. . . . The chaff and the wheat, weeds and plants, blight, rain, insects, sun,—it is a sacred emblem from the first furrow of spring to the last stack which the snow of winter overtakes in the fields."

From this idea of discipline in morals Emerson finds a transition to idealism through the thought of the "unity of nature,—the unity in variety which meets us everywhere." In fact, we find everywhere in this remarkable essay what may be called a dialectic, whereby one part joins to the next by a sort [349] of natural growth. Thus commodity becomes beauty through the idea of all society existing for the well-being of each member of it,—the whole existing in the part manifests beauty. So, too, beauty becomes language in its phase of presenting self-knowledge. Language in its highest form, wherein Nature as a whole reflects spirit as a whole, reveals the end of Nature as a discipline, and we reach an ultimate unity.

"So intimate is this unity that it is easily seen; it lies under the undermost garment of nature, and betrays its source in universal spirit." . . .

[353] In the six chapters that are devoted to this discussion we have progressed by a natural growth of the subject—by what would be called a dialectical evolution of the

idea of nature—to the doctrine of the first principle of the world as a personal being. In the seventh chapter . . . this result is made a special theme. It is the doctrine of Spirit as the absolute. "Idealism is a hypothesis to account for nature by other principles than those of carpentry and chemistry." But as merely negative it is a defective view. "If it only [354] deny the existence of matter, it does not satisfy the demands of the spirit. It leaves God out of me. It leaves me in the splendid labyrinth of my perceptions, to wander without end." . . .

Up to this point the doctrine of nature has been what we may call that of evolution, or at least in harmony with the modern doctrine of that name. Indeed, there is prefixed to the essay one of those oracular pieces of verse that Emerson often used to sum up his prose essays. The key-note which expresses the theme sounds forth:—

> A subtle chain of countless rings
> The next unto the farthest brings;
> The eye reads omens where it goes,
> And speaks all languages the rose;
> And, striving to be man, the worm
> Mounts through all the spires of form.

Here is the doctrine of evolution substantially set forth. It does not say that the lower produces the higher. Nor does the doctrine of evolution, when rightly understood. In saying "there is a survival of the fittest," it says that mind is the goal of nature. The farther from mind, the farther from survival. The chaotic and inorganic is an unstable [355] equilibrium which is continually changing and attempting some new form. But individuality begins when nature ascends to mind, and the power of self-preservation increases with the increase of mind. . . . Evolution of the fittest . . . points to man or spiritual being as the final cause of nature. All beings are on their way thither. In the result of the process of nature one may read the character of the supreme first principle revealed in it. If nature is so constituted that left to its own laws it does evolve and can evolve only rational creatures as the fittest, evidently the absolute Being must be rational. Here is the view of nature that Emerson had reached and announced in his own doctrine of evolution before 1836. While it is substantially the doctrine of evolution, it is spiritual evolution; being an insight into the fact that nature reveals spirit as its final cause, and into the fact that the universe is not alien to man, but throughout the projection of a being like man, or divine-human.

Turning from the contemplation of evolution to the final chapter of this treatise on "Nature," we come to the question of "Prospects." In the eighth chapter we rise to take a survey of the whole. "Prospects" shall mean both history and prophecy.

[356] He unfolds in this chapter an altogether new and surprising theory of the world,—a theory that one would pronounce incompatible with the evolutional theory developed thus far. It is no less than the theory of "Lapse," or Descent of the Soul, somewhat like that found in the fourth Ennead of Plotinus.

There are, indeed, a few notes in the preceding chapter on "Spirit," at the close, which form the transition to this remote doctrine of Lapse. The inadequacy or imperfection of the individual is the connecting link. "As we degenerate, the contrast between us and our house is more evident. We are as much strangers in nature as we are aliens from God. We do not understand the notes of birds. The fox and the deer run away from us; the bear and the tiger rend us. We do not know the uses of more than a few plants, as corn and the apple, the potato and the vine." . . .

[357] If man is the creator of the finite, then all imperfect beings have arisen through his agency. From this the doctrine of Lapse is easily deduced. But the doctrine of Evolution does not account for the existence of lower orders of being by supposing a lapse, or degeneration, of higher beings. It supposes that an All-Good Highest Being desires to share his blessedness with creatures, and therefore creates them by an eternal process, giving them the possibility of developing by freedom into all knowledge and goodness. All lower and lowest creatures belong to the process necessary in the Divine Wisdom for creating beings with free individuality. Such free individuality must be reached by the exercise of will power. Natural selection involves this exercise of such rudiments of will and intellect as belong to lowest organisms. Arrived at man, individuality is reached that can know universal truth, and will universal good; and thus the final type is attained.

As the view of evolution here described makes nature a process of creating new spirits, and thus of increasing the number of blessed beings, it is thoroughly optimistic in its character. The other view, that explains nature by the fall of spirits from an Eden of blessedness or by a lapse from holiness, is, on the contrary, pessimistic. . . .

[358] Either because he wishes to indicate that the theory is one delivered to him by tradition, and one which he has not fully verified in his own intuitions, or because he has a feeling of the discrepance between this theory and that of evolution already approved, he calls it "some traditions," and intimates that he received it from "a certain poet," whom he quotes or feigns to quote. Note especially the difference in style between the foregoing essay and these "traditions." There is a sort of poetic rhythm in the latter, and a sonorous balance of sentences quite in contrast to the epigrammatic style of the remainder of the treatise. . . .

[361] This form of the Lapse differs from the Oriental tradition of it, found in Neoplatonism and Gnosticism, in having two forms of paradise,—a past and a future. Since the soul lapsed from a past perfection, [362] how can it be assured against a future lapse if it recovers its state once more? More especially, how can it recover at all?

The inconsistency of Asiatic philosophy ever reappears in the mysticism of the Occident. But this special form of it,—one is piqued to ask: Does it belong to some earlier studies of Emerson which marked his first insights into Plato's Phædrus, or the Enneads of Plotinus, or Jacob Boehme? And did he feign to quote it in order (like a favorite device of Carlyle) to avoid the necessity of making a steep transition to such an Orphic style? Or, are the quotation-marks no mask, after all, and did he quote the substance of his friend Alcott's Orphic rhapsodizings? Perhaps, however, these words were written before the acquaintance with Alcott began; perhaps, too, before Alcott himself adopted the theory of the Lapse. But it is certain that nowhere else . . . could one find such a complete statement of the Lapse theory, held by Alcott ever since the Orphic sayings were written for "The Dial" in 1842.

I cannot think that Emerson ever held the doctrine of the Lapse, or believed it seriously to be the true view of the world. He makes occasionally a poetic allusion to it, and sometimes seems to be attracted by its intimation of a former union with God which the soul may attain again; but for his own genuine theory of the world one must look to his statement of evolution—an *ascent* rather than a lapse.

RECENT CRITICISM, 1930-1967

1930

"a little manual of pantheism"

by Regis Michaud

[133] In 1836 he published anonymously and under an azure cover a little manual of pantheism entitled *Nature*. Under the common ægis of Lamarck and Plotinus, this was a reply to his doubts in the Jardin des Plantes, a *De Rerum Natura*, a poem in prose. With his habitual serenity and without further ado, he gave here the quintessence of his meditations and reading. The outer world embarrassed him; it baffled his idealism. Emerson adroitly juggled it away. His tactics toward the universe might be called caressing. He began by adopting the outer world and doing it the honor of believing it real. In a series of contemplations entitled "Commodity," "Beauty," "Discipline," he declared that he embraced the universe. But he did [134] not remain faithful to it for long. In the chapter on language the outer world begins to evaporate. It is no longer anything but a dictionary of metaphors for the use of poets. And suddenly, disloyally, Emerson gives it the slip. Three final stages, where the lyricism ascends proportionally as we approach the dénouement, plunge us into the heart of pantheism, of mythology. The world is nothing more than a fiction of the mind. It is man who has created the sun, woman the moon. In the age of innocence the universe was the irradiation of our thoughts, but through our fault it has petrified on the surface. The universe crushes man, its inventor. Emerson does not consider this fall as definitive. In a final overflow of poetry he announces the eternal youth of the soul and of the universe. What the discursive reason has destroyed, let divine instinct reconstruct. Let the rejuvenated soul render to the world its primitive beauty and its unity. Let wisdom and love join hands and transfigure the ever youthful, the plastic universe.

There is recognizable beneath these beautiful myths a translation of the Christian

From *Emerson the Enraptured Yankee*, translated by George Boas (New York: Harper and Brothers, 1930), pp. 133–135. Reprinted with the permission of Harper & Row, Publishers.

dogma. It was Calvin set to music and transposed by Plato, [135] Plotinus, and Swedenborg. The theologians have not been mistaken on the bearing of this Purana and this new fashion of interpreting the dogma of the fall and the redemption. Emerson juggles away God as serenely as the world. For Jehovah he boldly substitutes Prometheus. In the land of the Puritans such audacity and poetry had never been seen, but a whole generation of youth thrilled at the voice of the Enchanter.

1952

The Angle of Vision

by Sherman Paul

[83] Even more than the distant vision it satisfied, astronomy gave Emerson a chance to speak for "the sovereignty of Ideas" (*JMN*, V, 146). As a student of thirteen, he chose astronomy for the subject of a free theme (*L*, I, 29), and astronomy—imaginatively interpreted—excited him during the long remainder of his life. Herschel's great astronomy was his source book, and his "The General Nature and Advantages of the Study of the Physical Sciences," as much as Emerson's own delight in the Jardin des Plantes, directed him to the natural [84] sciences (*L*, I, 343; *JMN*, IV, 238). In them, he was searching for the moral law, and astronomy—"thought and harmony in masses of matter" (*W*, I, 219)—seemed to Emerson its most grandiloquent expression. Calvinism and Ptolemaic astronomy lacked this moral grandeur for Emerson: they had yet to grasp the moral beauty of the Newtonian universe. They did not know "the extent or the harmony or the depth of their moral nature." Like the Unitarians, "they are clinging to little, positive, verbal versions of the moral law, and very imperfect versions too, while the infinite laws, the laws of the Law, the great circling truths whose only adequate symbol is the material laws, the astronomy, etc., are all unobserved" (*JMN*, IV, 83). For to observe the stars was, for Emerson, to "come back to our real, initial state and see and own that we have yet beheld but the first ray of Being" (*JMN*, V, 468). It was in the search for this experience that he began *Nature* (*W*, I, 7), and it was the end of all he said in *Nature* to bring men "to look at the world with new eyes" (*W*, I, 85). In viewing the stars he escaped into loneliness and health (*JMN*, IV, 267, 358), because alone in an atmosphere "transparent with this design" he felt "a perpetual admonition of God and superior destiny" (*JMN*, IV, 267). Again he undulated with the sea of being (*JMN*, V, 468), rested his immortality in the immortal stars, and found in their great circles the laws that merger transformed into ideas. Properly *distant*, the natural unarmed eye achieved an angle of vision in which perception had a destiny (*J*, VIII, 321). Properly distant, restored to its natural scope, the eye was no longer retrospective, but prospective (*J*, VI, 190).

II

Emerson's critics, understandably, seized the central and striking image of the, eyeball. Cranch has left us nothing that will give him as much fame, perhaps, as his good-natured sketch of this passage (L, II, 190 [see Plate II]). But the Very Rev. Henry [85] A. Braun, reviewing *Nature* in *The Catholic World*, cited the passage as evidence of insanity: "We wonder, when he wrote that, whether he was not bilious and his 'eyeball' bloodshot as he looked at it in the glass?" He was using this "critical" bludgeon to prove that "Nature is not the correlative of the mind." *The Westminster Review* of London also singled it out as full of familiar truths, but here too much relied on and simplified: "They are propounded as if they lay on the surface of truth and within the grasp of all men, and contained not problems . . . in the solution of which the lives of thoughtful men have gone by, leaving the giant contradictions of our moral being just as they were, standing face to face, irreconcilable." [Cf. p. 105, above, in the review by Richard Monckton Milnes.]

What these and other critics have often failed to see is that the transparent eyeball is only representative for Emerson of one aspect of the mind, and that the angle of vision as a metaphor of inspiration has its origins in Emerson's thought in the religious affirmation of compensation. For the problem of the mind, as it presented itself to Emerson, was that of a twofold process. Structurally, this process was represented by the two poles or termini of the mind: Intellect Receptive and Intellect Constructive (W, II, 334). They recreated in man-the-microcosm the cosmological dualism of the universe. Functionally, they presented the problems of inspiration and its control, of passivity or "pious reception" and concentration or form. Between these poles the life of the mind played like a sputtering spark, and Emerson's creative task was to prohibit a surplus of energy to store itself at either pole and thus intermit the circuit. "Human life," he wrote, "is made up of two elements, power and form, and the proportions must be invariably kept, if we would have it sweet and sound" (W, III, 65). Seen in another way, this mental equilibrium required innocence and sophistication, that is, the openness of response and mature judgment that modern critics of the arts often [86] remark on as impossible: "The lover of nature is he whose inward and outward senses are still truly adjusted to each other; who has retained the spirit of infancy even into the era of manhood" (W, I, 9). Although the receptive aspect of this process—certainly the more primary in Emerson's experience—was mystical merger, Emerson was not a mystic in the usual "visionary" sense of the word. He was not seeking in the angle of vision an escape from the world; as it formed, the angle of vision was to make *use* of the world. But mystical union, for him, was an epistemological necessity. Vision, he said of the inner seeing of the mind, "is not like the vision of the eye, but is union with the things known" (W, II, 325). The knowledge of merger, however, had its use only in the prudential world; if knowledge *began* in reception, it ended in action. Mysticism ended in rest. And

"Man," he wrote, "was made for conflict, not for rest. In action is his power; not in his goals but in his transitions man is great" (W, XII, 60).

The transitions, or better, the transmutation of mystical power into form was his best description of the life of the mind. In this process the mind was a transmitter, a conduit through which the infinite was funneled from the spiritual reservoir to the prudential tap. Or again, to switch the metaphor, mind was the lens converging the rays of spirit on the daily affairs of man. Standing between the worlds of spiritual laws and prudential affairs, man's "health and erectness," Emerson wrote, "consist in the fidelity with which he transmits influences from the vast and universal to the point on which his genius can act" (W, I, 208–209). The point of action was found in everyday life, just as the only way of making the mystical power of insight available was by conveying it to men in the "language of facts." The ray of spiritual light, he pointed out in illustration, "passes invisible through space, and only when it falls on an object is it seen." Similarly, "when the spiritual energy is directed on something outward, [87] then it is a thought" (W, II, 335). Speaking of his own experience of transition as ebb and flow, Emerson described the same process more "psychologically": "The daily history of the Intellect is this alternating of expansions and concentrations. The expansions are the invitations from heaven to try a larger sweep, a higher pitch than we have yet climbed, and to leave all our past for this enlarged scope. Present power, on the other hand, requires concentration on the moment and the thing to be done" (W, XII, 58).

In this twofold process of expansion and concentration, nature was instrumental both as the activator of insight and as the object of focus. Correspondence, therefore, as an inspirational means, was sympathy with nature, as well as the doctrine of its expression. . . .

1953

The Dream of Greatness

by Stephen E. Whicher

[52] Since *Nature* is written under several strong and not always harmonious influences—Coleridge, Swedenborg, and various varieties of Platonism—and since it discusses such an array of elaborately subdivided topics, one cannot always easily penetrate its rapid criss-cross of ideas and see its underlying intention. A comparison with the contemporary journals, however, makes plain that Emerson's inquiry into the meaning and purpose of nature is at bottom an effort to assimilate nature into himself, to reduce the NOT ME to the ME. The effort took two directions: one, toward the conquest of nature intellectually, by achieving her Idea or theory; the other, toward a practical conquest, a kingdom of man, by learning the lesson of power. Through most of the book the first is dominant; the aim of the book is to indicate an answer to the question, To what end is [53] nature? His chief weapon for this conquest of nature is idealism, a word he uses in two senses: the Ideal Theory of the Locke-Berkeley-Hume tradition; and a more Platonic conception.

The first five chapters are designed to establish the dominion of Platonic Ideas over nature. A soon discarded Swedenborgian notion of nature as a kind of divine cryptogram, a mute gospel which man is to decipher, somewhat obscures this purpose in *Nature*, but it emerges clearly in a summary entered in his journals at about the time he was putting the book together for the press. 'The delight that man finds in classification is the first index of his Destiny. He is to put nature under his feet by a knowledge of Laws. . . . The moment an idea is introduced among facts the God takes possession. . . . Thus through nature is there a striving upward. Commodity points to a greater good. Beauty is nought until the spiritual element. Language refers to that which is to be said. Finally; Nature is a discipline, and points to the pupil and exists for the pupil. Her being is subordinate; his is superior; Man underlies Ideas. Nature receives them as her God.'

Up to this point Emerson has not gone much farther than a Cambridge Platonist or a Unitarian might have gone, though he has undoubtedly expressed himself differ-

From Chapter Three of *Freedom and Fate: An Inner Life of Ralph Waldo Emerson* (Philadelphia: University of Pennsylvania Press, 1953), pp. 52–57. Copyright 1953 by the University of Pennsylvania Press. Used with the permission of the publisher.

ently. He has asserted the primacy of Ideas, has called this world a place of discipline, and has read man's moral values into his environment. He portrays a man, however, still in a state of pupilage, environed with a parentally superior nature, even if she is centered on him; and he has done little to suggest that the common God of man and nature is not the familiar external Creator, playing his master role in the drama of Christendom. From this subordination he breaks loose in the last three chapters, using the sceptical sense of idealism as a lever. Here he accomplishes his real revolution. Outside is subjected to inside; the huge world comes round to the man.

First, by means of the Ideal Theory, he would lead us 'to regard nature as [a] phenomenon, not a substance; to attribute necessary existence to spirit; to esteem nature as an accident and an effect.' Nature is brought within the sphere of the self; man [54] is finally cut adrift from the belief in any reality external to himself. But to affirm the lack of a reality outside was only half the truth, unless reality were rediscovered inside; so Emerson moves from idealism to spiritualism. 'The Idealist says, God paints the world around your soul. The spiritualist saith, Yea, but lo! God is within you. The self of self creates the world through you. . . .' Thus the final revelation, reached in the chapter 'Spirit,' is the oneness of man and the self of self, so that man, the self, can be considered in a certain sense not merely the pupil or the observer but the creator of nature. Here, of course, the distinction springs up between the universal man and the individual; as things are, the self of self seems infinitely to transcend the capacities of the individual. But the distinction is a secondary or relative one, between possibility and actuality, and not between two separate things; the thought that stirs Emerson is that God is essentially self, and that ideally or poetically the two should and can be identical.

This ultimate assimilation of God into the self is the vision of the orphic poet in 'Prospects.' Whatever the relation of these passages to the conversation of Alcott, they are clearly integral to Emerson's book and Emerson's thought. The orphic poet is a device for expressing certain of Emerson's insights too bold and visionary to be asserted in his own person. Where expository prose, tied down to common sense, falters, the freer and more irresponsible speech of the poet can complete the thought. And the thought the orphic poet expresses for his creator is the ideal identity of man and God.

'Nature is not fixed but fluid. Spirit alters, moulds, makes it. . . . Every spirit builds itself a house, and beyond its house a world, and beyond its world a heaven. . . . Build therefore your own world. . . . The kingdom of man over nature, which cometh not with observation,—a dominion such as now is beyond his dream of God,—he shall enter without more wonder than the blind man feels who is gradually restored to perfect sight.' At the same time the poet spins a myth of the fall of man, to account for man's present compound nature. Emerson regularly moves into mythology when speaking of this duality—necessarily, since [55] his philosophy denies it. Why is man not divine in fact as well as in nature? There is no answer from philosophy, but the poet can interpose a fable. 'A man is a god in ruins. . . . Once he . . . filled nature with his overflowing currents. Out from him sprang the sun and moon. . . . But, having made for himself this huge shell, his waters retired; he no longer fills the veins and veinlets; he is shrunk to a drop. . . . Yet sometimes he starts in his slumber, and wonders at himself and his house, and muses strangely at the resemblance betwixt him and it.'

In this chapter, also, the intellectual and the practical conquests of nature come together. Why can we not discover the secret of nature? 'The reason why . . . is because man is disunited with himself.' We shall find a theory of nature when we achieve the redemption of the soul. And the same self-fulfillment will solve the question of power. The momentary exhibitions of man's proper dominion over things that we now glimpse in acts of heroism, in art and poetry, in 'many obscure and yet contested facts, now arranged under the name of Animal Magnetism; prayer; eloquence; self-healing; and the wisdom of children,' will become steady and habitual when the work of culture is complete, and 'you conform your life to the pure idea in your mind.' Then will come about, intellectually and practically, the kingdom of man that, to the eye of Reason, is no mythological prophecy sung by a poet to beguile the understanding into faith, but is now.

The full revolutionary force of what Emerson in these later chapters is saying is obscured by his Platonic and moralistic language, even in the exposition of his least orthodox thoughts. He himself, perhaps, does not fully appreciate the newness of what he is trying to say and wavers ambiguously between transcendental egoism and Platonic idealism. His originality remains impressive. One cannot demonstrate any important influence of Fichte or of any other source of German idealism on Emerson, although hints and echoes of this way of thinking were of course in the air. Though presumably he would not have moved in this direction if he had not been prompted to do so by some indirect Germanic influences, he still comes to this faith independently, [56] his will to believe such doctrine allowing him, without altogether understanding his own thought, to expand a few imperfect hints into a whole worldview.

His contemporary Theodore Parker knows little of this egoism, nor Hedge, nor Ripley, all three good German scholars; the two latter cling to what vestiges of historical faith their Unitarianism and intuitionism together may leave them; the former is simply an intuitionary *philosophe*, deploying all his scholarship in support of his grand design to try the creeds of the churches and the constitutions of the states by the nature of mankind and the constitution of the universe. Brownson again, even at his most transcendental, has a social consciousness quite foreign to this self-centeredness. Nor is there anything really similar in Alcott's high-souled talk of Lapse and Birth and Personalism, nor in Margaret Fuller's enthusiasms, nor even in Thoreau, whose sensuous and spiritual self-immersion in nature is quite unlike Emerson's desire to put nature under his feet.

Though Coleridge more than anyone else helped him to this faith, his own religious experience and feeling is very different. Perhaps Carlyle, heavily influenced by

Fichte, provides the closest parallel, but even he sees a call to duty and discipline and *Entsagen* where Emerson, for all his moralism, sees the emancipation of man. Borrowing hints and phrases from all around him, responding with his uncanny sense for the key thought to the intricate cross-influences of his time, Emerson yet strikes one of the most startlingly new notes, all circumstances considered, ever to be struck in American literature, while hardly appearing to be aware that he has said anything unusual. The lesson he would drive home is man's entire independence. The aim of this strain in his thought is not virtue, but freedom and mastery. It is radically anarchic, overthrowing all the authority of the past, all compromise or coöperation with others, in the name of the Power present and agent in the soul.

This revolutionary reading of his discovery of the God within, as it is the most unsettling, so it is the most unstable. It could come into being at all, one feels, only because of his peculiar craving for self-dependence. And it is protected also by the [57] very fact that it is not the only element in Emerson's faith, but one member in an ambiguity. He could proclaim self-reliance because he could also advocate God-reliance; he could seek a natural freedom because he also sought a supernatural perfection; he could challenge society with his heresies because he considered himself closer to the true faith than they; he could assert that the individual is the world because, thanks to the moral law, we know that nothing arbitrary, nothing alien shall take place in the universe; the huge world, which he dared to defy, was really on his side and would not, as it were, spoil his game. The dual necessity, at once divergent and identical, to be free and invulnerable shapes much of his thinking.

1954

"the last of his apprentice exercises"

by Richard P. Adams

[121] Nature has always seemed to me, in spite of its many brilliant passages, a fundamentally unsatisfactory piece of work. However, for that reason, an examination of it yields important clues to Emerson's difficulty in arriving at a coherent statement of his thoughts and beliefs. Its lack of unity may be explainable partly by the persistence of the sermon structure, with its firstly, secondly, and so on, which is poorly suited to the subject. But a more important reason, it seems to me, is that its language also fails to assimilate the organic idea which it struggles to express.

One reason for both these weaknesses may be that the strategy of the book was determined too early, before Emerson had gained a clear understanding of the gospel he wanted to preach. In a sermon on "Summer," first delivered on 14 June 1829, he had discussed nature under four headings very like the first four he was to use in 1836: first, the utilitarian function of plants in assimilating nutritious elements from the earth and making them fit for human sustenance ("Commodity"); second, the beauty of nature, which is not necessary for our physical welfare and must therefore be "to give pleasure" to our souls ("Beauty"); third, the correspondence between us and nature which makes everything in it "an emblem, a hieroglyphic," and a means of communicating the soul's truth among men ("Language"); and fourth, a moral influence admonishing us to do our duty as well as the plants do theirs ("Discipline").[1] On 6 January 1832, when he put down in his journal an outline of a book he thought of writing, he used a somewhat similar list of topics [see p. 38 above, item 1]. And, when he finally began the work, at the end of his first European trip in September 1833, he was obviously still committed to the same general scheme. In these four headings, and more especially in the three he added, "Idealism," "Spirit," and "Prospects," he established only partly, and then in fragments, the desired sense of harmony with the world. His point of view was not steady enough; it shifted uncomfortably and unpredictably between something like Platonic idealism and something like romantic organicism, doing justice to neither.

Reprinted by permission of the Modern Language Association from "Emerson and the Organic Metaphor," PMLA, LXIX (March, 1954), 117–130.
[1] Young Emerson Speaks, ed. Arthur S. McGiffert, Jr. (Boston, 1938), pp. 43–45.

[122] The same awkwardness may be seen in the slight but irritating inappropriateness of diction that permeates the essay, especially in the chapter on "Language," where Emerson tried to make use of the Swedenborgian doctrine of correspondence, the theory that the world objectifies the mind of God and therefore also the similarly formed, though smaller, mind of man. The Swedenborgian correspondence, with its one-to-one ratio of idea and object, is not the same thing as the organic theory of functional and universal relationship, as Emerson himself later pointed out (*Works*, IV, 121). His eclectic use of it in *Nature* was as a stepping-stone to the pure organic idea for which he had not yet mastered an effective vocabulary.

The essay itself seems less like a stepping-stone than a stumbling-block in Emerson's career; the last of his apprentice exercises rather than the first of his mature works; a thing that had to be done before he could do something better, to be put behind him before he could go ahead. It belongs to 1829 more than to 1836, and its publication represents a clearing up and clearing away of Emerson's accounts with his teachers and his own journals to that point, and brings him up to date. It is partly for that reason, I suspect, that when the pressure of the Phi Beta Kappa invitation was applied he was ready, though not without difficulty and worrying delays, to say more cogently [in "The American Scholar"] what he thought in 1837.

1964

Two Remarks in *Nature*

by *Jonathan Bishop*

[9] Books of criticism, even those whose pretensions are necessarily ancillary, also imply a position on larger cultural issues, whether or not these appear overtly. To describe and explain is always also to advocate. And to talk on behalf of Emerson is to engage oneself in a war of values, in which judgments about the importance of certain literary figures in the American past are a way of talking about human preferences for the future. . . . Here I need only say that these speculations derive from an assumption that Emerson is a true ancestor: that *Nature* is our primal book, and that the tradition of prophecy and art descending from it leads not only through Emerson's later work and through Alcott and Thoreau to Dickinson and Frost, but most strongly through the vital center of Melville, Whitman, William James, Henry Adams, and Wallace Stevens; it thus constitutes, though not our only tradition, still our greatest, our one indispensable tradition. In an age in which the seminal claims of Hawthorne and Twain have had somewhat more than their due, this fact might be better understood than it is. If it were, we should now be able to make better use of the very untraditional welter we are in now. Emerson is still our good old cause.

Let me complete this necessarily rather abstract introduction by demonstrating in miniature the sort of thing I shall do in detail. There is a certain risk in incorporating long quotations in [10] books of criticism, but let me ask the reader to read this one and to determine which of the sentences in the following passage from *Nature* is the best and which the worst. Laying my own cards on the table, I should be willing to exaggerate and say there is one of each: one of the best remarks in Emerson and one of the silliest.

To speak truly, few adult persons can see nature. Most persons do not see the sun. At least they have a very superficial seeing. The sun illuminates only the eye of the man, but shines into the eye and the heart of the child. The lover of nature is he whose inward and outward senses are still truly adjusted to each other; who has retained the spirit of infancy even into the era of manhood. His intercourse with heaven and earth becomes part of his daily food.

In the presence of nature a wild delight runs through the man, in spite of real sorrows. Nature says,—he is my creature, and maugre all his impertinent griefs, he shall be glad with me. Not the sun or the summer alone, but every hour and season yields its tribute of delight; for every hour and change corresponds to and authorizes a different state of [the] mind, from breathless noon to grimmest midnight. Nature is a setting that fits equally well a comic or a mourning piece. In good health, the air is a cordial of incredible virtue. Crossing a bare common, in snow puddles, at twilight, under a clouded sky, without having in my thoughts any occurrence of special good fortune, I have enjoyed a perfect exhilaration. I am glad to the brink of fear. In the woods, too, a man casts off his years, as the snake his slough, and at what period soever of life is always a child. In the woods is perpetual youth. Within these plantations of God, a decorum and sanctity reign, a perennial festival is dressed, and the guest sees not how he should tire of them in a thousand years. In the woods, we return to reason and faith. There I feel that nothing can befall me in life,—no disgrace, no calamity (leaving me my eyes), which nature cannot repair. Standing on the bare ground,—my head bathed by the blithe air and uplifted into infinite space,—all mean egotism vanishes. I become a transparent eyeball; I am nothing; I see all; the currents of the Universal Being circulate through me; I am part or parcel of God. The name of the nearest friend sounds then foreign and accidental: to be brothers, to be acquaintances, master or servant, is then a trifle and a disturbance. I am the lover of uncontained and immortal beauty. In the wilderness, I find something more dear and connate than in the streets or villages. In the tranquil landscape, and especially in the distant line of the horizon, man beholds somewhat as beautiful as his own nature. (W, I, 8–10 [pp. 7–8, above])

Perhaps one's first impression as he reads along here is the undistinguished mildness of most of it. But the good and bad remarks do stand out. The bad one, presumably, is the "transparent eyeball" sentence, perhaps the best known sentence of Emerson's among readers who wish to make fun of him. I shall want [11] to look at it again in a moment, but first let us examine the good one. This, as I take it, is, "Crossing a bare common, in snow puddles, at twilight, under a clouded sky, without having in my thoughts any occurrence of special good fortune, I have enjoyed a perfect exhilaration," and its coda, "I am glad to the brink of fear." Suppose one agrees that this is the noticeably good place in the paragraph. Can its excellence be accounted for? The subject matter, in the broad sense, would not explain it; the whole paragraph is about the response of man to experience, and almost all the individual sentences attempt to express or recommend the joy of contact with nature. Such redundancy is a usual principle of order, indeed, in an Emersonian paragraph; the separate sentences are often more or less synonymous ways of saying "the same thing." Another sentence near by is an example: "Not the sun or the summer alone, but every hour and season yields its tribute of delight; for every hour and change corresponds to and authorizes a different state of the mind, from breathless noon to grimmest midnight." Here is the same point being made quite without distinction— except a little, a tiny amount, in the abstract comprehensiveness of the turn through "corresponds to and authorizes." "Breathless noon," "grimmest midnight," and "yields its tribute" are the stock properties of college rhetoric.

But, in a sharper sense, the motif is important. The good sentence repeats the touch of an actual experience or combination of experiences—the verb "have enjoyed" leaves it open whether the event has occurred more than once. The bareness of the common, the clouds, the puddles of melting snow, quickly identify a concrete image of winter thaw or early spring weather in a New England village. The wry trick the sentence plays depends in part on one's knowledge that those experiences are the least likely to seem occasions of joy at the time. New England weather is at its ugliest, the villages at their meanest, on such chill wet days, and walkers crossing the common are anxious to get home to change their shoes. Here of course is part of Emerson's point; the voice obliges you to take another look at the potential beauty of mean situations.

This brings us to the speaker. It is worth comparing him to the Victorian rhapsode of the other sentence, with the seasons and [12] hours spread out like cards before him. The man in the good sentence exists as an "I." He is calm and unhurried and makes no special requests of his imagined interlocutor, whom he addresses quietly: "we agree," says the tone, "that these are not matters to discuss in a loud voice, using terms we both suspect; we must see such things obliquely." He is modest, polite, reserved; listen to that "any occurrence of special good fortune." It is an educated voice, a little humorous. The modesty continues throughout: "enjoyed," "exhilaration," "glad," are all slightly lower in intensity than what one expects. The word "glad," for instance, acts as it does partly because it is *not* "joyful," and "perfect" means "perfected, that of the whole man," but is allowed to mean more because it might as well mean, to start with, "excellent of its kind, the same sort of exhilaration you get from a winter walk"—which this experience, after all, is.

The imaginative action for which one is searching, then, is at first a physical response to a natural environment and then the self-demonstration of a certain person, a speaker. The subject of action in this experience is alone, and the experience is casual; he is perhaps on his way home after doing an errand on the Milldam. How often has Emerson had this particular enjoyment? He is a connoisseur of such moments. "It is necessary to use these pleasures with great temperance" (W, I, 11), he says with prim irony a page later.

Even the rhythm stresses the ordinariness of the occasion. He is walking home, "crossing a bare common, in snow puddles, at twilight, under a clouded sky." The sentence is deliberately not going anywhere unexpected; the details of the natural context are there, each equidistant from the other, each an unemphasized portion of reality. The movement of the sentence imitates the unhurried stride of a walker. Hence the small shock when an announcement is casually made that the "original relation to the universe" desiderated in the opening paragraph of *Nature* has in fact occurred: "without having in my thoughts any occurrence of special good fortune, I have enjoyed a perfect exhilaration." The very casualness of the order forestalls the question, how did this joy occur? What is its cause? The rhythm implies, one cannot say; one can only accurately and modestly take notice and [13] remark that something has happened. A situation has become an event; but the exact course of the metamorphosis, the relation between the scene and the person in it, is inexpressible. "Let us inquire to what end is nature?" Emerson asked to begin his essay; here, unexpectedly, the question is answered. The "end," the purpose, is joy, the release of natural energy to enjoy the environment.

This large joy emerges half-paradoxically out of a clash between gladness and fear. These emotions are not quite polar opposites, since the antithesis of gladness is sorrow and the reverse of fear is security. But ordinarily one would not expect to entertain a state of feeling combining the two. At exceptional times, though, the element of physical alertness both feelings share may come to the fore. When we are afraid, our senses are sharpened, and our body becomes ready to fight or flee. We become more distinctly conscious of our environment as we prepare ourselves to meet something in it that may endanger us. Fear alerts us to reality. When we are glad, on the other hand, we are unusually satisfied with the way things are. We experience our circumstances as pleasurable and feel our own value as an enjoyer of these. A gladness that reaches the brink of fear would then presumably be a satisfaction borrowing some of the special intensity of frightened anticipation, an enjoyment in which complacency is replaced by a certain anxiety as to whether the world will continue pleasing. The exhilaration seems comparable to that of the mountain climber, say, whose pleasurable consciousness of his own physical powers and of the beauty and strangeness of the scene depends very much on the constant danger of life involved in the exercise of those powers. The right move is intensely satisfying because the wrong move is so easy and so fatal.

At such moments we feel our condition; we are vividly aware simultaneously of our environment and of our own life acting within it. We know reality—even the reality of snow puddles— and we know ourselves. Such experiences of physical contact with the world are at the root of what the romantic has always meant by "joy," from Wordsworth to Lawrence. Joy is the emotional and intellectual precipitate of a quick relation to things as they are. Through joy one recovers one's faith that there is a world [14] to be inhabited, a world one can touch at all points together. It is characteristic of Emerson that he should report an experience of this kind which he encountered in the midst of his daily affairs; he did not need, the implication runs, to seek out in extravagant situations opportunities to possess nature and himself.

So much one can say, I think, of the sentence just as it appears. But it also has a literary history. In Emerson's journal for December 8, 1834, is the following entry: "I rejoice in Time. I do not cross the common without a wild poetic delight notwithstanding the prose of my demeanour. Thank God I live in the country! Well said Bell that no hour no state of the atmosphere but corresponded to some state of the mind; brightest day, grimmest night" (*JMN*, IV, 355). It is interesting to observe that it is the paragraph's relatively banal sentence that comes closest to its final form in this, the first literary version; the editorial change from "brightest day, grimmest night" to "breathless noon" and "grimmest midnight" is not a significant step. Little else is present in the words—just enough to make us sure, on reading this entry, that it is a beginning, a germ. One can notice, for example, how the "prose of my demeanour" has become, in the final version, a matter of tone, not a stated entity.

In the next spring is another relevant entry: "The wild delight runs through the man in spite of real sorrows Nature says he is my creature & spite of all his impertinent griefs he shall be glad with me. Almost I fear to think how glad I am" (*JMN*, V, 24–25). This note bears the date March 26, [1835]; it too contributes a full sentence to the final paragraph and adds as well the essential notion of a paradox of feeling, a combination of fear and gladness. We cannot know how Emerson thought to make just the connections he did, but the result is surely a pivot for the whole paragraph in *Nature*. The achievement can represent the essay as a whole, an essay that is in its turn the plain foundation for everything Emerson publicly said thereafter.

It can be disconcerting, however, to observe the difference in quality between this good moment and its context. The very next remark in the finished paragraph of *Nature* is, "In the woods, too, a man casts off his years, as the snake his slough, and at what period soever of life is always a child." That "too" gives the case [15] away: "There are other advantages to afternoon walks, dear nature-loving reader, which I can think of readily," says the tone. The two sentences are, on one unfortunate level of the author's mind, of equal value.

Still worse is the parody of these excellences in the notorious eyeball sentence. "Standing on the bare ground,—my head bathed by the blithe air and uplifted into infinite space,—all mean egotism vanishes. I become a transparent eyeball; I am nothing; I see all; the currents of the Universal Being circulate through me; I am part or parcel of God." Christopher Cranch unerringly picked this image out to caricature; his drawing . . . [see Plate II] shows the one concrete picture these words irresistibly muster up, a preacherly eyeball staring into the heavens. The *doctrine* about the Soul's relation to Nature, so far as it is paraphrasable, is the same as that of the "bare common" sentence. But the speaker, the I, is innocently absurd at best; the rhythm is a coarse parody of the watchful casualness of the other sentence; and the language is vapid.

A reader's job, then, is plain: to distinguish the excellent moments for himself and, having distinguished, to appreciate the art of the saying he hears and, through the art, the truth said. It is thus that we learn what Emerson has to tell us regarding the Soul.

1966

Nature as Symbol: Emerson's Noble Doubt

by Joel Porte

[61] It is a curiosity of nineteenth-century literary and intellectual history that Emerson has earned the reputation of being a Romantic despite the fact that his major doctrine amounts unmistakably to a belief in the beautiful necessity of worshipping the human conscience. In Emerson's view, nature is completely ancillary to moral science and is best used when it serves to furnish rhetorical tropes with which to adorn a discourse. The business of the poet, as of the preacher and the scientist, is "to hunt out and to exhibit the analogies between moral and material nature in such a manner as to have a bearing upon practice" (*JMN*, III, 130). Nor, it might be suggested, was Emerson a typologist of nature, either in the literal fashion of an Origen—whose "extravagances" Emerson condemned outright in his journal (*JMN*, II, 307)—or, more importantly, in the mystical fashion of Jonathan Edwards, who saw nature as intrinsically valuable and true. For Emerson "every natural fact is trivial until it becomes symbolical or moral" (*J*, V, 421). And:

Whilst common sense looks at things or visible Nature as real and final facts, poetry, or the imagination which dictates it, is a second sight, looking through these, and using them as types or words for thoughts which they signify. (*W*, VIII, 19)

[62] Unlike Edwards, who, as Perry Miller tells us, quoted "Scripture to confirm the meaning of natural phenomena," Emerson argued from nature to Scripture: "All things with which we deal, preach to us. What is a farm but a mute gospel?" (*W*, I, 42). And, again unlike Edwards, Emerson had small use for that art which amounted to no more than an imitation or description of nature, since he considered the latter to be intrinsically of little value. Emerson, for example, continually criticized Wordsworth for being "foolishly inquisitive about the essence and body of what pleased him, of what all sensible men feel to be, in its nature, evanescent" (*J*, II, 108–9); and although the youthful desire to "abuse" Wordsworth which is apparent in the following early journal entry (1819) was to disappear, Emerson's attitude toward "nature in poetry" would not change substantially:

From Chapter Three of *Emerson and Thoreau: Transcendentalists in Conflict* (Middletown: Wesleyan University Press, 1966), pp. 61–67. Copyright © 1965, 1966 by Wesleyan University. Reprinted by permission of Wesleyan University Press. Footnotes are omitted.

He is the poet of pismires. His inspirations are spent light. It is one of the greatest mistakes in the [world] to suppose that that much abused virtue of nature in poetry consists in mere fidelity of representation. (*JMN*, I, 162)

Emerson had a different view, namely, that nature should be touched "gently, as illustration or ornament. Beds of flowers send up a most grateful scent to the passenger who hastens by them, but let him pitch his tent among them and he will find himself grown insensible to their fragrance" (*JMN*, III, 39). Emerson had no desire to glut his sorrow on a rose or die of it in aromatic pain; a quick whiff of the moral law was really what he wanted from the natural world, rather than a moment of sublime illumination. Unlike Edwards, who was a religious phenomenologist, Emerson was a pious Platonist who went to nature for confirmation and illustration of his a priori ethical system, not for mystic ecstasy inseparable from its ineffable meaning.

Emerson, in fact, thought he knew perfectly well what [63] nature meant and devoted his *Nature* to an assertion of that meaning. Indeed, Emerson's own sad admission that there was a "crack" in his first book between the chapters on "Discipline" and "Idealism" may appear to be overly harsh self-criticism to a reader who has come to terms with what Emerson's idealism really signifies—a simple denial of the inherent worth of matter and sense experience. All of *Nature* has one theme, and there is actually no disparity among its sections. In the chapter on "Commodity," for instance, we learn that "a man is fed, not that he may be fed, but that he may work" (*W*, I, 14). Nature serves to enable man to do his duty, not to allow him to rest slothfully in his pleasure. Nor does the section on "Beauty" contradict this stern dictum, although Emerson seems to suggest that aesthetic satisfaction is an end in itself when he states that "the world . . . exists to the soul to satisfy the desire of beauty. This element I call an ultimate end." He quickly adds the warning that "beauty in nature is not ultimate" (*Ibid.*, 24). Virtue, we realize, is what beauty really exists to imply. In the next section we find that language serves as the medium of expression for parables of moral truth, while nature functions as the symbol of spirit, which equals the human mind, which in turn implies ethical awareness. This reading is made explicit in the chapter on "Discipline," where Emerson tells us that "sensible objects conform to the premonitions of Reason and reflect the conscience." Things "hint or thunder to man the laws of right and wrong, and echo the Ten Commandments," and "the moral law lies at the centre of nature" (*Ibid.*, 40–41).

The connection between the sections on "Discipline" and "Idealism" is, then, by no means obscure if we consider that to a man enamored of his conscience, natural phenomena are indeed unimportant. Nature, which embodied Fichtean duty earlier in the essay, was scarcely real in a way which would be meaningful to a naturalist, scientist, or artist. It is therefore hardly inconsistent for Emerson to suggest that nature is less [64] substantial, less meaningful than "ideas"—by which he means not mere abstractions and disembodied essences, but Hegelian "concrete universals," such as truth and justice, incarnated in religion and ethics, church and state:

Whilst we behold unveiled the nature of Justice and Truth, we learn the difference between the absolute and the conditional or relative. We apprehend the absolute. As it were, for the first time, *we exist*. We become immortal, for we learn that time and space are relations of matter; that with a perception of truth or a virtuous will they have no affinity. (*Ibid.*, 57)

Emerson's idealism, then, is simply an affirmation of the supreme importance of the moral law and a restatement of the notion, expressed earlier in his essay, that nature exists (or ceases to exist) as a discipline in ethics. The essentially mundane nature of Emerson's idealism is perhaps made clearer in "Circles":

There are degrees in idealism. We learn first to play with it academically, as the magnet was once a toy. Then we see in the heyday of youth and poetry that it may be true, that it is true in gleams and fragments. Then its countenance waxes stern and grand, and we see that it must be true. It now shows itself ethical and practical. We learn that God *is*; that he is in me; and that all things are shadows of him. The idealism of Berkeley is only a crude statement of the idealism of Jesus, and that again is a crude statement of the fact that all nature is the rapid efflux of goodness executing and organizing itself. (W, II, 309–10)

God is clearly the conscience, which is certainly practical and efficient when it organizes the natural world in the service of an ordered society. Idealism, to return to *Nature*, "presents the world in precisely that view which is most desirable to the mind" (W, I, 59)—to the mind, we should add, of the moralist, for whom ethics is infinitely more important than sensuous [65] experience. "For seen in the light of thought, the world always is phenomenal; and virtue subordinates it to the mind" (*Ibid.*, 60). Crickets and crab apples are a distraction to a man in love with the moral law and, for him, may be said not to exist.

This theme of *Nature* is repeated almost exactly in Emerson's "Poetry and Imagination"; but there, as if to avoid from the start· the seeming "moonshine" of *Nature*, Emerson commenced with a solid assertion of the existence of the world:

The restraining grace of common sense is the mark of all the valid minds. . . . The common sense which does not meddle with the absolute, but takes things at their word,—things as they appear,—believes in the existence of matter, not because we can touch it or conceive of it, but because it agrees with ourselves, and the universe does not jest with us, but is in earnest, is the house of health and life. (W, VIII, 3)

Now it seems clearly nobler to believe in matter. However, Emerson has by no means become reconciled to matter in itself: "The primary ·use of a fact is low; the secondary use, as it is a figure or illustration of my thought, is the real worth" (*Ibid.*, 11). Nature simply serves as a source of tropes for the discourses of the moralist or, in this case, the poet (who turns out to be a moralist in disguise). Emerson then returns to his idealistic strategy, but this time obliquely:

This belief that the higher use of the material world is to furnish us types or pictures to express the thoughts of the mind, is carried to its logical extreme by the Hindoos, who, following Buddha, have made it the central doctrine of their religion that what we call Nature, the external world, has no real existence,—is only phenomenal. (*Ibid.*, 14)

"Logical extreme" may strike us as strange until we remember that idealism, at least in Boston and Concord, was "ethical and practical" and, far from having the immo-bilizing effect found in the East, was being approved by Emerson for the opposite [66] reason. At any rate, if idealism as a doctrine still seemed odd to Emerson's readers, it could be blamed on Buddha rather than on the writer. Emerson then made the characteristic leap to "symbolic nature," but this time with an interesting twist: "The poet discovers that what men value as substances have a higher value as symbols; that Nature is the immense shadow of man" (*Ibid.*, 23). Previously, nature had been symbolic of spirit; but the careful reader found out that spirit was equiva-lent to God, and God simply a way of talking about conscience. So nature is de-scribed here as the reflection of man's moral sense—which, by a characteristic kind of synecdoche that tells us much about his views, is certainly what Emerson means by "man." Furthermore, Emerson is quick to head off the dangers of egotism and subjectivity by defining his man:

Of course, when we describe man as poet, and credit him with the triumphs of the art, we speak of the potential or ideal man,—not found now in any one person. . . . He is the healthy, the wise, the fundamental, the manly man . . . (*Ibid.*, 26)

Like Hegel's "absolute self," Emerson's poet is a universal and not a particular man; this is an important qualification, at least for Emerson's argument, since he would appear to be unlike most poets the world has seen. Indeed, the poet soon reveals himself to be a moralist at heart, as Emerson implies when he quotes Ben Jonson: " 'The principal end of poetry is to inform men in the just reason of living' " (*Ibid.*, 38). Furthermore, the work of this man will be inspiring, affirmative, and ethical (*Ibid.*, 64); his poetry will be "the high poetry which shall thrill and agitate man-kind, restore youth and health, dissipate the dreams under which men reel and stagger, and bring in the new thoughts, the sanity and heroic aims of nations" (*Ibid.*, 73). The poet must be a moralist, for whom nature is a discipline in moral truth. Clearly, then, the sensuous experi-[67]ence of real nature is ruled out; it is simply too conducive to reeling and staggering.

In 1849, Emerson attempted to define the modern era in a journal entry which, perhaps better than anything else, helps us to summarize his attitude toward idealism and the true function of nature:

The Modern: When the too idealistic tendencies of the Christian period running into the diseases of cant, monachism, and a church, demonstrating the impossibility of Christianity, have forced men to retrace their steps, and rally again on Nature; but now the tendency is to marry mind to Nature, and to put Nature under the mind, convert the world into the instrument of Right Reason. Man goes forth to the dominion of the world by commerce, by science, and by philosophy. (*J*, VIII, 78)

Nature is certainly substantial here, yet it hardly seems important in detail. Commu-nion and ecstasy are replaced by progress, and art finds no honored place beside commerce, science, and philosophy. Instructed by such a passage, and bearing in mind that for Emerson "poetry and prudence should be coincident" (W, II, 231), the student may notice that *Nature* ends as a hymn to progress under the moral law. It predicts the "kingdom of man over nature" (W, I, 77), rather than the perfection of man in himself through a renewed contact with the physical world.

A naturalist might say that nature, viewed as Emerson views it in that essay, is not nature at all; and an artist might object that sense experience is intrinsically important to his life and craft. But for Emerson, who ultimately cared less for sense experience than for public morality, his theory of nature was a strategy of self-justification which his neighbors could understand. Nature as symbol was the kind of "Romanticism" that New England had lived with since its founding.

1966

I, Eye, Ay—Emerson's Early Essay "Nature": Thoughts on the Machinery of Transcendence

by Kenneth Burke

I

[3] An enemy might want to rate this early essay of Emerson's as hardly other than a Happiness Pill. But I admit: I find it so charming, I'd be willing to defend it even on that level, it is so buoyant.

Also, we need not confine our speculations to the one essay. I shall try to make clear what I take to be its salient traits, as considered in itself. But I also hope that what I say about it can be considered from the standpoint of symbolic action in general. Since Emersonian "transcendentalism" was quite accurately named, I shall discuss the work from the standpoint of "transcendence."

Though dialectical transcendence and dramatic catharsis have many areas in which the jurisdictions covered by the two terms overlap, there are also terministic situations in which they widely differ. And the simplicity of the procedures embodied in Emerson's essay is exceptionally useful in this regard, as a way to bring out the contrast between transcendence and catharsis.

Catharsis involves fundamentally purgation by the imitation of victimage. If imaginative devices are found whereby members of rival factions can weep together, and if weeping is a surrogate of orgiastic release, then a play [4] that produced in the audience a unitary tragic response regardless of personal discord would be in effect a transformed variant of an original collective orgy (such as the Dionysian rites out of which Greek tragedy developed). Here would be our paradigm for catharsis.

But transcendence is a rival kind of medicine. Despite the area of overlap, the distinction between the two is clear enough at the extremes. And Emerson's brand of transcendentalism is a thorough example of the difference.

Reprinted from *Transcendentalism and Its Legacy*, edited by Myron Simon and Thornton H. Parsons (Ann Arbor: The University of Michigan Press, 1966), pp. 3–24, by permission of The University of Michigan Press. Copyright © by The University of Michigan Press, 1966.

There are traces of victimage even here. Similarly, in the Platonic dialogue, there are traces of victimage, insofar as some speakers are sacrificed for the good of the dialogue as a whole (sacrificed in the sense of being proved wrong—yet their errors were a necessary part of the ultimate truths in which the dialogue, ideally, culminates). A similar "cathartic" element is indicated here in references to what has been called Hegel's "logonomical purgatory."

Though transcendence as we shall deal with it is a sheerly symbolic operation (quite as with catharsis by victimage), the process has an *institutional* base as well—and I can indicate my meaning quickly.

In the appendix to the revised edition of my *Attitudes Toward History*, there is an article, "The Seven Offices." It aims to decide how many, and how few, categories are needed to designate the functions that people perform for one another. The first six are:

> govern (rule)
> serve (provide for materially)
> defend
> teach
> entertain
> cure

But one further function still had to be dealt with. For a while, I thought of "console." After a person has been governed, provided for materially, defended, taught, and entertained, but has gone beyond the point where [5] he can be cured, there is nothing left to do for him but attempt to console him, as do the churches. But the priestly function could not be confined to consolation. A priesthood also assists in the processes of rule, insofar as promises of reward in the afterlife are matched by threats of punishment, though Gilbert Murray has pointed out that threats of punishment also have a consoling effect, insofar as we can tell ourselves that our unjust enemy must eventually suffer for his misdeeds—and revenge is sweet. But, in any case, I suddenly realized that, regardless of whether a priesthood is promising rewards in the afterlife or threatening punishment, or even if the priesthood is discussing some other realm without reference to ultimate reward or punishment, a realm HERE is being talked about *in terms of* a realm ELSEWHERE—and there is a terminology designed to *bridge* these disparate realms. So, for my seventh office, I chose the term:

> pontificate; that is, to "make a bridge."

Viewed as a sheerly terministic, or symbolic, function, that's what transcendence is: the building of a *terministic bridge* whereby one realm is *transcended* by being viewed *in terms of* a realm "beyond" it. Once you consider this process purely from the standpoint of *symbolic functions*, you will see that it is by no means confined to such "tender-minded" modes of expression as we find in the explicit transcendentalism of an Emerson.

Transcendence, as we shall see, is best got by processes of dialectic (quite as catharsis is best got through drama). And in borrowing so much from Hegel's dialectic, even so "tough-minded" a nomenclature as that of Karl Marx inevitably retained transcendental traces (as when conditions *here and now* are seen *in terms of* a broad historic sweep that quite *transcends* them, and thus imparts to them a kind of "ulterior" meaning).

II

The discussion of catharsis centers in speculations on the way in which an audience is purged by somewhat identi-[6]fying itself with the excesses of the tragic hero. There are two main meanings of *hubris:* "pride" and "excess." (Both translations fit Coriolanus superbly. He is arrogant—and in his arrogance he embodies with great intensity a moral tension of society as we know it, the distinction between the privileged and the underprivileged.)

We must also consider a non-Aristotelian kind of catharsis, as with the Crocean stress upon the cathartic nature of sheer expression, the relief of getting things said (of turning brute impressions into articulate expression). Perhaps the most effective instance of such gratification in *Coriolanus* is the way in which the play reduces to a clear narrative line the bundle of overlapping complexities among the motives of individual, family, class, and nation.

In many ways, drama and dialectic are alike. Both exemplify competitive coopera-tion. Out of conflict within the work, there arises a unitary view transcending the partial views of the participants. At least, this is the dialectic of the ideal Platonic dialogue. Both drama and dialectic treat of persons and their characteristic thoughts. But whereas drama stresses the *persons* who have the *thoughts,* and the dialectic of a Platonic dialogue stresses the *thoughts* held by the *persons;* in both forms the element of personality figures.

However, dialectic can dispense with the formal division into cooperatively compet-ing voices. The thoughts or ideas can still be vibrant with personality, as they so obviously are in the essays of Emerson. Yet we think of them as various aspects of the same but somewhat inconsistent personality, rather than as distinct *characters* in various degrees of agreement and disagreement, as in a Platonic dialogue.

Though the Hegelian dialectic lays much greater stress than Emerson's upon the cooperative *competition* (as with Hegel's pattern whereby antitheses become resolved in a synthesis that is the thesis out of which will arise a new antithesis, etc.), Emerson had his variant in his doctrine of "Compensation." (The scheme amounted to this: show how evils will have good results, but play [7] down the reciprocal possibility whereby good might have evil results. "There is no penalty to virtue, no penalty to wisdom; they are proper additions to being." In brief, work up a dialectic that would rule out an ironic concept such as Veblen's "trained incapacity," or the French proverbial formula, "the defects of its qualities.")

All told, however, at their extremes there is a notable difference between tragic catharsis and dialectical transcendence—and the Emerson essay serves as a delightful illustration of this difference. To be sure, the essay is a bit innocuous; but it is charmingly so. It has a kind of exaltation, thanks in large part to Emerson's profuse mixing of his ideas with ingratiating imagery. And we can readily understand why he was so enthusiastic about Whitman, before a more quizzical look at Whitman's poetic evangelism led him to see that it was beckoning "Come hither" to much more than a highly respectable vendor of uplift such as Emerson had bargained for. Both approached the conflicts of the century in terms that allowed for a joyous transcendental translation. To apply in a twisted way (and thereby twisting a twist) Rimbaud's demand for a poetics based on the "reasoned derangement of the senses," we might say that Emerson was as idealistically able as Whitman to look upon some traveling salesmen and see a band of angels. There can be transcendence upwards (as when Coleridge studies the constitution of Church and State "according to the idea of each"). There can be transcendence downwards (as when, thinking of a Church, one speaks of it in terms of the sewer upon which a Church is necessarily built). And there can be a fluctuating between the two. (Cf. in E. M. Forster's novel, A *Passage to India*, the wavering as to whether India is a "muddle" or a "mystery.")

III

Emerson's essay is definitely an idealistic exercise in transcendence up. (There is also a down implicit in such a [8] pattern—but as we proceed, we'll see how it differs from the angry or Beatnik downs.)

Since both tragic catharsis and dialectical transcendence involve *formal development,* by the same token both modes give us kinds of *transformation.*

In tragic catharsis (or, more generally, dramatic catharsis—for there are corresponding processes in comedy), the principle of transformation comes to a focus in *victimage.* The tragic pleasure requires a *symbolic sacrifice*—or, if you will, a *goat.* And the same is obviously true of the comic pleasure.

In dialectical transcendence, the principle of transformation operates in terms of a "beyond." It is like our seventh office, the "priestly" function, in that it pontificates, or "builds a bridge" between disparate realms. And insofar as things here and now are treated in terms of a "beyond," they thereby become infused or inspirited by the addition of a *new or further dimension.*

The Emerson essay is a delightful example of such a terministic process. But before we deal with it in particular, further preparatory considerations are in order, since they bear directly upon the distinction between tragic catharsis and dialectical transcendence. They concern Friedrich Nietzsche's *The Birth of Tragedy.* Though the histories of philosophy usually stress Plato's quarrels with the Sophists, Nietzsche was exercised rather with the difference between the Socratic medicine (as interpreted by Plato) and the medicine of the tragic playwrights. Celebrating the cult of tragedy, the cult of the kill, resolution in terms of extreme victimage, Nietzsche attacked Socrates for being a *reformer* whose policies implied the *death* of tragedy.

You might recommend a cause by tragic dignification (by depictiing people of worth who are willing to die for it). Or (along the lines of Aristotle's *Rhetoric*) you might recommend it by showing the advantages to be gained if the cause (or policy) prevails (that is, you might argue in terms of expediency). Or there are the resources of dialectical transcendence (by seeing things in terms of some [9] "higher" dimension, with the spirit of which all becomes infused). In Nietzsche's case the situation was further complicated by the fact that, even while attacking Plato, Nietzsche attributed to Plato a large measure of tragic dignification, owing to the stress that Nietzsche placed upon the figure of the "dying Socrates" who willingly sacrificed himself as a way of bearing witness to the virtues of the Socratic (Platonic, dialectical) method.

Essentially, the dialectical operations in the Emerson essay are to be built around the traditional One-Many (unity-diversity) pair. Emerson states it succinctly: "ascent from particular to general"; for if we say "furniture" instead of "tables, chairs, and carpets," we spontaneously speak of the more general term as in some way "higher." The process is completed when one has arrived at "highly" generalized terms like "entities" or "beings"—whereupon all that is left is a further step to something like "Pure Being," or the One, or First, or Ultimate, or some such. When we arrive at this stage, the overall term-of-terms or title-of-titles is so comprehensive it is simultaneously nowhere and everywhere. Hence, mystics can select just about anything, no matter how lowly and tangible, to stand for it (for instance, the enigmatic role of the wasp, as seen by Mrs. Moore and imagined by Professor Godbole, in *A Passage to India*). Dialectical transcendence depends upon these quite pedestrian resources of terminology.

In the case of Emerson's essay, the underlying structure is as simple as this: the everyday world, all about us here and now, is to be interpreted as a *diversity* of *means* for carrying out a *unitary purpose* (or, if you will, the *principle* of purpose) that is situated in an ultimate realm *beyond* the here and now. The world's variety of things is thus to be interpreted *in terms of* a transcendent unifier (that infuses them all with its single spirit). And by this mode of interpretation all the world becomes viewed as a set of *instrumentalities*. (Emerson more resonantly calls them "commodities.") For we should bear it in mind that Emerson's brand of transcendentalism was but a short step ahead of out-and-out pragmatism, which would retain [10] an unmistakable theological tinge in William James, and furtive traces even in Dewey. I have in mind the ambiguity whereby, when Dewey pleads that people use their "capacities" to the fullest, he secretly means their "*good* capacities." He thus schemes to make a quasi-technical term serve a moralistic purpose—money being a kind of universal purpose (since it can serve for an almost endless variety of purchases); whereas one might ask, "Give our lives *meaning*," or "Give our lives *purpose*," you are more likely to hear the pragmatic reduction, "*Give us jobs*."

It is well to keep such developments in mind when we read the Emerson essay. While affirming much the kind of moralistic utilitarianism that one finds in the

Discourses of Epictetus, and with hankerings after the kind of moralistic "Progress" that one finds in Bunyan's idea of pilgrimage, the essay must now be seen as inevitably, inexorably placed along the way towards the confusions that beset the current combinings of technological and monetary rationalization. "Under the general name of commodity," Emerson writes, "I rank all those advantages which our senses owe to nature." Thus, under the head of "Commodity," he can refer to "Nature, in its ministry to man." While reading that section we should, perhaps, not merely be sure to interpret "commodity" in a moralistic sense that has since dropped away, but also have in mind the poignancy of the fact that—as we can now readily discern, since history is by nature a Damoclean sword—Emerson's use of the term already held in suspension the narrower contemporary meaning.

Where, then, are we? I am trying to do at least three things at once. I am trying to build up a contrast between transformation by victimage (dramatic catharsis) and transformation by dialectical "transcendence" (modes of "crossing" whereby something here and now is interpreted in terms of something beyond). I am trying to discuss precisely how these operations are performed in one particular essay, by Emerson, on Nature. (In brief, he so sets up "Nature" that it is to be interpreted in terms of Supernature.) And I further hope to indicate that the design [11] here being discussed is employed in all sorts of terministic schemes. For the same principle is involved (there are tiny "transcendences") every time an author, no matter how empirical his claims, mounts to a "higher" level of generalization and, in effect, asks that "lower" levels of generalization be interpreted in its terms.

The third thesis should especially concern anyone who, while spontaneously shifting back and forth between different levels of generalization, might incline not to see that all such procedures are operating within the same rules, but in a fragmentary way.

So, if one feels that Emerson's essay is not tough-minded enough (and I'd be the last to assert that it is, for all my love of it), I'd contend that such a judgment is not enough to dismiss it.

If only like loving a pleasant dream, love him for his idealistic upsurge. For *it reads well*. It is medicine. Even in those days, I feel sure, both he and Whitman suspected that they might be whistling in the dark. But they loved the gesture (if whistling is a gesture)—and it is an appealing gesture. Albeit a gesture much more plausible then than now. Emerson's scheme for transcendence (like Whitman's variant) was propounded before his fellow-townsmen had lost their sense of a happy, predestinated future. There was not yet any crying need to turn, rather, and begin hoarding relics of the ancestral past, like an unregenerate Southerner, with the trunkload of Confederate money in his attic.

IV

Here is what I take to be the underlying form of the essay: it treats of Society in terms of Nature—and it treats of Nature in terms of the Supernatural. Thereby, even the discussion of Society in its most realistic aspects becomes transcendentally tinged (somewhat as though you had made a quite literal line-drawing with pen and ink and had covered it with a diaphanous wash of cerulean blue).

In keeping with such an approach to the everyday [12] materials of living, note how even the realm of the sensory can be interpreted as a kind of *revelation*. For whatever the world is, in its sheer brute nature as physical vibrations or motions it *reveals itself* to us *in terms of* sights, sounds, tastes, scents, touch, summed up as pleasure or pain. Thus, you already have the terministic conditions whereby even the most material of sensations can be called "apocalyptic" (since the word but means "revealing")—and Emerson does apply precisely that word. In this respect, even the crudest of sensory perceptions can be treated as the revealing of nature's mysteries, though the revelations are confined to the restrictions imposed upon us by the physical senses that reveal them. Also, the resources of dialectic readily permit us to make a further step, insofar as particulars can be treated in terms that transcend their particularity. Within the Emersonian style, this convenience indigenous to terminology would be more resonantly stated: "when the fact is seen in the light of an idea."

If Nature is to be treated in terms of Supernature, another possibility presents itself. There could be stylistic procedures designed to serve as *bridges* (or intermediaries) between the two sets of terms. The simplest instance of such a bridging device is to be seen in the dialectic of Christian theology. If you make a distinction between "God" and "Man," you set up the terministic conditions for an intermediate term (for bridging the gap between the two orders); namely, "God-Man." Similarly, in the dialectic of psychoanalysis, one might be advised to inquire whether the term "preconscious" can serve (at least on some occasions) as a bridge between the terms "conscious" and "unconscious." Fittingly, the major bridge of this sort in Emerson's essay comes in the chapter halfway through, containing the homily on "Discipline."

We'll discuss later how the chapter on Discipline operates as a bridge, a "pontificator." Meanwhile, we should note another kind of bridge: the *imagistic*. There is such a profusion of images in the essay that at first I was puzzled as to how I might discuss the imagery in the [13] summarizing way needed for a presentation of this sort. For to deal with the images in their particularity, one would need the kind of line-by-line analysis that is possible only to a succession of sessions in the classroom.

So I propose a makeshift. Near the start of the essay, Emerson writes, "if a man would be alone, let him look at the stars." Then he continues:

The rays that come from those heavenly worlds will separate between him and what he touches. One might think the atmosphere was made transparent with this design, to give man, in the heavenly bodies, the perpetual presence of the sublime. Seen in the streets of cities, how great they are! [I fear that that line has become a victim of technological progress.] If the stars should appear one night in a thousand years, how would men believe and adore; and preserve for many generations the remembrance of the city of God which had been shown! [This passage presumably refers to a spot in the Introduction: "The foregoing generations beheld God and nature face to face; we, through their eyes." And at that point, of course, one might turn aside to mention the favored role of eye-imagery in Emerson's transcendental vision.] But every night come out these envoys of beauty, and light the universe with their admonishing smile.

Perhaps we should add the opening sentence of the next paragraph: "The stars awaken a certain reverence, because though always present, they are inaccessible; but all natural objects make a kindred impression, when the mind is open to their influence."

On the basis of these sentences, I would propose for purposes of essayistic efficiency to suggest that Emerson's imagery in general is "starry-eyed." Recall that all three canticles of *The Divine Comedy end* on references to the stars, and put that thought together with the fact that Emerson's essay thus *begins.* Note also that, in keeping with the quality of Emersonian individualism, he equates [14] the stars with a desire to be *alone.* And when he refers to the atmosphere as being "made transparent with this design," we are advised to note the several other incidences of the term, thus:

I become a transparent eye-ball.

. . . the universe becomes transparent, and the light of higher laws than its own shines through it.

If the Reason be stimulated to more earnest vision, outlines and surfaces become transparent, and are no longer seen; causes and spirits are seen through them.

The ruin or the blank that we see when we look at nature, is in our own eye. The axis of vision is not coincident with the axis of things, and so they appear not transparent but opaque.

And in his essay "The Poet," with reference to reading a poem which he confides in "as an inspiration," he says: "And now my chains are to be broken; I shall mount above these clouds and opaque airs in which I live,—opaque, though they seem transparent,—and from the heaven of truth I shall see and comprehend my relations."

Here is what I am aiming at: first, the essay involves a definite *crossing,* via the middle section on "Discipline," so far as the development of the *ideas* is concerned. But in the starry-eyed visionary imagery (as epitomized in the notion of the "transparent") the transcendence is *implicitly* or ambiguously there from the start, and permeates the style throughout the entire essay. To pick some instances almost at random:

. . . like an eagle or a swallow . . . the pomp of emperors . . . the live repose of the valley behind the mill . . . spires of flame in the sunset . . . the graces of the winter scenery . . . this pomp of purple and gold . . . the dewy morning, the rainbow, mountains, orchards in blossom, stars, moonlight, shadows in still water . . . the spells [15] of persuasion, the keys of power . . . like travellers using the cinders of a volcano to roast their eggs . . . the azure sky, over whose unspotted deeps the winds forevermore drive flocks of stormy clouds . . . a leaf, a drop, a crystal, a moment of time . . . not built like a ship to be tossed, but like a house to stand . . . This transfiguration which all material objects undergo through the passion of the poet . . . the recesses of consciousness . . . faint copies of an invisible archetype . . . [Nor should we omit mention of this resonant set in his Introduction: "language, sleep, madness, dreams, beasts, sex." And, characteristically, at one point he gives us the equation: "the eye,—the mind."]

And here would be the place to cite from the transitional chapter on "Discipline," and at almost the mathematical center of the essay, his central bit of Uplift. In these tough times, I'd not even have the courage to repeat the passage, if I could not immediately hasten to propose a non-Emersonian translation:

Sensible objects conform to the premonitions of Reason and reflect the conscience. All things are moral; and in their boundless changes have an unceasing reference to spiritual nature. Therefore is nature glorious with form, color, and motion; that every globe in the remotest heaven, every chemical change from the rudest crystal up to the laws of life, every change of vegetation from the first principle of growth in the eye of a leaf, to the tropical forest and antediluvian coal-mine, every animal function from the sponge up to Hercules, shall hint or thunder to man the laws of right and wrong, and echo the Ten Commandments. Therefore is Nature ever the ally of Religion.

Going beyond the specifically theological level here, one might note the sheerly "logological" fact that a strategic feature of the Decalogue is its urgent sprinkling of Negatives. Elsewhere I have dealt with the all-importance [16] of the Negative in the development of language, in connection with the complex property-structures that depend upon the codifications of secular law (and its species of "thou-shalt-nots"), and with the modes of thinking that arise from the resources of Negativity (Alienation, or "Negativism," for instance).

But for present purposes I might offer a shortcut of this sort: you know of the great stress upon Negativity in much contemporary Existentialist philosophy. And you know of the ingenious talk about "Nothingness" (the Heideggerian concern with *nichten* and the Sartrean concern with *le Néant*). Well, in the last analysis, when Emerson grows edified at the thought that all things, for man, are permeated with the spirit of the "thou shalt not," is he not talking about the same situation, except that his particular dialectic allows him to discuss it in the accents of elation, thereby (if we may apply one of his own words) endowing his statements with the quality of the "medicinal"?

Indeed, once the pattern gets established, you will find Emerson doing with his transcendentalism much the same thing as Whitman does with his infectious cult of the glad hand. Accordingly, since Nature is viewed as disciplinary, and since (as we have already noted) the Social Structure is viewed in terms of Nature, it follows that even the discords of "Property and its filial systems of debt and credit," can be welcomed transcendentally as a primary mode of moral discipline, thus:

Debt, grinding debt, whose iron face the widow, the orphan, and the sons of genius fear and hate;—debt, which consumes so much time, which so cripples and disheartens a great spirit with cares that seem so base, is a preceptor whose lessons cannot be foregone, and is needed most by those who suffer from it most.

V

But I have not yet made wholly clear how the chapter on "Discipline" serves as a bridge between the Hic et [17] Nunc and the "Beyond." To appreciate the dialectical maneuvers here, we should lay great stress upon the strategic sentence in the Introduction: "Let us inquire, to what end is nature?" This question sets the conditions for the pattern of development. Of all the issues that keep recurring in the maneuvers of dialectic, surely none is more frequent than the theme of the One and the Many. As I have said, I feel that it is grounded in the logological fact that terms for particulars can be classified under some titular head. And thus, when we say "the Universe," we feel that we really are talking about the Universe, about "everything," though the term certainly includes an awful lot that we don't know anything about.

Be that as it may, given the typical resources of terminology, the question, "To what end is nature?" allows for a one-many alignment of this sort: the world of our Empirical existence can be viewed not just as a great variety of *things*, but as a great variety of *means*, all related to some ultimate *end*. In this regard we can see how Emerson's dialectic pattern (of *manifold means* in the world of everyday experience emblematically or hieroglyphically announcing some *unitary end* in a realm beyond everyday experience) set up the conditions for transcendentalizing maneuvers that would be progressively transformed into William James's pragmatism and John Dewey's instrumentalism. Though work, in its *utilitarian* aspects, amasses *material* powers, in its *ethical* aspects work can be felt to *transcend* utility. Hence, "Discipline" serves as the means of crossing from sheer expediency to edification.

Before the bridge, Emerson's stress is upon *uses* (a subject dear to his countrymen, who were to build, by their technology, the highest Babylonian Tower of useful things the world has ever known, though many of the uses were to prove worse than useless). In his case, of course, the many resources of utility are moralized in terms of a transcendental purpose, itself in the realm *beyond* the bridge. On this side the bridge, there are "Commodities," "Beauty," and "Language." "Beauty" endangers the de-[18]sign, inasmuch as it is an end in itself. But Emerson preserves the design by his concluding decision that "beauty in nature is not ultimate. It is the herald of inward and eternal beauty."

Nothing could more quickly reveal the terministic resources of the Emersonian dialectic (or, if you will, the Emersonian unction) than a contrasting of his views on language with Jeremy Bentham's "theory of fictions." Bentham laid major stress upon the fact that all our terms for spiritual or psychological states are initially terms for sheerly physical things and processes. And by "fictions" he had in mind the thought that all moral or psychological nomenclatures are essentially metaphors carried over from the physical realm and applied analogically. But Emerson's transcendental dialectic allows him to apply a tender-minded mode of interpretation, thus:

Words are signs of natural facts. The use of natural history is to give us aid in supernatural history; the use of the outer creation, to give us language for the beings and changes of the inward creation. Every word which is used to express a moral or intellectual fact, if traced to its root, is found to be borrowed from some material appearance. *Right* means *straight; wrong* means *twisted. Spirit* primarily means *wind; transgression,* the crossing of a *line; supercilious,* the *raising of the eyebrow.* We say the *heart* to express emotion, the *head* to denote thought; and *thought* and *emotion* are words borrowed from sensible things, and now appropriated to spiritual nature.

And so on. In any case, once you thus turn things around, you see why, if the things of nature are to serve us by providing us with terms which we can apply analogically for the development of a moral terminology, then the whole subject would come to a focus in a chapter on nature itself as a source of moral "discipline." Fittingly, the chapter begins by reference to the "*use* of the world" as a discipline. And at the beginning of the [19] next chapter, "Idealism," we read: "To this one *end* of Discipline, all parts of nature conspire." (Italics in both cases ours.) Thus, when the chapter on "Discipline" is over, we have gone from the realm of *means* to the realm of *ends,* or more specifically, one unitary end (or, if you will, the sheer *principle* of purpose).

Now that we have crossed the bridge, into the realm of "Reason" and "Spirit," Nature appropriately suffers what Emerson himself calls a "degrading." For whereas Nature rated high when thought of as leading towards the Supernatural, in comparison with the Supernatural it comes into question, even as regards its material existence. (Incidentally, this change of rating in Emerson's dialectic corresponds, in the Marxian dialectic, to a step such as the transformation of the bourgeoisie from the class that is the bearer of the future to the class that is to be buried by the future. In a ladder of developments, rung five is "progressive" with regard to rung three, but "reactionary" with regard to rung seven.) However, in this later "degrading" of Nature, he pauses to admonish: "I do not wish to fling stones at my beautiful mother, nor soil my gentle nest." He wishes, in effect, but to complete the tracking down of the positions implicit in his dialectic.

One final development should be mentioned, since it throws a quite relevant light upon the essay's methods. In his final chapter, "Prospects," while zestfully reciting the many steps that man has taken through the course of history towards the affirming of what Emerson takes to be the ultimate supernatural Oneness, the essay has so built up the promissory that we scarcely notice how airily the problem of evil is dismissed:

Build therefore your own world. As far [fast] as you conform your life to the pure idea in your mind, that will unfold its great proportions. A correspondent revolution in things will attend the influx of the spirit. So fast will disagreeable appearances, swine, spiders, snakes, pests, mad-houses, prisons, enemies vanish; they are tempo-[20]rary and shall be no more seen. [This comes close to the line in "Lycidas": "Shall now no more be seen."] The sordor and filths of nature, the sun shall dry up and the wind exhale. As when the summer comes from the south the snow-banks melt and the face of the earth becomes green before it, so shall the advancing spirit create its ornaments along its path, and carry with it the beauty it visits and the song which enchants it.

He envisions in sum: "The kingdom of man over nature."

One can't do anything with that, other than to note that it disposes of many troublesome things in a great hurry. But the Marxist dialectic is not without an analogous solution, in looking upon the socialist future as "inevitable."

Two asides: as regards "the thinking of the body," there are strong hints of a fecal motive near the end of the section on "Language":

"Material objects," said a French philosopher, "are necessarily kinds of *scoriae* of the substantial thoughts of the Creator, which must always preserve an exact relation to their first origin; in other words, visible nature must have a spiritual and moral side."

I have found that readers seldom look up the word *scoriae*. It comes from the same root as "scatological." Here it conceives the realm of matter as nothing other than God's *offal*. Such images are likely to turn up somewhere in the dialectics of transformation, especially where there is talk of "discipline." And, thanks to an ambiguous use of the verb "betrays," I'd incline to see traces of it in Emerson's statement that the principle of Unity "lies under the undermost garment of Nature, and betrays its source in Universal Spirit." In his later and shorter essay on "Nature," where we are told that the universe "has but one stuff," the same tricky usage appears thus: "Compound it how she will, star, sand, fire, water, tree, man, it is still one stuff, and betrays the same properties." Surely [21] "stuff" here is synonymous with matter in the reference to Nature as God's *scoriae*. And thinking along the same lines, we find it noteworthy that, though Unity is the best of words when applied to the realm of the Supernatural, in the chapter "Prospects" it is called "tyrannizing" when applied to the earthly animal kingdom.[1]

VI

At the end of the chapter on "Discipline," just before we cross to the realm of the Beyond, we find traces of victimage, in his solemnizing references to separation from a friend:

When much intercourse with a friend has supplied us with a standard of excellence, and has increased our respect for the resources of God who thus sends a real person to outgo our ideal; when he has, moreover, become an object of thought, and, whilst his character retains all its unconscious effect, is converted in the mind into solid and sweet wisdom,—it is a sign to us that his office is closing, and he is commonly withdrawn from our sight in a short time.

Is not this passage a euphemism for the death, or near-death, of a close friend? And thus, does not the bridge that carries us across to the Beyond end on strong traces of tragic dignification of victimage?

Similarly, I have tried elsewhere to show that James Joyce's story, "The Dead,"

[1] The grounds for my speculations here are made clearer in my essay on "Thinking of the Body" (*The Psychoanalytic Review*, Autumn 1963), particularly the section on the symbolism of "matter" in Flaubert's *La Tentation de Saint-Antoine*. Similar connotations flit about the edges of an expression such as "purge the eyes."

should be analyzed primarily in terms of transcendence.[2] But the very title indicates that the purgative force of victimage also figures here.

Without considering the story in detail, we might note this much about it: the "transcending," or "beyond," concerns the final transformation whereby the situation of the living is viewed in terms of the dead. For if the world of conditions is the world of the living, then the transcending of conditions will, by the logic of such terms, equal the world of the dead. (And the Kantian transcendental dialectic could get in the idea of God by [22] this route: if God transcends nature, and nature is the world of conditions, then God is the realm of the unconditioned.)

The final twist, what Joyce would call an "epiphany," is contrived by the transforming of "snow" from a *sensory* image to a *mythic* image. That is, in the first part of the story, the references to snow are wholly realistic ("lexical" snow, snow as defined in a dictionary). But at the end, snow has become a *mythic* image, manifesting itself in the world of conditions, but standing for transcendence above the conditioned. It is a snow that bridges two realms—but, as befits the behavior of snow, this Upward Way is figured in terms of a Downward Way, as the last paragraph features the present participle, "falling."

There is an interesting variant in Chaucer's *Troilus and Criseyde*. The poem tells a pagan story in a pagan setting. But in the telling, Chaucer infuses the story with the medieval terminology of Courtly Love. Now, it so happens that this terminology is a *secular* analogue of the language applied to *religious* devotion. Accordingly, the story as so told sets up the conditions for the use of this language in ways that transcend its application to a pagan love affair. The book closes on the picture of slain Troilus looking down upon "This litel spot of erthe" in the traditional Christian attitude of the *contemptus mundi,* in contrast with "the pleyn felicite / That is in hevene above"—thence finally to an outright Christian prayer involving the Mary and the Trinity.

In the early part of his trip to the Underworld, Virgil encountered those of the dead who could not cross Cocytus and the Stygian swamps. Charon would not ferry them to their final abode because they had not been buried. Then comes the famous line:

> *Tendebantque manus ripae ulterioris amore*
> (And they stretched forth their hands, through
> love of the farther shore).

That is the pattern. Whether there is or is not an ultimate shore towards which we, the unburied, would [23] cross, transcendence involves dialectical processes whereby something HERE is interpreted *in terms of* something THERE, something *beyond* itself.

These examples involve modes of "beyonding" that overlap upon connotations of victimage where symbolic fulfillment is attained in the ambiguities of death and

---

[2] See the section from "Three Definitions" reprinted in my *Perspectives by Incongruity,* edited by Stanley Edgar Hyman (Bloomington, Ind., 1964).

immortality (with technical twists whereby, if "death" means "not-life," "immortality" compounds the negative, giving us "not not-life"). Obviously, Emerson's dialectic of a transcendent End involves similar operations. But I would here stress the fact that the principle of transcendence which is central to his essay is not confined to its use in such thorough-going examples.

The machinery of language is so made that, either rightly or wrongly, either grandly or in fragments, we stretch forth our hands through love of the farther shore. The machinery of language is so made that things are necessarily placed in terms of a range broader than the terms for those things themselves. And thereby, in even the toughest or tiniest of terminologies—terminologies that, on their face, are far from the starry-eyed transcendentalism of Emerson's essay—we stretch forth our hands through love of a farther shore; we consider things in terms of a broader scope than the terms for those particular things themselves. And I submit that, wherever there are traces of that process, there are the makings of Transcendence. [24]

1967

The Architectonics of
Emerson's *Nature*
by Richard Lee Francis

[39] In his otherwise sensitive and sympathetic reading of Emerson's essays, Stephen Whicher once observed of *Nature* that "the style is stiff and naif, the organization is overelaborate, the thought gowned in unbecoming borrowed terminology," and yet it remained for him, "one of the most extraordinary pieces of writing yet to come from an American." This ambivalent response is familiar to readers of Emerson's essays in general and of *Nature* in particular. Our efforts to come to terms with Emerson's essays in an analytic way tend to flounder in a morass of "linear logic" that Emerson was at such pains to have us avoid. We frequently seek in his essays the very qualities they do not contain, and we evaluate them in stylistic terms that are not always illuminating. This mis-perception is especially injurious in regard to Emerson's first major written essay; for *Nature* is a work that partakes of both the oral and the written stylistic traditions and is influenced in its structure and development by other modes of expression besides those of the conventionally rhetorical and oratorical. To comprehend *Nature* we need to consider its architectonics, the artful system of construction by which Emerson put together this principal statement of his transcendental vision.

The basic element of Emerson's style we usually assume is an outgrowth of his pulpit experience, and we further assume that it resembles a sermonic style that stresses what Cotton Mather once described as "easy conveyance of ideas." But Emerson, in abandoning the pulpit, gave up not only the conventional expression of the Unitarian creed but the "easy conveyance" as well. In search of a new creed, he was also of necessity in search of a new style. Yet, for all his rebellious assertions, Emerson was essentially conservative by nature; and, whether by design or not, he returned to an older style whose principal character had been stated a century earlier by Cotton Mather in *Manuductio ad Ministerium* (1726). As Howard Mumford

From *American Quarterly*, XIX (Spring, 1967), 39–53. Copyright, 1967, Trustees of the University of Pennsylvania. Reprinted with the permission of *American Quarterly* and the author. A footnote is omitted.

Jones has reminded us, Mather was not en-[40]tirely happy with the new rhetorical style and wished to preserve something of the older, more elaborate manner. He observed in his manual for preachers:

There is a way of writing, wherein the author endeavors, that the reader may have something to the purpose in every paragraph. There is not only a vigor sensible in every sentence, but the paragraph is embellished with profitable references, even to something beyond what is directly spoken. Formal and painful quotations are not studied; yet all that could be learnt from them is insinuated. The writer pretends not unto reading, yet he could not have writ as he does if he had not read very much in his time; and his composures are not only a cloth of gold, but also stuck with as many jewels, as the gown of a Russian ambassador. (*M. ad M.*, p. 44)

This double function of style, of substantial matter enriched with highly conscious ornamentation, is characteristic of an artistic style that Emerson had visually absorbed on his European tour in 1833—the baroque. If we may appropriate the term from the visual arts and music, we might say that the style of *Nature* is "baroque." And while this appropriation from other art-forms runs that risk of mis-application which any term of analogy invites, there is some precedent for it in Emerson's own thinking at the time.

To examine Emerson's journals for the years 1833–36 is to encounter his frequent preoccupation with architectural images and with the relation of these to his germinating theories of the soul. For example, in the *Q Journal* kept during his European trip, he notes Mme. de Stael's famous remark (later cited in *Nature*): "Architecture is frozen music" (*JMN*, IV, 40). And while staying in Milan on June 10, 1833, Emerson recorded in the same journal that "it is in the soul that architecture exists and Santa Croce and this Duomo are far-behind imitations," and continued, "I would rather know the metaphysics of architecture as of shells and flowers than anything else in the matter" (*JMN*, IV, 75). Further on in this same entry he adds a paraphrase of Mme. de Stael ("Architecture, said the lady, is frozen music"). More than a year later, back home in Concord, he ruminated in the *A Journal*:

If one should seek to trace the genealogy of thoughts, he would find . . . Mme. de Stael's "Architecture is frozen music," borrowed from Goethe's "Architecture is dumb music," borrowed from Vitruvius, who said, "The Architect must not only understand drawing but also music. . . ." (*JMN*, IV, 337)

[41] This preoccupation with the fine arts did not end with his journal entries for 1833, for even in the *B Journal* of 1835, kept during the year of composition and refinement of *Nature*, Emerson frequently invoked the visual arts as metaphor. "May I say with presumption," he noted in an early entry for that year, "that like Michael Angelo I only block my statues" (*JMN*, V, 14). On November seventh, he remarked most revealingly: "Give me one single man and uncover for me his pleasures and pains, let me minutely and in the timbers and ground plan study his architecture and you may travel all around the world" (*JMN*, V, 107).

Even the public lectures that Emerson gave in 1836 reveal this preoccupation with art and as such reflect something of the cast of Emerson's mind as he completed *Nature* and was beginning to expand and develop what it enunciates both in terms of statement and style. These orations were examples of what Emerson called "eloquence" in a lecture on "Art" that he delivered in December 1836, three months after the publication of *Nature*. In placing eloquence among the "fine arts" of music, poetry, painting, sculpture and architecture, Emerson observed:

Eloquence, as far as it is a fine art, is modified how much by the material organization of the orator, the tone of the voice, the physical strength, the play of the eye and countenance! All this is so much deduction from the merit of Art, and is the attribute of Nature. (*EL*, II, 46)

Eloquence is a kind of acting, a performance, in which auditory and visual effects are just as much a part of the endeavor as are the thoughts expressed. Eloquence is an art-form with a double function, as Emerson noted earlier in the same lecture when he observed that "architecture and eloquence are mixed arts, whose end is sometimes beauty and sometimes use" (*EL*, II, 45). While this epigrammatic assertion might at first appear to be a variation on Horace's classic dictum of *utile dulce*, it is not simply so; for in discussing beauty, Emerson was pervasively concerned with the order and harmony that we perceive in the correspondence between the human and the divine and with the particular use to which we put that perception. Though he appears merely to enumerate the "uses" of nature in his essay, Emerson was ultimately concerned with the cumulative effect of such uses, which created for him a beautiful harmony. Eloquence, then, is no casual entertainment; it endeavors, like all art, to make the actual meaningful by giving it an ideal order. Perhaps Emerson put this matter most lucidly in a journal entry for October 1836: "It is the constant endeavor of the mind to idealize the actual, to accommodate the show of things to the desires of the mind. Hence architecture and all art" (*JMN*, V, 221). The concept of duality, and particularly [42] of an interpenetrating duality, is essential to Emerson's views here and is reflected in the chapters of *Nature* which he had just completed. *Nature* is, then, Emerson's first exuberant attempt after the tentative testing of the initial lectures to delineate the complexities of the actual by seeing the inherent order in the structure of the whole. To that extent he emulates the baroque; for as some art critics have suggested, the baroque was an effort to approximate nature by bringing it under the discipline of reason, to reconcile the picturesquely romantic with classical order. What Emerson envisioned from the beginning (as he later expressed it while preparing the essay for republication in 1849) was a rebirth of Nature freed from the excesses both of pagan and Christian assumptions. In his journal at that time, Emerson noted a very Renaissance-oriented attitude. He observed that there have been three stages in history: the Greek, when men deified Nature; the Christian, when they craved a heaven out of Nature and above it; and the Modern, when "the Tendency is to marry mind to Nature, and to put Nature under the mind, convert-[ing] the world into the instrument of Right Reason" (*J*, VIII, 78). Though a late observation such an evolutionary concept in *Nature* is implicitly enforced by the motto chosen for the 1849 edition which ends: "And striving to be man, the worm/

Mounts through all the spires of form." The *recovery* of nature was to be accomplished by the *discovery* of mind. Thus the metaphor of "renaissance," so vigorously appropriated by Matthiessen, is even more precise than he perhaps intended. A closer examination of *Nature*, its structure, strategies and progression, will suggest more fully the architectonics of Emerson's baroque renascent style.

At first glance few essays could look so transparent. *Nature* begins with an "Introduction" and has a final chapter called, "Prospects." Between the beginning and end, there are seven chapters, respectively entitled: "Nature," "Commodity," "Beauty," "Language," "Discipline," "Idealism" and "Spirit." Yet on closer examination we discover that the chapters are of radically unequal length and that in terms of conventional logic we find it difficult to discover the transition from one chapter to the next. Beyond these problems we observe that one chapter, "Language," seems to command more attention than the others, undoubtedly because its organization and development seem more transparent and conventional than in the other chapters. Its very centrality in the essay and the nature of its definitions have led some critics to argue that the platonic aspect of the essay, underscored by the original motto of 1836, creates a division at this point between the first five chapters and the last four, that with this chapter we cross over the famous divided line of Plato from the world of impressions to the world of ideas. But there is a particular aspect of the chapter, "Language," which provides us with a clue to [43] Emerson's strategy in the essay. For while the entire essay is an elaborate exercise in definition of the sort that the chapter, "Language," enumerates—that is, a movement from phenomenal experience to symbolic comprehension of noumenal experience in the phenomenal world— the specific gesture toward syllogistic formulation that is so conspicuously part of the chapter hints at a "scientific" approach. Part of the author's strategy in defining the "uses" of nature is to present himself not merely as spiritual philosopher but also as scientific naturalist. Once more we find precedent for this assumption in Emerson's early lectures. In 1833, in a lecture on "The Uses of Natural History," Emerson gave initial expression to the central concept of "Language."

The strongest distinction of which we have an idea is that between thought and matter. The very existence of thought and speech supposes and is a new nature totally distinct from the material world; yet we find it impossible to speak of it and its laws in any other language than that borrowed from our experience in the material world. We not only speak in continual metaphors of the morn, the noon and the evening of life, of dark and bright thoughts, of sweet and bitter moments, of the healthy mind and the fading memory; but all our most literal and direct modes of speech—as right and wrong, form and substance, honest and dishonest . . . are, when hunted up to their original signification, found to be metaphors also. And this, because the whole of Nature is a metaphor or image of the human Mind. (*EL*, I, 24)

The scientific naturalist begins by classifying and defining data, but he is ultimately engaged in ordering the human mind's conception of its own existence. To that end the naturalist becomes philosophic; he becomes poetic as well as systematic. This mode of defining is highly fluid, partaking of the interaction of matter and thought, of natural facts and spiritual facts. It creates in Emerson's style a quality that M. W. Croll has defined in his classic essay on "The Baroque Style in Prose" (1929):

> There is a constant swift adaptation of form to the emergencies that arise in an energetic and unpremeditated forward movement; . . . these signs of spontaneity and improvisation occur in passages loaded with as heavy a content as rhetoric ever has to carry. That is to say, they combine the effect of great mass with the effect of rapid motion; and there is no better formula than this to describe the ideal of the baroque design in all the arts. (*Studies in English Philology*, pp. 442–43)

If we examine the first two sections of the essay, we confront a series of definitions characterized by great fluidity. The "Introduction" contains four paragraphs. The first two constitute a general approach to the [44] large topic of the essay. The first is interrogative and evocative; the second is declarative and imperative. The first begins with an assertion about the past and concludes with an injunction for the future. The second paragraph begins with a sweeping generalization and concludes with the crucial question of the essay. The third and fourth paragraphs are quite concrete. The third approaches the topic from the perspective of science; the fourth from the perspective of philosophy. The third poses a series of value judgments concerning the scientific approach to nature; the fourth undertakes a series of definitions of the central term and its subcategories. Thus the "Introduction" moves from a series of oratorical flourishes to some rhetorical distinctions and definitions. In contrast to this introduction, the first chapter of the essay makes a highly personal statement about how we perceive what has just been defined. The approach here is in contrast to the striving for objectivity at the end of the introduction. We sense a strong personal voice which is not that of a mere impersonal scientific naturalist or quite that of the universal Orphic Poet, for it expresses itself in a series of highly metaphoric statements about the phenomenal world that culminates in that metaphor of vital spatial vision—the transparent eyeball (still maligned, even by Jonathan Bishop in his otherwise sensitive reading of Emerson on the Soul). The voice moves from the familiar and concrete (the speaker is scuddling through the winter puddles of a common) to a bizarrely vivid attempt at a universal symbol appropriate both to natural anatomy and spiritual insight which is the climax of the fourth paragraph. Then the "occult relation" between man and his world is treated subjectively in the fifth paragraph; and finally in the sixth paragraph that relationship is objectively crystallized in the epigram: "Nature always wears the color[s] of the spirit." Thus in the first two sections of the essay, we encounter two kinds of definition. In the "Introduction" nature is defined as "essence unchanged by man" and art as "the mixture of man's will with those essences." These are essentially substantive definitions that operate near the "ground line of familiar facts." In contrast to these the final large observation of the first chapter, "Nature," does not operate as a substantive definition; it appears to be a highly poetic assertion that is epigrammatic but illusive. Yet, as Chapter VII, "Spirit," will reveal, such a mode of defining is as essential to Emerson as the more conventional way. Between these two modes of definition the remaining chapters of the essay modulate.

The next six chapters, as Emerson makes clear in the opening paragraph of Chapter II, partake of this essentially dialectical mode of development. Chapter II, "Commodity," deals with "those advantages which our senses owe to nature," in which Emerson sees nature not only [45] as material substance but as process and result as well: "The wind sows the seed; the sun evaporates the sea; the wind blows the vapor to the field; the ice, the other side of the planet, condenses rain on this; the rain feeds the plant; the plant feeds the animal; and thus the endless circulations of the divine charity nourish man." The catalogue of such commodity and utility is, as Emerson notes, "endless." Chapter III, "Beauty," bears the same analogous relation to Chapter II that Chapter I bore to the "Introduction." Its opening line makes clear the more theoretical dimension of this section: "A nobler want of man is served by nature, namely the want of Beauty." A similar relationship is established between the chapter on "Language" and the chapter on "Discipline." The former is basically specific, like the section of definitions in the "Introduction" and like the concern with natural phenomena in "Commodity." On the other hand, "Discipline" defines a more theoretical concept and to that extent is more like "Beauty." This relationship of the specific to the theoretical also exists between the chapters on "Idealism" and "Spirit"; for idealism as an *ism* lends itself to specific definition and classification, whereas spirit must be intuitively and poetically apprehended.

In terms of its structure *Nature* moves through a series of chapters in which not only a relationship between the specific and the theoretical is established but each pair of chapters leads to an increasingly more complex set of concepts. For example, though "Language" might be said to be more complex in its definitional structure than the stipulative terms in the "Introduction," and while "Idealism" might be said to be even more complex than "Language" in the nature and scope of its definitions; yet each, in retrospective relation to what follows, seems relatively simple. What we experience is a definitional escalation. In this fashion Emerson is able to move from the minutiae which are principally the concern of the scientific naturalist to the metaphoric speculations which are the primary concern of the artist as Orphic Poet. From what we glean in Emerson's letters and journal entries, we can recognize his structural intentions in these terms. We know, for example, that when he decided to add to his "little book" the essay, "Spirit," on which he was working separately, he was troubled by the transition from "Discipline" to "Spirit." The chapter on "Idealism" which he then wrote, serves as a specific concrete bridge and completes the pattern of complementary chapters. In such a structural scheme, the final chapter, "Prospects," stands as a summation of the whole work. This sense of mounting dialectic definition is also supported by the motto of 1849, with its clear emphasis on the evolving, upward aspiration of the worm to be man. Indeed this later motto suggests that the chapters are not merely a series of ladder rungs but constitute demarcations on a helixical spire of form which the [46] 1849 motto vividly describes. Accordingly we are invited both to pair the chapters and to see them in some sort of helixical evolutionary scheme, moving from very finite data to the larger realms of spirit and to the prospects beyond about which the Orphic Poet, the final voice of the author, sings so prophetically.

This principle of double reading—of "double vision" as Whicher called it—is analogically related to those multi-dimensional art-forms that Emerson discusses in "Art": music, sculpture and architecture. Indeed he may well have unconsciously absorbed the principle from observing the constructional technique of Michelangelo, whose work he admired on his trip abroad in 1833, and on whom he lectured in 1835. For Emerson's style partakes of the same technique that Henry Moore described in Michelangelo's "Moses" when he observed that Michelangelo built up a mass of detail yet kept the same vision throughout. To walk around a Michelangelo statue or to see photographs of one taken from various sides but in the same light is to encounter what appear to be different statues. So with Emerson's essay: the individual chapters may be said to constitute different perspectives, though the subject—and particularly the vision that defines the subject—remains the same. What we stylistically encounter is what Emerson cites in "Discipline" when he speaks of architecture as "frozen music." That is, we recognize not only the parts, the notes, the members, but the manner in which the parts flow into the whole that is the church or the cantata or the composition.

This "double vision" is most evident in the more theoretical chapters of *Nature*: "Beauty," "Discipline" and "Spirit." In the chapter "Beauty," for example, Emerson first tried to suggest the complex possibilities of beauty in a single paragraph; but he wisely recognized that such an approach was too abstract, too illusive. What the first paragraph tries to convey is the eye's response to several aspects of beauty simultaneously. But Emerson must intuitively have sensed that the reader might need to recognize the parts first before he could see the whole, and so he began the next paragraph: "For better consideration, we may distribute the aspects of Beauty in a threefold manner." As we analyze the three separate aspects, we see that they are delight, virtue and intellect. Returning then to the observation of the first paragraph, we see how the eye should see these three aspects of beauty simultaneously in cosmic harmony. Each represents a single dimension of the whole; but they are ordered in relation to their increasing complexity. That is, delight is essentially simple sensuous response; virtue is sensuous response combined with human will; and intellect is sensuous response related to thought that is itself related to human will. Consequently for Emerson "Beauty, in the largest and profoundest sense, is one expression for the universe. . . . Truth, [47] goodness, and beauty are but different faces of the same All." In the final paragraph Emerson returns to where he began, weaving the three strands back together and leaving the reader with a more articulated sense of that first formulation, beyond which the chapter has not really gone. Again, M. W. Croll has described quite clearly this particular mode of baroque progression:

The first member is likely to be a self contained statement of the whole idea. . . . It is so because writers in this style like to avoid prearrangements and preparations; they begin, as Montaigne puts it, at *le dernier poinct* [sic], the point aimed at. The first member therefore exhausts the mere fact of an idea; logically there is nothing more to say. But it does not exhaust its imaginative truth or the energy of its conception. It is followed, therefore, by other members, each with a new tone or emphasis, each expressing a new apprehension of the truth expressed in the first. We may describe the progress . . . therefore, as a series of imaginative moments occurring in a logical pause or suspension. (p. 433)

The chapter "Discipline" reflects a similar mode of progression. Here the division of the initial assertion ("The use of the world [as discipline] includes the preceding uses, as parts of itself") is two-fold rather than three. The assertion of the first section is: "Nature is a discipline of the understanding in intellectual truths." And the assertion of the second section is: "Sensible objects conform to the premonitions of Reason and reflect the conscience." The principle of discipline is singular; but it affects the human organism in two different ways that Emerson can best illustrate by adopting the Neoplatonic, Coleridgean distinction between the Understanding and Reason. To delineate the two assertions and the concepts they embody is again to sort out the parts for the sake of the inexperienced eye. In actuality both the assertion and the concepts are interlocked and indeed take their definitions from this fact. In terms of the geometric metaphor that Emerson employs in this chapter, it would not be possible to define center without circumference or to comprehend circumference without some comprehension of center. As so often in Emerson, the geometric metaphor becomes the only way in which the author can convey some sense of the divisions within the whole. What is Unity?

It is like a great circle on a sphere, comprising all possible circles; which, however, may be drawn and comprise it in like manner. Every such truth is the absolute Ens [Being] seen from one side. But it has innumerable sides.

The geometric metaphor is adroitly chosen, for it enables Emerson to [48] distinguish in the subsequent two chapters between the limitations of idealism and the infinitude of spirit. In the final paragraph of the chapter on "Idealism" we are told that it "beholds the whole circle of persons and things, of actions and events, of country and religion." Idealism is inclusive of phenomena; but it answers, as the next chapter reminds us, only the question, "What is matter?" To that extent it is like that "great circle on a sphere." It may have scope, but it does not encompass the whole. Or, as Emerson expresses it in "Spirit," such views "do not include the whole circumference of man." Without spirit we may see a circularity to our existence, but we do not see the sphericity that constitutes its symmetry. Without spirit we may ascertain the *line* of existence, but we do not comprehend its *volume*. Without spirit our geometry is plane, not solid. That is the ultimate implication of the seemingly bizarre symbol of the transparent eyeball with which Emerson began in the first chapter. Indeed that crucial fourth paragraph of the first chapter, on which Jonathan Bishop rightly has dwelled, presents in brief the structural components of these later chapters. For to "return to reason and faith" in nature is a circular journey, while to be "glad to the brink of fear" is a spheral insight. The former undertaking is logically clear; the latter is paradoxical. And it is a resolution of this paradox which the chapter "Spirit" proposes. Idealism attempts to resolve the paradox of existence by seeing "the world in God," but that solution is for Emerson to "leave God out of me." The paradox can only be resolved by seeing—in a phrase Emerson almost uses but shies away from for reasons of obvious Christian theological import—"God with us." In such a phrase we would grammatically recognize two separate entities; but in effect the connective says that the distinction is of no real significance because the connective implies unity. Through spirit there is no separateness between the infinite and the finite. Emerson makes this point quite clear in his natural metaphor near the end of the chapter: "The Supreme Being does not build up nature around us, but puts forth through us, as the life of the tree puts forth new branches and leaves through the pores of the old." The chapter "Spirit" dissolves the fluidity by which so much of the essay has moved and presents us with the mass of unity that is to be seen in the prospects before us. It achieves the condition of "frozen music."

Before that great coda is sounded we might note another distinction that exists in the pairing of the chapters. We need to consider again the question of voice, not so much as strategy but as mode. We observe a notable distinction between the kinds of voices heard in the individual chapters. If we turn to the musical metaphor for a moment we might liken the various chapters of the essay to the parts of a baroque cantata. [49] The theoretical chapters we have examined are like chorales, intricately contrapuntal but moving toward a great harmonic final unity (which in this case is the final chapter). Intermingled with these chorales are the recitatives, which as the term itself denotes, are linear statements essentially singular in voice. Such an analogy is not alien to Emerson's thought, as an entry in the B Journal for March 11, 1836 suggests, when Emerson juxtaposes de Stael and Goethe with Haydn's Creation, immediately preceding a passage he later incorporated into Nature. An examination of "Language" and "Idealism" will illuminate this sort of analogy. In "Language" each section of the syllogistic formulation at the beginning of the chapter is taken up individually and separately; each one grows out of the previous one. The same might be said of "Idealism," which though more abstract than "Language" is also linear in progression. The five-fold effects of culture are carefully and sequentially listed. Thus we encounter a series of chapters that modulate between rather singular, linear statements and extremely complex contrapuntal ones. Just as the baroque chorales are more exciting and memorable than the recitatives, so too the chapters devoted to mind are more intricate, more challenging and revealing, than those recitative passages devoted to aspects of matter. The weight of our interest is thrown stylistically toward those chapters whose ideas Emerson, for all his meticulous dialectical construction, more fully valued.

This fact should not surprise us. Acknowledging that matter and mind are essential to one another, Emerson always makes clear where his commitment lies. Indeed his analysis is intended as a corrective to the existing situation, as he makes quite clear in his final chapter, "Prospects": "At present man applies to nature but half his force. He works on the world with his understanding alone." For Emerson the task confronting man was not merely scientific but poetic—to apply his Reason imaginatively to the world. This is the task of the Poet-Naturalist, who must restore unity to nature by first restoring unity to himself: "The reason why the world lacks unity, and lies broken and in heaps, is because man is disunited with himself. He cannot be a naturalist until he satisfies all the demands of the spirit." To this extent the task of the Poet-Naturalist is the task of the artisan learning the intangible dimension of his craft that will aid him intuitively in shaping the phenomena before him into a meaningful whole. Emerson anticipated something of this conclusion in his lecture on "The Naturalist," in 1834, when he observed:

It is fit that man should look upon Nature with the eye of the Artist, to learn from the great Artist whose blood beats in our veins, whose taste is upspringing in our own perception of beauty, the laws by which our hands should work that we may build St. Peter'ses or paint [50] Transfigurations or sing Iliads in worthy continuation of the architecture of the Andes, [of] the colors of the sky and the poem of life. (*EL*, I, 73)

What is truly significant about *Nature* is what Emerson did with this rather conventional Romantic notion. For what, as we now see in "Prospects," the Poet-Naturalist creates is not merely churches or paintings or poems but no less than Man himself. The Poet-Naturalist becomes the architect of Man. We should have guessed this fact from the beginning; for quite early, in "Commodity," Emerson quoted two lines from George Herbert's poem, "Man." Here, in "Prospects," he quotes five stanzas. The first line is prophetic of the whole Emersonian perspective: "Man is all symmetry." The ending to the essay, which is no conclusion in the conventional rhetorical sense, is simply but grandly the recognition of symmetry, the shaping of the capstone to the broken arch. *Nature* is, then, a blueprint, an architectonic, for the construction of the self out of the world's body, of the *me* out of the *not me*. This imaginative act of creation is an affirmation of the transcendent truth of man's divine nature. Hence the injunction of the coda to the essay:

Know then that the world exists for you. For you is the phenomenon perfect. What we are, that only can we see. All that Adam had, all that Caesar could, you have and can do. Adam called his house heaven and earth; Caesar called his house, Rome; you perhaps call yours, a cobbler's trade; a hundred acres of ploughed land; or a scholar's garret. Yet line for line, and point for point your dominion is as great as theirs, though without fine names. Build therefore your own world. As far [fast] as you conform your life to the pure idea in your own [*sic*] mind, that will unfold its great proportions.

The entire coda is more intricate stylistically, more eloquent verbally, but not really very different in kind from the ending to one of the lectures on natural history two years earlier. Emerson concluded "On the Relation of Man to the Globe" by observing of man,

. . . That not only a perfect symmetry is discoverable in his limbs and senses between the head and the foot, between the hand and the eye, the heart and the lungs,—but an equal symmetry and proportion is discoverable between him and the air, the mountains, the tides, the moon, and the sun. I am not impressed by solitary marks of designing wisdom; I am thrilled with delight by the choral harmony of the whole. Design! It is all design. It is all beauty. It is all astonishment. (*EL*, I, 49)

It may well be that Emerson is merely astonished here at his own oratory; [51] but since he was later to use these very members of the human body as metaphoric titles of his lectures on "Human Culture," it is more probable that he here expresses that profounder astonishment that is implicit in the historical experience of western man. It is the astonishment that the Greeks knew when Sophocles' Theban chorus exclaims: "Wonders are many on the earth and the greatest of these is man"; it is the astonishment that was rediscovered by the Italians in the Renaissance as reflected in Leonardo's famous circular emblem of Man the Measure. It is this same astonishment that Emerson faced rather ingenuously for the first time in 1834, but then was to express two years later with the self assurance and skill that is the intricate baroque style of *Nature*.

If Emerson's terminology happens to be borrowed, that should not distract us. For what should interest us is not so much from whom it was borrowed, but rather what Emerson did with it. In the baroque tradition there is ample precedent for such borrowings. Some of the best of Bach's work is based on motifs that he borrowed from other composers and from common musical sources; and the architecture of the Renaissance, as Geoffrey Scott has persuasively argued, is not poorer but richer for its tasteful borrowings. What is important in all these borrowings is the manner in which they have been reshaped and given the personal signature of the artist who did the borrowing. To that extent it is difficult to see how we can view the Emersonian style in *Nature* as either stiff or naive. It may be that we do not care for an architecture of "frozen music"; but that is a matter of personal taste and should not enter into our efforts to determine Emerson's style. As Emerson's most sustained single effort, *Nature* stands as his most baroque endeavor because it has about it those qualities which were the concern of baroque renaissance artists—mass and largeness of scale. It remained until the end of his career Emerson's most ambitious undertaking. It was in the words of Galen that Emerson noted in his *Q Journal* of 1832, "a solemn hymn to the great architect of our bodily frame . . ." (*JMN*, IV, 11).

To that extent, *Nature* works toward that important end of baroque art—the active sense of exultation. In an interesting canceled passage from the original notes for his lecture on "Art," Emerson commented in those terms:

As thus in architecture the mass, so in music the qualities of the atmosphere & the vibration of sonorous bodies; in painting, colour; in sculpture, the marble or bronze; in poetry the language; in oratory the voice & person of the orator & the accidents of time, place, topic, & other circumstances, are all adventitious fountains of pleasure independent of the spiritual arrangement in which alone the art resides. Art is thus ever impure & secondary. Nature paints the best part of the [52] picture, carves the best part of the statue, builds the best part of the house, & speaks the best part of the oration. (*EL*, II, 386)

Nature is the divine order; art is man's effort to make that order spiritually comprehensible. Not only then in terms of its subject matter but by means of its artfully structured style, *Nature* is a sophisticated anticipation of the world that Emerson was to build for himself in the lectures and the essays that followed, a spheral world of transparent symmetry.

SCHOLARSHIP OF THE 1970's

The Composition of *Nature*

by Merton M. Sealts, Jr.

The first in time and the first in importance of the influences upon the mind is that of nature. . . .
The scholar must needs stand wistful and admiring before this great spectacle. He must settle its
value in his mind. What is nature to him?—"The American Scholar" (CW, I, 54)

I. "A TRUE THEORY OF NATURE & MAN"

The common misconception that Emerson wrote all or most of *Nature* before 1836,
the year of its publication, is traceable in part to "The Old Manse," Nathaniel Hawthorne's prefatory sketch opening his *Mosses from an Old Manse* (1846), in which
"The Author Makes the Reader Acquainted with His Abode." There Hawthorne recalls the small writing room at the rear of the old house at Concord to which he had
brought his wife in 1842. It was "the most delightful little nook of a study that ever
afforded its snug seclusion to a scholar," he declares, adding that in the very same room
"Emerson wrote 'Nature'" while he was an earlier inhabitant of the house.[1] The implication is that *Nature* was composed during that period of roughly eleven months when
Emerson and his mother were living with Dr. Ripley in Concord, from October of
1834 until Emerson's second marriage on September 14, 1835. But in 1887, after
Emerson's death, James Elliot Cabot in his *Memoir of Ralph Waldo Emerson* "conjectured" that the first five chapters of *Nature* had "been for some time in hand" even
before the removal to Concord, where the seventh and eighth chapters "seem to have
been written" next and "the sixth, Idealism, last of all, as the connection of the two."[2]
Cabot's conjectures about the writing of *Nature*, tentative as they were, have been
widely accepted as fact even in recent years, when the editing of new scholarly texts of

"The Composition of *Nature* by Merton M. Sealts, Jr., is drawn from a book-length work in
progress, *Emerson on the Scholar*, begun in 1975 when the author was a Senior Fellow, National Endowment for the Humanities. All rights reserved.

[1] Nathaniel Hawthorne, "The Old Manse," in *Mosses from an Old Manse* (Columbus: Ohio
State University Press, 1974), p. 5.

[2] James Elliot Cabot, *A Memoir of Ralph Waldo Emerson*, 2 vols. (Boston: Houghton Mifflin
Company, 1887), I, 259.

Emerson's writings has uncovered information unavailable to earlier commentators. In our own day, for example, the editors of an anthology of American literature widely used in colleges and universities have gone well beyond Cabot, stating without qualification that Emerson had "already written five chapters" of *Nature* by the time he settled in the Manse, so that what he did "in the very room in which Hawthorne later wrote his *Mosses from an Old Manse*" was to complete "the first draft."[3]

The facts about the origin and growth of *Nature* as we now know them are considerably different from this account and its antecedents in both Hawthorne and Cabot. It is true that by 1835, in his journal and early lectures, Emerson had worked out major ideas and even some of the actual phrasing that he later incorporated in parts of the book, but he had not composed any one of the chapters as they now stand. What became the fourth chapter, "Language," was the furthest advanced; one can see its central ideas taking substantial form in the lectures on natural history in 1833 and 1834 and continuing to grow by accretion in the series on English literature of 1835–1836. But the lectures on literature were not written until the fall and winter of 1835, after Emerson had remarried and moved from the Manse into his own house in Concord, and there *Nature* itself was shaped and composed, partly from existing journal and lecture materials and partly in newly written chapters or sections of chapters, during the first eight months of 1836. The manuscript from which the book was printed has not survived, and we have no preparatory outline or series of preliminary notes comparable to the material Emerson assembled in Notebook L before he wrote the Historical Discourse of 1835, the lectures on English literature, and other later writings. But a number of benchmark references in his journal of 1836 make possible a new analysis of Emerson's progress with the book during that year,[4] and we can now say with assurance that most of *Nature* other than "Language" first took its present form between January and June of 1836, with minor additions and revisions following in July and a significant change taking place early in August to produce what are now the penultimate Chapters VI and VII, "Idealism" and "Spirit."

Emerson's desire to write a book went back at least to his days as a parish minister, and it was specifically a "book about nature" that he had in mind when he returned from Europe in 1833. But he was in no position to begin a book-length work at that

---

[3] Sculley Bradley, Richmond Croom Beatty, E. Hudson Long, and George Perkins, editors, *The American Tradition in Literature*, 4th edition, 2 vols. (New York: Grosset & Dunlap, 1974), I, 1040, n. 1.

[4] Journal and lecture passages used in the successive chapters of *Nature* are listed and dated above, pp. 46–65, and tabulated more briefly in CW, I, 269–273. Sealts and Ferguson quote in full the earlier formulations of material used in the chapter on "Language" in order "to bring out their central importance in Emerson's emerging conception of the book he wanted to write" (p. 46). As Spiller and Ferguson explain, "a given passage or reference could appear several times" after its initial entry in Emerson's journal or other manuscript. "Sometimes the used passage would appear in the new context almost verbatim, but more frequently it would be edited in varying degrees. . . . A prose work by Emerson must therefore be regarded as *a composition*—in the sense that one speaks of a musical composition or the composition of a painting—rather than as a piece of exposition or argument developed logically at a single sitting" (CW, I, 269; emphasis added).

time, and in 1834, still wrestling with his problem of vocation, he was occupied with his new experiment of lecturing and with composition in verse. In the spring of 1835, after he had brought his mother to Concord and revived his old ambitions of prose authorship, his first thought had been of writing a "book of Nature whereof 'Howitt's Seasons' should be not so much the model as the parody. It should contain the Natural history of the woods ⟨for⟩ around my shifting camp for every month in the year. It should tie their astronomy, botany, physiology, meteorology, picturesque, & poetry together. No bird, no bug, no bud should be forgotten on his day & hour" (*JMN*, V, 25). Later in the year, as we also know, he was entertaining somewhat different ideas about the book: it might be written "on spiritual things" (*JMN*, V, 40); it might be made up of "Essays chiefly upon Natural Ethics" (*L*, I, 447); it might include a chapter on "the Duty & Discipline of a Scholar" (*JMN*, V, 84). During the summer of 1835, when Emerson was making plans for his marriage, buying and remodeling his house in Concord, and preparing for a busy schedule of addresses and lectures that extended into the fall and winter, he had little time for other writing of any kind, but early in 1836, within scarcely more than a week after his lectures on English literature had closed in Boston, he was actively planning a new composition. It was probably on January 22, 1836, on a page of his current Journal B, that he began to assemble a collection of extracts from his earlier writings that concern the scholar (*JMN*, V, 116–117).[5] Most of these items had already been collected in Notebook L (Literature) during the previous summer and fall: the initial observation about the scholar as working "with invisible tools to invisible ends" had been set down in slightly different words among the preliminary notes for his lectures on English literature, and several of the other extracts had been used there or in later pages of the notebook to characterize the scholar in his alternative role as man of letters. Here the figure under discussion is not "the writer" or "the Thinker" but simply "the Scholar."

Although these notes may well have been intended as an outline for some or all of the projected "chapter" or "sermon" on the scholar and his ethics that Emerson kept reminding himself to write, there is a significant addition that sounds the keynote for the "book about Nature" itself. Holding that literature is the concern not merely of a few persons but of mankind in general, Emerson had said in 1835 that in setting other men "to think" the scholar as writer must "convert for them the dishonored facts which they know, into trees of life, their life into a garden of God by suggesting the principle which classifies them." Now, after repeating these words, Emerson adds a new question which the scholar is evidently to answer with an affirmative demonstration: "We ⟨stand⟩ ↑build↓ the sepulchers of our fathers: can we never behold the Universe as new and ↑feel↓ that we have a stake as much as our predecessors[?]" In this challenging question of 1836 is the germ of that characteristically Emersonian paragraph that stands at the very beginning of the published book, calling for a direct vision of God and nature and "an original relation to the universe."

[5] The passage from Journal B is reproduced as Plate I, p. 4 above. For the development of Emerson's conception of "the Scholar," see Merton M. Sealts, Jr., "Emerson on the Scholar, 1833–1837," *PMLA*, LXXXV (March, 1970), 185–195.

Our age is retrospective. It builds the sepulchres of the fathers. It writes biographies, histories, and criticism. The foregoing generations beheld God and nature face to face; we, through their eyes. Why should not we also enjoy an original relation to the universe? Why should not we have a poetry and philosophy of insight and not of tradition, and a religion by revelation to us, and not the history of theirs? Embosomed for a season in nature, whose floods of life stream around and through us, and invite us by the powers they supply, to action proportioned to nature, why should we grope among the dry bones of the past, or put the living generation into masquerade out of its faded wardrobe? The sun shines to-day also. There is more wool and flax in the fields. There are new lands, new men, new thoughts. Let us demand our own works and laws and worship. (*Nature*, p. 5)

Since the years of his Boston pastorate, when Emerson had complained that "we worship in the dead forms of our forefathers" (*JMN*, IV, 27), he had been preaching "a religion by revelation," emphasizing not institutions, creeds, and past miracles but the perpetual miracle of man's being itself, inspired in the living present by the God Within. This notion of man's "infinitude" is the essential teaching of his "first philosophy." In 1833 and 1834 he had lectured on nature as "a metaphor or image of the human Mind" (*EL*, I, 24) and had written verse about nature that deserves to be called "a poetry of insight," as in his book he intended to offer "a philosophy of insight." The new book would be his most comprehensive report to date of what as "Watcher" he had learned to see in nature since his decision that to be a good minister he must leave the ministry. Throughout the 1830's Emerson repeatedly turned away from institutions and works of the past in favor of new creation in the present with an eye to the future. A "true theory of nature & man," he wrote in 1836, first in his journal and again in *Nature*, must have in it something "progressive" (*JMN*, V, 182; *Nature*, p. 5), something that looks to the future; so in an early sermon he had declared it to be "the blessed law of heaven" that "our nature should be progressive" (*YES*, p. 54), and in his recent lectures he had said that "a great genius" will "guide the future, not follow the past" (*EL*, I, 232). "The American Scholar" in 1837 characterizes as "progressive" the "active soul" of the true scholar, not content to "stop with some past utterance of genius" but original and creative in its own right (*CW*, I, 56–57); and the Divinity School Address of 1838 declares that in religion "a true teacher" will likewise "show us that God is, not was; that He speaketh, not spake" (*CW*, I, 89). The most radical expression of this aspect of Emerson's thought was to come in 1841: as "an endless seeker with no past at my back," he declares, "I unsettle all things." This is in "Circles," which gives fair warning to the timid: "Beware when the great God lets loose a thinker on this planet" (*W*, II, 318, 308).

The scholar, as Emerson had repeatedly said by 1836, is not only a thinker himself but the cause of thinking in others; he is able to "set men upon thinking" by converting or transforming "dishonored facts," and he does so "by suggesting the principle which classifies them." Emerson amplifies the point in his journal, returning again and again to the idea of *classifying* facts through the application of *principles*. "Every man must live upon a principle," he wrote in 1835. "I have seen the adoption of a principle transform a proser into an orator. Every transgression that it makes of routine makes man's being something worth. . . . Every principle is an eye to see with" (*JMN*, V, 70, 71). When Emerson began urging his contemporaries to "behold the Universe as new" instead of building "the sepulchers of our fathers" he was asking them to shift their "angle of vision" (*JMN*, X, 133, 173; W, XII, 10)[6] in order to look at their world with what he liked to call the eye of Reason. Here he was once more making the Coleridgean distinction between the Reason and the Understanding. "Every fact studied by the Understanding is not only solitary but desart. But if the iron lids of Reason's eye can once be raised, the fact can be classified immediately & seen to be related to our ⟨school⟩ nursery reading & our profoundest Science" (*JMN*, V, 85). Although ready-made systems of classification are offered us under various titles, such as history, science, religion, economy, and taste, "in every man the facts under these topics are only so far efficient as they are arranged after the law of *his* being" (*JMN*, V, 89). "Instead of studying things without the principles of them," Emerson had written in 1833, "all may be penetrated unto within him" (*JMN*, IV, 84). Within himself, within the sphere of his own experience, lies the existential answer to his questions about himself and his world. Emerson developed this idea in his Introduction to *Nature* following a conversation on March 5, 1836 with his brother Charles, who "instructed" him that "every man has certain questions which always he proposes to the Eternal, and that his life & fortune, his ascetic, are so moulded as to constitute the answers, if only he will read his consciousness aright" (*JMN*, V, 135). In Emerson's own phrasing, "Every man's condition is a solution in hieroglyphic to those inquiries he would put. He acts it as life, before he apprehends it as truth. In like manner, nature is already, in its forms and tendencies, describing its own design" (*Nature*, p. 5).

The scholar's task, then, is to understand his own experience in nature by learning to see it with the eye of Reason and so to classify it, arrange it, and ultimately convert it into living thought and art for the benefit of other men and women. "The scholar of the first age," Emerson was to say in 1837, "received into him the world around; brooded thereon, gave it the new arrangement of his own mind, and uttered it again. . . . It was—dead fact; now, it is quick thought" (*CW*, I, 55). Given "an eye to see with," the scholar of any age will follow the same procedure. Emerson's "book about nature" as it finally took form during 1836 contains no chapter treating the scholar; in fact even the word "scholar" occurs only once, in an incidental reference to "a scholar's garret" (*Nature*, p. 35). The focus of the argument is rather on "what thought, what Revelation," the scholar as "Watcher" sees (*JMN*, V, 135)—or rather on *how* he sees, and how others through his teaching and example may learn to see as well. *Nature* is in large part a book about vision, the process of vision, the uses of vision. Metaphors of sight and seeing both open and close the discussion, which begins with Emerson's charge that in a "retrospective" age we behold God and nature only through the eyes of our forefathers but which ends, in a forward-looking chapter called "Pros-

---

[6] Sherman Paul, *Emerson's Angle of Vision* (Cambridge: Harvard University Press, 1952), offers a comprehensive treatment of Emerson's patterns of visual imagery. An extract from Chapter Three is reprinted above, pp. 131–133.

pects," by invoking the wonder that "the blind man feels who is gradually restored to perfect sight" (*Nature*, p. 37). The component chapters—even subdivisions of chapters —are arranged so as to appeal in turn to the senses of the reader (particularly his visual sense), then to his Understanding, and ultimately to his Reason, and in this way to foster that movement from sight to insight which Emerson took as the sign of a man's spiritual growth and self-fulfillment. "A man is a method, a progressive arrangement," he liked to say with Coleridge;[7] in both its form and its function a book setting forth a new vision of the universe, "a true theory of nature & man," must also be progressively arranged.

II. TRANSPARENCE AND OPACITY

"Our American literature and spiritual history," Emerson once said, are "in the optative mood" (*CW*, I, 207), and his own Introduction to *Nature* is an illustration. "Undoubtedly we have no questions to ask which are unanswerable," according to this sanguine declaration of faith. "We must trust . . . that whatever curiosity the order of things has awakened in our minds, the order of things can satisfy." Recognizing in 1836 that men are still "so far from the road to truth, that religious teachers dispute and hate each other," as he had long been noting with regret, and that "speculative men"—presumably in the Latin sense of Watchers on a tower, as Emerson saw himself —"are esteemed unsound and frivolous," as the scholar had been said to pass "for an idler or worse," he is nevertheless confident that "the most abstract truth is the most practical." "The truth of truth," he had written, is "that it is selfevident[,] selfsubsistent" (*JMN*, IV, 45); here he declares that "a true theory," including that theory of nature which is the aim of all science, "will be its own evidence," and once it is discovered it "will explain all phenomena" (*Nature*, p. 5).

The customary distinction between subject and object made by philosophers becomes in Emerson's phrasing the difference between ourselves and "all that is separate from us, all which Philosophy distinguishes as the NOT ME, that is, both nature and art, all other men and my own body." He minimizes the popular differentiation between nature and man's art, arguing that all of mankind's operations on external nature taken together "are so insignificant . . . that in an impression so grand as that of the world on the human mind, they do not vary the result." This deliberate passing over of human artifice means that Emerson intends to concentrate in *Nature* on "essences unchanged by man; space, the air, the river, the leaf" (*Nature*, p. 5). But although he does not explicitly say so in the Introduction, his real concern is less with external nature in itself than with nature in relation to man—that "original relation" he was seeking to foster—and the "impression" it makes on the human observer. "The scholar," as he

---

[7] The quoted sentence comes from Coleridge's "Preliminary Discourse on Method"; see *JMN*, V, 114, and compare *Nature*, p. 19 ("progressive arrangement") and "Spiritual Laws," *W*, II, 144. On Emerson's indebtedness to Coleridge, see also Barry Wood, "The Growth of the Soul: Coleridge's Dialectical Method and the Strategy of Emerson's *Nature*," *PMLA*, XCI (May, 1976), 385–397 (reprinted in part below).

put it in 1837, must settle the *value* of nature *"in his mind.* What is nature *to him?"* (*CW*, I, 54; emphasis added). The orientation of *Nature* is unabashedly subjective. "Montaigne said, himself was all he knew," Emerson had remarked while in Italy. "Myself is much more than I know, & yet I know nothing else" (*JMN*, IV, 68). To study nature, he would argue in "The American Scholar," is to understand human nature, so that "the ancient precept, 'Know thyself,' and the modern precept, 'Study nature,' become at last one maxim" (*CW*, I, 55).

The basic difficulty is that most men and women cannot or do not really *see* the world around them, even with their natural eyes, let alone with the insight that Emerson wished to demonstrate. "To speak truly, few adult persons can see nature," he writes in his initial chapter. "Most persons do not see the sun. At least they have a very superficial seeing. The sun illuminates only the eye of the man, but shines into the eye and heart of the child." Here Emerson is repeating a point he had been making since his lectures on science: both the senses and the affections must be brought into play if one would deal adequately with nature. "The *lover* of nature is he whose inward and outward senses are still truly adjusted to each other; who has retained the spirit of infancy even into the era of manhood. His intercourse with heaven and earth, becomes part of his daily food" (*Nature*, p. 7; emphasis added). Emerson is not merely repeating here the commonplaces of Romantic theory about nature and childhood he could have picked up in reading Wordsworth and Coleridge; he is speaking out of his own experience, as he does again and again throughout *Nature*. As both naturalist and poet, "in the sense of a perceiver & dear lover of the harmonies that are in the soul & in matter" (*L*, I, 435), he drew sustenance from living in a country town, where so prosaic an experience as crossing the Concord common on a December day had brought him "a wild poetic delight" (*JMN*, IV, 355). The occasion is recalled in *Nature* to demonstrate that men and women of Emerson's generation in New England villages can also "enjoy an original relation to the universe" without merely existing on the accumulated spiritual capital of their forefathers: "Crossing a bare common, in snow puddles, at twilight, under a clouded sky, without having in my thoughts any occurrence of special good fortune, I have enjoyed a perfect exhilaration" (*Nature*, p. 8). As Jonathan Bishop has remarked, the episode as described in *Nature* comprises "a concrete image" of a time when "New England weather is at its ugliest, the villages at their meanest," while the voice of the speaker "obliges you to take another look at the potential beauty of mean situations."[8]

That is finely said; Bishop has exactly captured both Emerson's intention and his rhetorical strategy. But "the 'bare common' sentence," as Bishop calls it, is only part of what Emerson is driving at. Moving out of the village into the nearby woods, he goes on to say in the same paragraph that there, beyond the streets and houses, is "perpetual youth," and within these unsettled "plantations of God" an adult, whatever his age, "casts off his years, as the snake his slough," and returns "to reason and faith."

[8] For Bishop's discussion, quoted here and below, see his *Emerson on the Soul* (Cambridge: Harvard University Press, 1964), pp. 10–15 (reprinted above, pp. 140–144).

Nature, in other words, effects a transformation, restoring that true adjustment of the "inward and outward senses" Emerson had associated with childhood and thereby bringing about a recovery of religious faith as well as renewed psychological wholeness. It is in this context that he makes a celebrated personal declaration:

> There I feel that nothing can befal me in life,—no disgrace, no calamity, (leaving me my eyes,) which nature cannot repair. Standing on the bare ground,—my head bathed by the blithe air, and uplifted into infinite space,—all mean egotism vanishes. I become a transparent eye-ball. I am nothing. I see all. The currents of the Universal Being circulate through me; I am part or particle of God. The name of the nearest friend sounds then foreign and accidental. To be brothers, to be acquaintances,—master or servant, is then a trifle and a disturbance. I am the lover of uncontained and immortal beauty. In the wilderness, I find something more dear and connate than in streets or villages. In the tranquil landscape, and especially in the distant line of the horizon, man beholds somewhat as beautiful as his own nature. (*Nature*, p. 8).

Within this latter portion of the paragraph is "the notorious eye-ball sentence," as Bishop calls it, which is "perhaps the best known sentence of Emerson's among readers who wish to make fun of him." Among his own contemporaries Christopher Cranch "unerringly picked this image out to caricature"; Cranch's drawing "shows the one concrete picture these words irresistibly muster up, a preacherly eyeball staring into the heavens," Bishop writes. "The *doctrine* about the Soul's relation to Nature, so far as it is paraphrasable, is the same as that of the 'bare common' sentence. But the speaker, the I, is innocently absurd at best; the rhythm is a coarse parody of the watchful casualness of the other sentence; and the language is vapid."[9]

Bishop is right in saying that readers have had difficulties with Emerson's "transparent eye-ball"—especially unsympathetic readers; any classroom teacher of *Nature* has encountered his share of them. But Bishop has surely erred in arguing that in the latter part of his paragraph Emerson is merely repeating what he had already said about the implications of the preceding experience on the bare common. There his speaker is still in the village; when he is made to leave the village for the woods the level of discourse is significantly shifted along with the setting, and the ensuing episode takes place on what Emerson would later call another "platform" of experience. With these developments the speaker himself is transformed. He is now "uplifted into infinite space"; he becomes what he has not previously been as consciousness of personal identity gives way to a new sense of identification of the perceiver with what he sees; there are no longer the usual impediments between the "I" and "the Universal Being"; in short, he declares himself "part or particle of God."[10] The "eye-ball" may well be

[9] For Cranch's drawing, see Plate II, p. 9 above. As Bishop notes, p. 233, n. 14, there is a "source" for the eye image—or at least an analogue—in Plotinus, who held that in the intelligible world "everybody is pure, and each inhabitant is, as it were, an eye": see John S. Harrison, *The Teachers of Emerson* (New York: Sturgis & Walton Company, 1910), p. 105. On the *tone* of Emerson's passage on "the transparent eye-ball," see Barbara Packer's comments in "Uriel's Cloud: Emerson's Rhetoric," *Georgia Review*, XXXI (Summer, 1971), 327–328.

[10] In an 1856 printing Emerson substituted "parcel" for "particle"; CW restores the "particle" of the 1836 and 1849 printings.

an unfortunate image for what Emerson seeks to convey here. But this part of the paragraph clearly involves more than "exhilaration," and the clue to the further transformation he wishes to suggest is in the single word "transparent"—a word which plays a significant role in other passages of *Nature* that also treat moments of supreme vision.[11] The paragraph is arranged to build upward to an epiphany, or what Emerson himself liked to call, with Xenophanes, Cudworth, and Goethe, "an εν και παν."[12]

Emerson repeatedly uses images drawn from sense-experience as analogies for psychological processes that transcend the operations of the senses themselves. There is an apposite example in a journal passage of June 1836 characterizing his new friend Bronson Alcott, whose inflexible self-centeredness Emerson contrasted unfavorably with his own openness and receptivity. Alcott, he said, was constitutionally unable to interest himself in the ideas of others, spoken or written, and therefore could not "delight in Shakspear" as Emerson himself did. "I go to Shakspear, Goethe, Swift, even to Tennyson, submit myself to them, *become merely an organ of hearing*, & yield to the law of their being. I am paid *for thus being nothing* by ⟨a new⟩ an entire new mind & thus a Proteus I enjoy the Universe through the powers & organs of a hundred different men" (*JMN*, V, 178; emphasis added). The speaker in *Nature* has an analogous experience, except that he becomes "merely an organ of *seeing*"—the "eye-ball"; he too is "nothing" himself as "all mean egotism vanishes," and for the time he also "yields" himself to "powers & organs" not his own. What Emerson means in the journal passage is that he could be stimulated and invigorated by surrendering himself to the thinking of other minds, though even inspiring books, as he was to say in "The American Scholar," are "for the scholar's idle times" (*CW*, I, 57). "Hearing" the words of Shakespeare requires receptivity; speaking for one's self demands active creation. For his scholar Emerson wanted both: "The alternations of speaking & hearing," he believed, "make our education" (*JMN*, V, 98).

When Emerson employed sight imagery he carried the same ideas still further. Essential truth, self-evident truth, "is light," he had written in 1832—and "You don't get a candle to see the sun rise" (*JMN*, IV, 45). *Light* is his characteristic sign of the

---

[11]"Have you not thoughts & illustrations that are your own?" Emerson had asked himself in 1835, citing—among other motifs he was to use in *Nature*—"the reason why the atmosphere is transparent" (*JMN*, V, 40). On "the notion of the 'transparent'" as signifying *transcendence* in *Nature*, see Kenneth Burke, "I, Eye, Ay—Emerson's Early Essay 'Nature': Thoughts on the Machinery of Transcendence," in Myron Simon and Thornton H. Parsons, editors, *Transcendentalism and Its Legacy* (Ann Arbor: The University of Michigan Press, 1966), pp. 13–14 (reprinted above, pp. 156–157). For another discussion of Emerson's terminology, which appears to derive in part from his reading of David Brewster, *The Life of Sir Isaac Newton* (1831), see Barbara Packer, "The Instructed Eye: Emerson's Cosmogony in 'Prospects'" (printed below).

[12]"One and all"—that is, a single event or fact epitomizing the universe (*JMN*, V, 128 and n. 393), "an Epiphany of God" (*JMN*, VII, 29). The scholar, Emerson had recently written, "knows all by one" (*JMN*, V, 117); like Michelangelo, he sees—or forms—"*il piu nell' uno*," or Multitude in Unity (*EL*, I, 101). Emerson quotes the Italian phrase in Chapter III, "Beauty," echoing his own poem "Each and All" in adding that "Nothing is quite beautiful alone: nothing but is beautiful in the whole" (*Nature*, p. 14); in Chapter V, "Discipline," again alluding to Xenophanes, he recurs to the idea of nature's "Unity in Variety" (*Nature*, p. 21).

divine presence: "God is, not was," is what he means by saying in the Introduction to *Nature* that "The sun shines to-day also" and in Chapter I that "every night" the stars "light the universe." "One might think the atmosphere was made *transparent* with this design," he writes, "to give man, in the heavenly bodies, the perpetual presence of the sublime" (*CW*, I, 89; *Nature*, pp. 5, 7; emphasis added). As for man himself, Emerson had remarked in a sermon of 1832 that "the genuine man" assumes no veil and needs none: "He is transparent" (*YES*, p. 185). A man of true perception is endowed with a mind that operates like "a lens formed to concentrate the rays of the Divine laws to a focus which shall be the personality of God," according to a journal entry of 1835, which adds that this focus "falls so far into the infinite that the form or person of God is not within the ken of the mind" (*JMN*, V, 83–84). In *Nature* that same perceiving lens appears as the "transparent eye-ball," which is directed toward the infinite as the see-er is figuratively "uplifted into infinite space" to become "part or particle of God." When the outward senses are dominant, as a later chapter of *Nature* has it, the universe seems wholly impenetrable and opaque, but when the inward eye of Reason is opened then both perceiver and perceived become wholly transparent, "and the light of higher laws . . . shines through." The transformation from opacity to transparence takes place whenever the eye is "instructed" (*JMN*, IV, 96); that is, when the perceiver grasps the true "relation between the mind and matter," as Emerson writes in "Language" (*Nature*, p. 18); in an earlier version of the same sentence he had said "between thought and the world" (*EL*, I, 226). "All things" are transparent, according to the journal; to the perceiving eye they "show God through every part & angle" (*JMN*, V, 176). The idea is further elaborated in a key passage of Chapter VI, "Idealism," which emphasizes the role of Reason in the process of learning to see man and nature as they exist beyond the realm of the senses.

To the senses and the unrenewed understanding, belongs a sort of instinctive belief in the absolute existence of nature. In their view, man and nature are indissolubly joined. Things are ultimates, and they never look beyond their sphere. The presence of Reason mars this faith. The first effort of thought tends to relax this despotism of the senses, which binds us to nature as if we were a part of it, and shows us nature aloof, and as it were, afloat. Until this higher agency intervened, the animal eye sees, with wonderful accuracy, sharp outlines and colored surfaces. When the eye of Reason opens, to outline and surface are at once added, grace and expression. These proceed from imagination and affection, and abate somewhat of the angular distinctness of objects. If the Reason be stimulated to more earnest vision, outlines and surfaces become transparent, and are no longer seen; causes and spirits are seen through them. The best, the happiest moments of life, are these delicious awakenings of the higher powers, and the reverential withdrawing of nature before its God. (*Nature*, p. 24)

"Grace and expression," Emerson says here, "proceed from imagination and affection." As early as his lecture on "The Uses of Natural History" in 1833 he had spoken of the "power of *expression*" in nature that makes it a resource for metaphorical language (*EL*, I, 24), and in 1834 he had insisted in "The Naturalist" that nature would reveal its ultimate laws only to the man who approaches her with "Love and Faith," not with an indiscriminate appetite for undigested facts (*EL*, I, 80). In 1835, beginning his lectures on English literature, he had explained that the poet, by "converting" natural objects into "symbols of thought," makes the outward creation "merely a convenient alphabet to express thoughts and emotions. This act or vision of the mind is called Imagination" (*EL*, I, 224). Now in "Idealism" Emerson defines imagination as "the use which the Reason makes of the material world" (*Nature*, p. 25),[13] and in "Prospects" he goes on to assert once again that nature demands affection as well as perception from those who would see her truly. Here he writes in terms of restoration and recovery, both of natural vision and of spiritual wholeness:

> The problem of restoring to the world original and eternal beauty, is solved by the redemption of the soul. The ruin or the blank, that we see when we look at nature, is in our own eye. The axis of vision is not coincident with the axis of things, and so they appear not transparent but opake. The reason why the world lacks unity, and lies broken and in heaps, is, because man is disunited with himself. He cannot be a naturalist, until he satisfies all the demands of the spirit. Love is as much its demand, as perception. Indeed, neither can be perfect without the other. In the uttermost meaning of the words, thought is devout, and devotion is thought. Deep calls unto deep. But in actual life, the marriage is not celebrated. There are innocent men who worship God after the tradition of their fathers, but their sense of duty has not yet extended to the use of all their faculties. And there are patient naturalists, but they freeze their subject under the wintry light of understanding. Is not prayer also a study of truth—a sally of the soul into the unfound infinite? No man ever prayed heartily, without learning something. But when a faithful thinker, resolute to detach every object from personal relations, and see it in the light of thought, shall, at the same time, kindle science with the fire of the holiest affections, then will God go forth anew into the creation. (*Nature*, pp. 34–35)

III. DISCIPLINE

"To write a very little takes a great deal of time," Emerson remarked to his friend Hedge in a letter of March 14, 1836. Although he had been doing more writing than reading during the winter months, he had "little to show for his solid days," chiefly because he had been unable to satisfy his desire for "the beautiful in composition" (*L*, II, 7). By this date he had drafted many isolated passages that would later be transferred from the journal to the book, but he still needed a basis for organizing its component chapters and arranging them in a functional sequence. The scholar, he had said in January, employs "the principle which classifies the facts," but it was late in March before he hit upon a classifying principle that would enable him to compose the existing materials for Chapters II–V: "Commodity," "Beauty," "Language," and "Discipline." He found his principle by applying to nature itself his conception of a dynamic ascent of spirit by way of successive levels, or platforms, of significance. "Thus through Nature," he wrote, "is there a striving ⟨for⟩ upward."

[13] "The Imagination is Vision," Emerson wrote in a journal entry of August 1, 1835; it "regards the world as symbolical & pierces the emblem for the real sense, & sees all external objects as types" (*JMN*, V, 76). Following Emerson's death his friend Bartol spoke of him as "a perceiver" who used "his imagination for an eye"; see C. A. Bartol, "Emerson's Religion," in *The Genius and Character of Emerson*, edited by F. B. Sanborn (1885; rpt. Port Washington, N.Y.: Kennikat Press, 1971), p. 145.

Commodity points to a greater good. Beauty is nought until the spiritual element. Language refers to that which is to be said. . . .

Finally; Nature is a discipline, & points to the pupil & exists for the pupil. Her ⟨nature⟩ being is subordinate; his is superior. Man underlies Ideas. Nature receives them as her god. (*JMN*, V, 146, 147)

In other words, the order of chapters in his book should reflect that principle of "progressive arrangement" that Emerson saw operating in nature as in human nature. "Man," he wrote in this same entry, "is an analogist," and the delight he finds in classification is "the first index of his Destiny," which is "to put Nature under his feet" by knowing her laws, or "to apprehend Nature in Ideas[.] The moment an idea is introduced among facts the God takes possession. Until then, facts conquer us. The Beast rules Man" (*JMN*, V, 146).

As we know, Emerson had already worked out much of Chapter IV, the long discussion of "Language," in his earlier lectures, developing the thesis that external nature serves man as "the vehicle of thought" (*Nature*, p. 15). Although he no doubt found it necessary to reshape some of the existing material of "Language" to its new context, it is probable that most of his work on *Nature* during 1836 went into other parts of the book. By early April, as his journal entries indicate, he was beginning to address the issues to be covered in later chapters, particularly "Idealism" and "Spirit," which deal with nature in its ultimate relation to Deity; at the same time he was reflecting not only on the general topic of "Discipline," the subject of Chapter V, but also on "the Ascetic of the man of letters" (*JMN*, V, 149)—in effect his old project of a chapter on the particular "Duty & Discipline of a Scholar."[14] When read in the light of later events his brief comment here seems portentous. "A persistent & somewhat rigorous temperance," Emerson wrote on April 2, cannot well be avoided by the man of letters—the scholar. "Saved from so many hurts & griefs, he must impose a discipline on himself. He must out of sympathetic humanity wound his own bosom, bear some part of the load of wo, and ⟨so to⟩ the most convenient & graceful to him is a quiet but unrelaxing self-command. If he accept this & manfully stablish it, it shall stablish him." But Emerson did not complete the entry, being more concerned with the larger project of his book about nature. Opening his planned sequence of four chapters with a short discussion of "Commodity," he began on the lowest of his successive "platforms" by considering "those advantages which our senses owe to nature." How he intended to proceed in the chapters to follow is suggested by his assurance that this "benefit" of nature "is temporary and mediate, not ultimate, like its service to the soul" (*Nature*, p. 10).

According to the next chapter in the sequence, "Beauty," the sight of natural forms is itself a delight, but the beauty to be seen in virtuous actions of men introduces a

[14]From Friedrich Schleiermacher, by way of his friend Hedge, Emerson had picked up the term "Ascetic," defined as "the discipline of life produced by the opinions" (*JMN*, IV, 360). "I think the Scholar's Ascetic ought to be systematically and gen[era]lly taught," he told Hedge on March 14, 1836 (*L*, II, 7).

higher "spiritual" element, and finally, on a still higher level, perception of the beauty of the world as "an object of the intellect" is a necessary prerequisite to artistic creation (*Nature*, pp. 11–13). This analysis is of course designed to prepare the reader for the following chapter on "Language," which illustrates in terms of Emerson's doctrine of correspondence between spirit and matter what it means to see nature as sages and poets do: as an object of the intellect, a transparent manifestation of higher laws made visible to the eye of Reason. But the actual composition of Chapter III in accordance with these "three aspects of Natural Beauty" was delayed until some time after May 30, 1836, when the triparite division of his topic occurred to Emerson during a walk "in the wood" (*JMN*, V, 166), and it was not until mid-June that he drafted key passages of the following chapter, "Discipline." For approximately six weeks of April and May he was obliged to suspend work on his book under the pressure of unexpected events. Since January, when he gave the last lecture of his course on English literature, he had been repeating selected lectures by invitation at Salem and also at Concord and Cambridge. On April 18 he had gone to Salem for what was to be a two-week course of lectures on biography and literature, drawn from his two Boston series of the previous year. But word from Concord of Charles Emerson's sudden illness obliged him to interrupt his lecturing on April 22 in order to accompany his brother as far as New York on a projected trip southward to a warmer climate. Leaving Charles with William and their mother in New York, he returned to lecture in Salem on May 2 only to learn that Charles, after seeming to improve, had taken a turn for the worse. He again set out for New York a few days later, this time escorting Charles's fiancée, Elizabeth Hoar of Concord, but his brother died suddenly on May 9 before their arrival, another victim of tuberculosis like Ellen and Edward.

Waldo Emerson was deeply affected by the new loss, as various friends attested after seeing him at the funeral and in ensuing weeks at home; he and Charles had been particularly close, especially during their residence in Concord, and Waldo was remodeling his new house to provide quarters for Charles and Elizabeth after their marriage. He himself wrote his wife from New York that Charles had been a soul "so costly & so rare that few persons were capable of knowing its price. . . . I determined to live in Concord, as you know, because he was there, and now that the immense promise of his maturity is destroyed, I feel not only unfastened there and adrift but a sort of shame at living at all." The best of his own strength, he said, had come from Charles. "How much I saw through his eyes. I feel as if my own were very dim" (*L*, II, 90). Returning to Concord with his mother and Elizabeth Hoar, he slowly found himself again, as he wrote in the journal, remembering "states of mind that perhaps I had long lost before this grief" (*JMN*, V, 160). He set about collecting his reminiscences of Charles and attempted to assess what their close companionship had meant to him, acknowledging once more that Charles had sharpened his own vision: "The eye is closed that was to see Nature for me, & give me leave to see," he wrote on May 16 (*JMN*, V, 152). Ideas discussed by the two brothers often found their way into Waldo Emerson's writing, which "borrowed color & sometimes form" from Charles, Waldo felt, to the degree that "it would not be possible for either of us to say, This is my thought, That is yours" (*JMN*, V, 151). Now with Charles gone he must take what consolation he could from balancing his gains and losses according to his stoical doctrine of compensation (*JMN*, V, 171).

Elizabeth Hoar came to stay for a time with the Emersons, and in attempting to insulate one another against their grief she and Waldo agreed in conversing that "we are no longer permitted to think that the presence or absence of friends is material to our highest states of mind." Emerson's characteristic comment on their talk is close to what is said in the "transparent eye-ball" passage of *Nature* about one's necessary detachment from even the name of his nearest friend and brother. "In those few moments which are the life of our life when we were in the state of clear vision, we were taught that God is here no respecter of persons[,] that into that communion with him which is absolute life . . . our dearest friends are strangers. There is no personëity in it" (*JMN*, V, 170). Such an observation anticipates what Emerson would say in his later writings about the impersonality of the Deity and the fugacity of human relationships.[15] But meanwhile there was work to be done. It is the scholar's duty to apply his philosophy to his own condition, and as a writer to convert facts and events into truth, Emerson had held; now it was his task once again to draw what wisdom he could from knowing and losing a loved one, as in that other dark period following his loss of Ellen five years before. The turning point came on June 14, 1836, as he walked in "the oracular woods" near Concord and formulated a lesson seemingly taught by Nature herself: that Man can and must "conform to his character" not only "particular events but classes of events & so harmonize all the outward occurrences with the states of mind" (*JMN*, V, 174). Obviously he was searching for some spiritual principle that would show him the meaning of events—not just the death of Charles but the untimely passing of Ellen and Edward as well—and so enable him to transform even the fact of their loss into some tree of life, as he said the scholar must do for the good of other men and women.

This idea of "conforming" whole classes of events so as to harmonize them with one's mind and character is carried over into Chapter V of *Nature*, the discussion of "Discipline" he had projected in April before the death of Charles, and there his thesis is both echoed and expanded (*Nature*, p. 20). At the beginning of the chapter he reaffirms what he had said earlier, after returning to Boston from Europe in 1833: that Providence, through "the simple occurrences of every day," is "always instructing those who are in the attitude of scholars" (*YES*, pp. 194, 197); thus the conditions of earthly life, according to *Nature*, "give us sincerest lessons, day by day," that "educate

[15]Whether in kitchens and cottages or parlors and fashionable society, Emerson had written on May 22, 1836, "the talk is exclusively occupied with . . . the sickness, crimes, disasters, airs, fortunes of persons; never is the character of the action or the object extracted." Among "the cultivated class," however, "in proportion to their cultivation," there is "a studious separation of personal history from their analysis of character & their study of things. Natural History is elegant, astronomy sublime for this reason, their impersonality. And yet when cultivated men speak of God they demand a biography of him as steadily as the kitchen & the bar room demand personalities of men" (*JMN*, V, 162).

both the Understanding and the Reason" (*Nature*, p. 19). The chapter as a whole comprises his considered response to even the harsher facts of life as he had come to know them, from the remembered poverty of his childhood to the recent death of Charles. For its conclusion (*Nature*, p. 23) Emerson drew upon a long paragraph of "pleasing sober melancholy truth" entered in the journal following his meditations in the woods on June 14. Then he had both posed and answered the renewed question of what it means to have—and inevitably to lose—a beloved friend, "a real person" sent by God "to outgo your ideal." Once "enamoured" of that person and inspired by him to "a new measure of excellence" and "a confidence in the resources of God,"

you will readily see when you are separated, as you shortly will be[,] the bud, flower, & fruit of the whole fact. As soon as your friend has become to you an object of thought, has revealed to you with great prominence a new nature, & has become a measure whereof you are fully possessed to guage & test more, ⟨then expect⟩ as ⟨t⟩his character becomes solid & sweet wisdom it is already a sign to you that his office to you is closing[;] expect thenceforward the hour in which he shall be withdrawn from your sight. (*JMN*, V, 174)

In "Discipline" and again in other chapters of *Nature* are a number of revised journal passages originating in recollected hardship or grief, but all are rewritten, as this one was, in the impersonal terms that Emerson used in his published writings to mark a conversion from particular facts of an individual life into general truths pertaining to all men and women.[16] "It were a wise inquiry for the closet," runs a sentence in the chapter called "Prospects," "to compare, point by point, especially at remarkable crises in life, our daily history, with the rise and progress of ideas in the mind" (*Nature*, p. 35). This sentence too was originally drafted on June 14, 1836 (*JMN*, V, 175), when he returned from the woods to practice a scholar's duty and discipline by resuming his work on *Nature*.

IV. SPIRIT

Late in June of 1836, in a letter to his brother William, Emerson was able to announce that his "little book" was at last "nearly done" although still not ready for publication. "Its title is 'Nature.'" The contents being brief, as he explained, his intention was "to follow it by & by with another essay, 'Spirit'; and the two shall make a decent volume"

[16] When the two concluding paragraphs of "Discipline" are read in connection with their immediate sources in the journal it becomes clear that Emerson was acknowledging his indebtedness not only to his brother but to other men and women as well. On May 19, 1836, he named eight of that "scattered company" who had "ministered to my highest wants": "Theirs is the true light of all our day. They are the argument for the spiritual world for their spirit is it" (*JMN*, V, 160–161). But in "Discipline" he says only that from such "forms, male and female," does "the spirit" draw "joy and knowledge." They show us "the power and order that lie at the heart of things," he affirms, but he does not "follow into detail their ministry to our education." Instead he draws on the journal entry of June 14, 1836, quoted above, writing that when a particular friend has "become an object of thought, and, whilst his character retains all its unconscious effect, is converted in the mind into solid and sweet wisdom,—it is a sign *to us* [not "to you"] that his office is closing, and he is commonly withdrawn from *our* sight in a short time" (*Nature*, pp. 22–23; emphasis added).

(L, II, 26). Since mid-June, beside finishing the chapter on "Discipline," he had also composed a concluding chapter, "Prospects," which expresses the fundamental Emersonian conviction that empirical science alone "is apt to cloud the sight, and, by the very knowledge of functions and processes, to bereave the student of the manly contemplation of the whole." Elaborating on themes first explored in his earlier lectures on science, Emerson argues that man learns of his relation to the world not "by any addition or subtraction or other comparison of known quantities, but . . . by untaught sallies of the spirit, by a continual self-recovery, and by entire humility." Physiologists and naturalists in their preoccupation with means rather than ends are too often content with facts rather than principles, Emerson charges; he himself, he declares, "cannot greatly honor minuteness in details, so long as there is no hint to explain the relation between things and thoughts; no ray upon the *metaphysics* of conchology, of botany, of the arts"; no effort to show the relation of natural and artistic forms to the mind and to "build science upon ideas." The "half-sight of science" must therefore be supplemented by the insight of poetry, and "a wise writer" will seek to answer "the ends of study and composition . . . by announcing undiscovered regions of thought, and so communicating, through hope, new activity to the torpid spirit" (*Nature*, pp. 31–33).

The opening paragraphs of "Prospects," which epitomize Emerson's earlier reasons for identifying himself as a poet rather than the naturalist he had once thought of becoming, serve to introduce a longer section of the chapter ascribed chiefly to an unnamed "Orphic poet" who has written in praise of spirit and its remedial force (*Nature*, pp. 33–34, 35–37). This material had first taken form in Emerson's journal between June 22 and 24, immediately following a visit from Bronson Alcott (see Plate IV, p. 36 above), who returned again to Concord for three days on June 25. Some readers have identified Alcott as the "Orphic poet" of these pages,[17] which were obviously composed while Emerson was under his immediate stimulus, as even their phrasing suggests: for example, a journal entry for June 22 refers to Alcott as "a world-builder" who studies not "particular" facts but "the Whole" (*JMN*, V, 178), and in "Prospects" Emerson himself not only calls for "contemplation of the whole" but also admonishes his reader to "Build, therefore, your own world" (*Nature*, p. 35). But Emerson regarded Alcott's mind as essentially narrower and less flexible than his own, as we have seen, and was later to refer to him as monotonously "onetoned" (*JMN*, V, 457). Although the visit of his friend certainly moved Emerson himself to write in the Orphic vein, there is nothing in "Prospects" out of harmony with his own thought and style; indeed the exaltation of spirit in the chapter is in keeping with the book's central idea, that nature is the symbol of spirit, and its theme of vision lost and recovered is poignantly close to his recent experience following the death of Charles Emerson, already reflected more somberly in "Discipline."

---

[17] See Odell Shepard's note as editor of *The Journals of Bronson Alcott* (Boston: Little, Brown and Company, 1938), p. 78, n. 3, and the counterargument of Kenneth W. Cameron, "Emerson's Daemon and the Orphic Poet," *Emerson the Essayist*, 2 vols. (Raleigh, N.C.: The Thistle Press, 1945), I, 361–399.

It was on June 28, just after Alcott left Concord, that Emerson wrote of his book as virtually complete, and in another letter to William early in the next month he reported that from Boston booksellers he had received an estimate of "a little more than a hundred dollars to make a handsome little book" (*L*, II, 28). There are relatively few entries in his journal during July, when he must have been busy putting the finishing touches on his manuscript, probably by adding more recent extracts from the journal at strategic points, as he did for example in Chapter I, and by supplying new transitional material, in his usual manner, wherever it seemed to be needed. By July 20, immediately before Margaret Fuller was to arrive for her first visit with the Emersons, he informed his friend Hedge that he now "had a Chapter which I call 'Nature' in solid prose." To Hedge as to William he expressed his intention of also writing "another chapter called 'Spirit'" but only after first printing *Nature* as it then stood (*L*, II, 30). The manuscript of *Nature* was not released to the printer until mid-August, however. "There is, as always, one crack in it not easy to be soldered or welded," Emerson had written to William on August 8, hoping that "if this week I should be left alone . . . I may finish it" (*L*, II, 32). Alcott had recently made another visit, Miss Fuller was not to leave the Emersons until August 12, Lidian Emerson was expecting their first child in October, and Waldo himself was occupied as executor of Charles Emerson's estate, which was then being probated. The "crack" he complained of was soon mended by unspecified revision of whatever stood in the manuscript between "Discipline" and "Prospects" so as to form one or both of the chapters now entitled "Idealism" and "Spirit" (VI and VII in the published text); Emerson did not write the separate essay under the latter title that he had projected earlier. With this last problem in continuity solved, he dispatched the manuscript for printing in time to receive his first proof sheets on August 27 (*JMN*, V, 190).

Why Emerson was dissatisfied with *Nature* as it stood in early August and exactly what he did to the manuscript by way of remedy have been topics for speculation. Cabot, as we know, conjectured in 1887 that "Idealism" was the last chapter to be written, but "Spirit" may well have an equal claim; Rusk apparently inferred that Emerson incorporated into his manuscript the material he had previously intended for a separate essay on "Spirit."[18] Both "Idealism" and "Spirit" are mosaics of old and new writing: in "Idealism" the range of material that can be dated is from journal passages first written as early as 1834 and already used in lectures of 1835 to other journal material as recent as June of 1836; in "Spirit" there are slightly later journal passages, from July and even early August of 1836. But this evidence is not conclusive, since a large portion of both chapters has no specific source or parallel in the journal or lectures, and there is no way to date the component material even approximately. It is possible that during August, feeling pressed for time, Emerson simply divided an existing chapter into two, added enough new material to sharpen his distinction between traditional philosophical idealism and what he and his friends like to call "Spiritual-

---

[18] See Cabot, *A Memoir of Ralph Waldo Emerson*, I, 259, and Rusk in *L*, II, 26, n. 76: "'Spirit' became the seventh chapter of *Nature*."

ism," [19] and titled the resulting chapters accordingly. He had been formulating ideas about idealists and spiritualists in scattered journal entries at least as early as the previous February (*JMN*, V, 124), and in June he had asked himself "Whether the Ideal Theory is not merely introductory to Spiritual views. It diminishes & degrades matter in order to receive a new view of it, namely this, that the world is the new fruit of Spirit evermore" (*JMN*, V, 183; see Plate III, p. 29 above). This question anticipates passages in what is now Chapter VI, "Idealism," concerning the "degrading" of material nature and asserting its "dependence on spirit" (*Nature*, p. 27). A related entry of July 30 similarly looks forward to the key paragraph of "Spirit": "Man," according to the journal, "is the point where matter & spirit meet & marry. The Idealist says, God paints the world around your soul. The spiritualist saith, Yea, but lo! God is within you. The self of self creates the world through you & organizations like you. The Universal Central Soul comes to the surface in my body" (*JMN*, V, 187; cf. *Nature*, pp. 30–31, quoted below).

In *Nature* itself, taking up his familiar theme of "the senses and unrenewed understanding" giving way to the higher perceptions of Reason, Emerson holds in "Idealism" that by "the effects of culture" the reflective individual will gradually incline toward philosophical idealism as he considers the relation between man and nature. Even mechanical shifts in his literal point of view will suggest differences between man the observer, who remains stable, and the world of nature, which appears to him as a moving and changing spectacle. The poet's imagination makes use of this spectacle to communicate his thoughts and feelings, as Emerson had repeatedly said in his lectures and again in "Language." The philosopher and the theoretical scientist work in a realm of abstraction, the world of Ideas, preferring intellectual analysis to empirical observation, and so "transfer nature into the mind," while an exaltation of spirit over matter has long been characteristic in the teachings of religion and ethics. Hence that "noble doubt" which perpetually arises in the mind, "whether nature outwardly exists" (*Nature*, p. 23). The Idealist's hypothesis that "matter is a phenomenon, not a substance," is adequate "to account for nature by other principles than those of carpentry and chemistry," Emerson then goes on to say in his companion chapter, but such a theory is incapable of dealing with first and final causes: "Whence is matter? and Where to?" If Idealism "only deny the existence of matter, it does not satisfy the demands of the spirit": "It leaves God out of me," thus providing no grounding in religion for ethical self-reliance; it makes the solipsistic perceiver a lone wanderer in "the splendid labyrinth" of his perceptions, balking his·affections by "denying substantive being to men

---

[19] In a sermon of 1833 Emerson had described Christ's teaching as "a brave stand made for man's spiritual nature against the sensualism, the forms, and the crimes of the age in which he appeared" and again as "a defence of spiritualism against sensualism" (*YES*, pp. 195, 198–199); in 1834 he thanked Carlyle for "the brave stand you have made for Spiritualism" in *Sartor Resartus* (*CEC*, p. 98). Charles Emerson had spoken of "the nimbleness & buoyancy which the conversation of a spiritualist awakens; the world begins to dislimn" (*JMN*, V, 99, 124). Bronson Alcott called *Nature* "the production of a spiritualist, subordinating the visible and outward to the inward and invisible"; see *The Journals of Bronson Alcott*, p. 78.

and women" and making nature "foreign" to him without accounting for "that consanguinity which we acknowledge to it" (*Nature*, p. 30).

In the teachings of Spiritualism Emerson finds his answer to these objections against
the "useful introductory hypothesis" of Idealism. Out of "the recesses of consciousness," according to a climactic paragraph of "Spirit," the student may learn

that the highest is present in the soul of man, that the dread universal essence, which is not
wisdom, or love, or beauty, or power, but all in one, and each entirely, is that for which all
things exist, and that by which they are; that spirit creates; that behind nature, throughout nature, spirit is present; that spirit is one and not compound; that spirit does not act upon us from
without, that is, in space and time, but spiritually, or through ourselves. Therefore, that spirit,
that is, the Supreme Being, does not build up nature around us, but puts it forth through us,
as the life of the tree puts forth new branches and leaves through the pores of the old. As a plant
upon the earth, so a man rests upon the bosom of God; he is nourished by unfailing fountains,
and draws, at his need, inexhaustible power. Who can set bounds to the possibilities of man?
(*Nature*, pp. 30–31)

This view of Spirit "admonishes me where the sources of wisdom and power lie"—
within, as Emerson had long been saying. Man, he declares, "has access to the entire
mind of the Creator, is himself the creator in the finite." Such a confident belief, in
keeping with the optative mood of the Introduction to *Nature*, "carries upon its face
the highest certificate of truth"; not only does it constitute a progressive "theory of nature & man" but it also provides a basis for the ethical conduct of life—that individual
world-building Emerson calls for in "Prospects": "it animates me to create my own
world through the purification of my soul" (*Nature*, p. 31).

The Growth of the Soul:
Coleridge's Dialectical Method
and the Strategy of Emerson's *Nature*

by Barry Wood

[386] The uniqueness of *Nature* among Emerson's other works (including the recently published *Early Lectures*, some of which predate *Nature*) has tended to invite a self-contained discussion. The principal motive for the present study is that *Nature* remains somewhat opaque apart from the rest of Emerson's work, particularly his early journals. The fact is that *Nature* stands at the end of eighteen years of journal and letter writing on scores of different topics and issues. Quite apart from passages in his journals which were deliberately culled for inclusion in *Nature*, a number of elements central to his thinking were combined in this work in a surprising way. By 1836 Emerson had nearly two hundred manuscripts stored in his study (including 171 sermons), none of which were published during his lifetime. His decision to write and publish *Nature* implies that this work stands at the exact center of his thinking, even if that centrality is not exactly clear. The radical achievement of the work, however, rests upon Emerson's discovery, so far unnoticed, of a detailed dialectical method in the writings of Coleridge. This method supplied Emerson with a strategy for the presentation of ideas developed well before 1836. The place to begin, then, is with those few major ideas that were consistently formulated in the earlier journals, for *Nature* represents the first synthesis and summation of those ideas—and they turned out to be pivotal ones for Emerson's time.

I

Emerson's doctrines of self-reliance and compensation are usually associated with specific essays published in 1841, but a full reading of his early journals reveals that these subjects had engaged his interest many years before *Nature* appeared. Indeed, while the journals prior to about 1833 are disappointing on the subject of nature, discussions of self-reliance and compensation make better reading in the journals than in the 1841 essays where personal experiences have been carefully pruned away, leaving only generalities.

Reprinted by permission of the Modern Language Association from *PMLA*, XCI (May, 1976), 385–397; adapted for the present volume by Professor Wood. Footnotes not pertaining directly to Emerson have been omitted.

As early as 1823 Emerson was formulating a doctrine of self-reliance, though not without considerable difficulty. One early image for the notion is suggested on the first page of his "Wide World 12" journal where he wrote "Δος που στω"—the first words of Archimedes' statement, "Give me a place to stand on and I will move the earth" (*JMN*, II, 187). This quotation images the primacy of the self in terms of the attainment of some position or Archimedean point apart from the world at such a distance that the self could, metaphorically, balance the world. The attainment of the Archimedean point would be, of course, the attainment of God-like power; Emerson was interested in power, particularly power gained through an increase in perspective, and so he developed his Archimedean point with metaphors of vision. No matter what metaphors might be chosen, of course, the image contains a problem, for while it captures the independence involved in the notion of self-reliance it also suggests that self-reliance leads to separation, even alienation. Thus, in a letter to his Aunt Mary in 1824, he wrote: "I think I could have helped the monks to belabour Galileo for saying the everlasting earth moved" (*J*, I, 359). For Galileo's telescope had resulted in an Archimedean point of sorts, a position with sufficient perspective that men now knew the earth moved. Emerson understood this as an enlargement of man, so that cognitively he was capable of balancing the world, indeed, the universe. At the same time, the telescope diminished man and his planet by reducing the earth to a minute speck of dust in the Milky Way. Increased knowledge of the world could indeed bring increased freedom for man by enlarging his "perspective" on the world, but Emerson felt the gain to be a loss which was "casting man back into a cold & comfortless solitude" (*JMN*, II, 252).

In strictly mechanical terms, of course, the world may be "balanced" at two points: at the distant end of the Archimedean lever and at the precise center of gravity of the world. This second balance point corresponds to things Emerson [387] has to say about the soul later in his journals. Thus, in 1827 he noted that "the soul has a divine power of assimilating all its acquisitions to its own nature" (*JMN*, III, 98–99). This power of assimilation forestalls any possibility of separation between the soul and the world it balances, specifically ruling out the idea that self-reliance leads to alienation. What Emerson needed, however, was a formulation that encompassed *both* notions of balance; that is, an Archimedean point at the exact center of the world which would retain the "leverage" of distance. From such a central point, presumably, both "perspective" and "assimilation" would occur and, perhaps, coincide.

The metaphor that captured *this* Archimedean perspective appeared in another letter Emerson wrote to his Aunt Mary, in 1827: "Now and then the lawless imagination flies out and asserts her habit. I revisit the verge of my intellectual domain. How the restless soul runs round the outmost orbit and builds her bold conclusion as a tower of observation from whence her eyes wander incessantly in the unfathomable abyss" (*J*, II, 223). Here the assimilation of the world by the self-reliant soul takes place from a central point from which the world is visually suspended or balanced. At the same time, the very act of assimilation "builds" the central point into a high "tower of observation" from which further assimilation can take place. Ascending this tower is not a movement away from the world but rather the attainment of enough height to sweep in the largest horizon possible. The higher the ascent the larger the sweep; the vaster the horizon assimilated by the Soul the greater its self-reliance and freedom. It is not surprising that Emerson attributes precisely this kind of self-reliance to Coleridge while reading *The Friend* in 1829: "What a living soul, what a universal knowledge! I like to encounter these citizens of the universe, that believe the mind was made to be spectator of all, inquisitor of all, and whose philosophy compares with others much as astronomy with the other sciences, taking post at the centre and, as from a specular mount, sending sovereign glances to the circumference of things" (*J*, II, 277). A variant of this visual metaphor is found in *Nature* where Emerson speaks of the "integrity of impression" resulting from a truly poetical kind of seeing. Most farmers own a field of the landscape; but "none of them owns the landscape. There is a property in the horizon which no man has but he whose eye can integrate all the parts, that is, the poet" (*Nature*, p. 7).

The imagery of ascent, combined with the notion that the soul assimilates its world, suggests that self-reliance involves two related actions of the soul. One is a metaphorical "distancing" of the soul from the world, as the Archimedean point implies; the other is a metaphorical "balancing" of the world by sweeping in the largest orbit possible from a central point. Within the framework of eyesight—which operates as an analogue for the higher vision of the soul—the central point is the top of a high tower of observation or "specular mount." Once assimilation from a given perspective is complete the ascent begins again, so that increasing self-reliance entails an alternation of ascent and assimilation. This alternation suggests a dialectical process, though Emerson does not describe it dialectically at this early point in his development. Instead he adopts another metaphor, that of growth.

As early as 1826 he observed that mental progress occurs in spurts rather than as "a perpetual & equable expansion." His illuminating metaphor is drawn from the growth process: "Corn grows by jumps. The ordinary growth of mind especially till the old age of man, depends on aliment procured from without" (*JMN*, III, 24). The biological process of procuring aliment provides a more exact metaphor for the assimilative power of the soul but it loses the dialectical flavor of the visual metaphor. The growth metaphor, however, attests to Emerson's originality, for it appears in his work several years before the release of Sampson Reed's *Growth of the Mind* (August, 1829) and well before Emerson had read Coleridge's notes on the assimilative power of plants in the "Conclusion" to *Aids to Reflection*. The growth of the soul was something he experienced rather than simply read about.

Along with these early explorations of self-reliance is found another doctrine central to Emerson's mature thought: the idea of compensation. In 1826, for example, he wrote that "the whole of what we know is a system of Compensations," by which he meant the "strange & awful story" of "the history of retributions" (*JMN*, II, 341). Indeed, throughout the years of his Unitarian ministry and his marriage to Ellen Tucker, Emerson understood compensation as a temporal [388] balancing of events such that the extremes of today (whether good or bad) would be equalized in the future. It was this necessary equalization that led Emerson during these years to his belief in immortality. As he put it in his first sermon, "Pray without Ceasing"—which was delivered twelve times from October, 1826, to November, 1828 (*YES*, p. 263)—"after death there is life. After death in another state . . . a world of remuneration. . . . Of one thing be certain, that if the analogies of time can teach aught of eternity, if the moral laws taking place in this world, have relation to those of the next . . . then the riches of the future are dealt out on a system of compensations" (*YES*, pp. 9–10). After the death of Ellen in 1831, Emerson gradually rejected the doctrine of immortality. Thus, while returning from Europe in 1833, he wrote: "They ask me whether I know the soul immortal. No. But do I not know the now to be eternal? . . . I believe in this life. . . . I plainly read my duties as . . . woven of immortal thread" (*JMN*, IV, 88).

But while Emerson rejected the doctrine of immortality, compensation remained. A remark penned in 1831 documents the shift to a new concept of compensation and puts forth a basic principle of his mature thought: "As religious philosophy advances, men will cease to say 'the future state' & will say instead 'the whole being'" (*JMN*, III, 304). Compensation here has shifted from a notion about temporal equalization to a doctrine of balance always evident in the present moment. For Emerson, balance—the idea of compensating polarities—was the "open secret" of the universe, the "soul's law": "It is only the feebleness & dust of the observer that makes it future, the whole *is* now" (*JMN*, IV, 87).

The idea of the balanced whole provides a general formulation for a more specific idea: the assimilative soul. It seems clear, for example, that one important meaning of compensatory balance centers on the perceptual transactions occurring between the self and the world. It seems clear, too, that the alternation between ascent and assimilation necessary for increasing self-reliance relates to the notion of balanced polarities. Emerson's emphasis on this twofold action of the soul provides us with a clear example of how compensatory balance might operate as a working principle in his thought. But while Emerson had arrived at these formulations in isolated journal entries well before 1836, he had not discovered a satisfactory *method* for their presentation. Thus, in the various lectures delivered between 1833 and 1836 the notion of compensation is present, but only very vaguely. A case in point is "On the Relation of Man to the Globe" (*EL*, I, 21–59), which assumes compensation as a fundamental truth without a single mention of the word. Similarly, the notion of self-reliance shines through many of his biographical lectures—for example, those on Luther, Milton, Fox, and Shakespeare (*EL*, I, 118–182, 287–319)—but usually under the rubric of "heroism." The central ideas of self-reliance and compensation keep shifting out of focus in these early lectures precisely because Emerson lacked a method suited to their presentation.

Emerson's development of a method is therefore the crucial factor of the middle 1830's, defining exactly the remarkable achievement of *Nature* over against the lectures immediately preceding it. Here too the importance of Coleridge for Emerson is brought into sharp relief, particularly when we keep in mind how far Emerson's own thought had developed before he read him. Almost every study of Emerson has fastened upon the obvious influence: his use of Coleridge's distinction between Reason and Understanding. Sherman Paul alone has gone beyond this to look at Coleridge's Essays on Method in *The Friend*, but he fails to demonstrate exactly how Emerson appropriated this material. His remark that Emerson "adopted the dialectic as a method of expression"[1] seems accidental, for he apparently overlooks the extended discussions of dialectical method in both *The Friend* and *Aids to Reflection*. Yet at precisely this point the influence of Coleridge was the most profound. Emerson's letters and journals suggest a renewed interest in Coleridge after their meeting in Europe; by May, 1834, Emerson was immersed again not only in Coleridge's discussions of Reason and Understanding (*L*, I, 412–413) but also in his Essays on Method (*JMN*, IV, 290). Principally, what seems to have ordered Emerson's thinking was Coleridge's discussions of dialectical method, which were so clear and well exampled that Emerson was led directly to a method for the presentation of his own thought. By 1836 he had appropriated the method and turned it to a use that went quite beyond anything Coleridge had imagined. *Nature* [389] was the first manifestation of it in Emerson's work.

II

Emerson's interest in compensation presumably led him to pay particular attention to Coleridge's discussion of polarity in *The Friend* and *Aids to Reflection*. Coleridge's formulation added an important dimension, however, by specifically linking polarity to the concept of development. Thus, in a long footnote in *The Friend*, Coleridge wrote, "EVERY POWER IN NATURE AND IN SPIRIT *must evolve an opposite, as the sole means and condition of its manifestation*: AND ALL OPPOSITION IS A TENDENCY TO REUNION."[2] The words *evolve* and *tendency* suggest the dynamic processes implicit in what Coleridge called "the universal Law of Polarity or essential Dualism." The footnote goes on to develop this law using terms usually associated with Hegel, though Coleridge derived them from Schelling: "The Principle may be thus expressed. The *Identity* of Thesis and Antithesis is the substance of all *Being*; their *Opposition* the condition of all *Existence*, or Being manifested; and every *Thing* or Phaenomenon is

---

[1] Sherman Paul, *Emerson's Angle of Vision: Man and Nature in American Experience* (Cambridge: Harvard University Press, 1952), p. 112. The presence of dialectics in Emerson's work was noted as early as 1884 by William T. Harris, "The Dialectic Unity of Emerson's Prose," *Journal of Speculative Philosophy*, CVIII (1884), 195–202, who argued that "the closest unity of the logical kind is the dialectic unity that begins with the simplest and most obvious phase of the subject, and discovers by investigation the next phase that naturally follows. It is an unfolding of the subject according to its natural growth in experience" (p. 195). While Harris emphasized the importance of a dialectical method in any essay that "expounds the genesis of the subject" (p. 196), his demonstrations failed to disclose this method at work. The same lack of rigor is apparent in his essay "Emerson's Philosophy of Nature," *The Genius and Character of Emerson*, ed. F. B. Sanborn (1885; rpt. Port Washington: Kennikat, 1971), pp. 339–364, where claims about "dialectic" appear again. Michael H. Cowan, *City of the West: Emerson, America, and Urban Metaphor* (New Haven: Yale University Press, 1967), utilizes the language of dialectics repeatedly as a way of talking about polar tensions in Emerson's thought, but fails to demonstrate anything like Coleridge's dialectical method in specific works.

[2] *The Collected Works of Samuel Taylor Coleridge*, ed. Barbara E. Rooke (Princeton: Princeton University Press, 1969), IV, 94, n. Hereafter cited as *Works*.

the Exponent of a Synthesis as long as the opposite energies are retained in that Synthesis" (*Works*, IV, 94, n). This principle can be seen, Coleridge argues, in the chemical synthesis of oxygen and hydrogen to form water; elsewhere in *The Friend* he illustrates it by referring to numerous eighteenth-century theories of electricity which have in common "the idea of *two—opposite—forces*, tending to rest by equilibrium" (*Works*, IV, 478). Philosophy, too, was "necessarily bi-polar," dealing with truth both subjectively and objectively, and Coleridge felt that Plato and Bacon treated truth from the subjective and objective poles respectively (*Works*, IV, 492). An adequate science of method could unify these two approaches; as he put it later in *The Friend*, "All method supposes a union of *several* things to a common end, either by disposition, as in the works of man; or by convergence, as in the operations and products of nature" (*Works*, IV, 497).

Coleridge's numerous remarks about polarity add up to a comprehensive theory embracing every realm of existence. In *Aids to Reflection* he carried the notion into a discussion of the Trinity: "I am clearly convinced that the Scriptural and only true God will, in its development, be found to involve the idea of Tri-unity." [3] This theological statement leads into an extended discussion and a long footnote culminating in a rigorous account of dialectical logic. That Emerson grasped Coleridge's linkage between the "development" of God and the development of thought is clear from an 1835 entry in his journal:

The Germans believe in the necessary Trinity of God,—the Infinite; the finite; & the passage from inf[inite] into Fin[ite]; or, the Creation. It is typified in the act of thinking. Whilst we contemplate we are infinite; the thought we express is partial & finite; the expression is the third part & is equivalent to the act of Creation. Unity says Schelling is barren. Duality is necessary to the existence of the World." (*JMN*, V, 30)

The footnote appended to the discussion in *Aids to Reflection* leads directly into the problem of method by establishing firm connections between the notions of polarity, development, logic, and growth. Diagrammatically, thesis and antithesis may be represented by opposite ends of a line, while its midpoint represents "the indifference of the two poles":

T	I	A
Thesis	Indifference	Antithesis

Coleridge then outlines what he calls the "Noetic Pentad":

	1. *Prothesis*	
2. *Thesis*	4. *Mesothesis*	3. *Antithesis*
	5. *Synthesis*	

[3] *Aids to Reflection: With a Preliminary Essay by James Marsh, D.D.*, edited by Henry Nelson Coleridge, 4th ed. (1840; rpt. Port Washington: Kennikat, 1971), p. 183.

[4] *Ibid.*, 184, n. My discussion in the next two paragraphs is summarized from the same note, pp. 185–186.

Drawing on geometrical analogies originating among the Pythagoreans, Coleridge suggests that "the line [is] generated, or, as it were, radiated, by a point not contained in the line but independent, and . . . transcendent to all production, which it caused but did not partake." The language here implies a doctrine of emanation. By analogy Coleridge identifies this "transcendent" point with the prothesis, or the starting point in any logical process. Then he goes on to describe how the prothesis ("identity or co-inherence of act and being") generates a thesis ("expressing thing"), which implies an antithesis ("expressing act"); when these are combined in a mesothesis or composed in a synthesis an "indifference" or "equilibrium" is reached.

[390] A good deal of this theoretical discussion remains opaque until Coleridge provides specific illustrations. First he applies the pentad to grammatical forms, suggesting that language is "generated" from a primordial "Verb substantive" which is conveniently illustrated in the Latin word *sum* ("I am"), the primary name of the Godhead. The complete range of correlations he suggests are: 1. Prothesis = Verb substantive (*sum*); 2. Thesis = Substantive (*res*); 3. Antithesis = Verb (*ago, patior*); 4. Mesothesis = Infinitive (*agere*); 5. Synthesis = Participle (*agens*). No matter what we may think of Coleridge's "generative" grammar, the illustration does clarify the theory, particularly in distinguishing between a mesothesis and a synthesis. Moreover, from Emerson's point of view it establishes a powerful linkage between logical thought and the method of language, a connection that Emerson, as fledgling poet, develops in his own way in the "Language" chapter of *Nature* (pp. 15–19). In his second illustration, Coleridge suggests that "the germinal power of every seed might be generalized under the relation of identity [prothesis]." The growth of a plant involves a seed in position (thesis), a nourishing environment in op-position (antithesis), an equilibrium of the two (mesothesis), and the composition (synthesis) of a plant out of this dialectic. The importance of this illustration for Emerson can hardly be overstated, for it not only reinforced his earlier notion about the growth of the soul by assimilation, but also forced upon him the crucial connection between the growth of the soul and the logical method of thought. At one stroke the importance of the organic metaphor became clear: organic growth was a dialectical process; logical thought was dialectical thought; therefore, a dialectical method was the appropriate method not only for tracing the growth of the soul but also for promoting it. The method of the essayist and the concern of the poet coalesced.

Emerson's interest in compensation may well have set him on the road to a dialectical method well before 1835. A dialectical pattern of thinking seems to lie behind the quotation from Dugald Stewart that Emerson copied onto the first page of "Blotting Book III" in June, 1831: "Our first and third thoughts coincide" (*JMN*, III, 265). A long discussion of the law of compensation follows immediately (pp. 265–268). In May, 1834 (*JMN*, IV, 292), Emerson recopied Stewart's quotation to follow his discussion of Coleridge's method (p. 290). Equally suggestive are the dialectical implications of an entry for December 10, 1831. Having paraphrased Stewart's quotation— "Write upon the coincidence of first & third thoughts"—he metaphorically adopts a synthesis position: "I should like to know if any one every went up a mountain so high as that he overlooked right & wrong & . . . saw their streams mix" (*JMN*, III, 310). Here again is the Archimedean point at the center, the "specular mount" from which the soul assimilates its world. "Opposition of first thoughts & common opinion. God has the first word. The devil has the Second but God has the last word. We distrust the first thought because we can't give the reason for it. Abide by it, there is a reason, & by & by long hence perhaps it will appear" (*JMN*, III, 310–311). Well before 1835, then, Emerson had explored a dialectical view of the world, summarized in his 1834 remark that "Extremes meet" (*JMN*, IV, 383). . . .

III

Evidence in Emerson's journals suggests he had been interested in the subject of nature for a number of years. In 1825 he had made the following notation: "No information transmitted from one man to another can be more interesting than the accurate description of this little world in which he lies; and I shall deserve the thanks of every knowing reader, if I shall shew him the colour, orbit, and composition of my particular star" (*JMN*, II, 317). The prospectus for a book that he set down in 1835 [391] stressed those facts of nature revealed only to one bent on acute observation: "If life were long enough among my thousand & one works should be a book of Nature. . . . It should contain the Natural history of the woods around my shifting camp for every month in the year. It should tie their astronomy, botany, physiology, meteorology, picturesque, & poetry together. No bird, no bug, no bud should be forgotten on his day & hour" (*JMN*, V, 25). Emerson's language here seems to anticipate the minute descriptions of the natural world found in Thoreau—in the "Brute Neighbors" or "Pond in Winter" chapters of *Walden*—rather than the smooth, generalized language of the 1836 publication. *Nature*, however, is not so much a contradiction of such a method as an expansion of it. The modes of this expansion are perhaps suggested in a self-accusatory entry in Emerson's journal for May 14, 1835: "When will you mend Montaigne? When will you take the hint of nature? Where are your Essays? . . . Have you not thoughts & illustrations that are your own; the parable of geometry & matter; . . . the power of Composition in nature & in man's thoughts; . . . the law of Compensation; . . . the sublimity of Self-reliance?" (*JMN*, V, 40). The "parable of geometry & matter" may be a vague, almost unrealized nod toward Coleridge's elaborate pentad, but there can be little doubt that "the power of Composition in nature & in man's thoughts" reflects exactly what Emerson had learned from him about the growth of the seed into a plant and the dialectical growth of thought. The concerns listed add a new dimension to Emerson's proposed "natural history of the woods"; and in the book itself physical nature is treated in the light of the fact that it can be treated only by the assimilative soul. Moreover, this necessary assimilation in the equation leads Emerson by a dialectical process to an idea quite beyond the "Nature" of the title.

The strategy of *Nature* is governed by the principle that Nature provides the soul with a systematic method for approaching spirit. The Introduction establishes the preliminary dichotomy between the soul and nature (p. 5)—the same division between subjective and objective reality that Coleridge postulated as the starting point in his dialectical method. Thus, in outlining an approach to the highest ideas, Coleridge writes: "What is an idea? In answer to this I commence with the absolute Real as the *prothesis*; the subjectively Real as the *thesis*; the objectively Real as the *antithesis*; and I affirm, that Idea is the indifference of the two" (*Aids to Reflection*, p. 186, n.). Thus, while Emerson's title suggests a study of something "objectively Real" (nature), Emerson treats it in conjunction with the "subjectively Real" (soul) in order to synthesize an Idea (spirit). The central concept of *Nature* can be described dialectically and the essay itself follows a rigorous dialectical logic. Thus, the strategy of its method duplicates the dialectical growth of the soul toward spirit which forms its central argument. Beginning with the question, "Why should not we also enjoy an original relation to the universe?" (p. 5), the essay advances from Emerson's own "original relation" (Ch. I), through an ascending progression of "uses" of nature (commodity, beauty, language, discipline, idealism), arriving finally at the source and goal of nature, spirit (Ch. VII).

The first chapter (pp. 7–8) moves toward a synthesis of nature and soul in Emerson's account of "perfect exhilaration" (p. 8). The chapter progresses from "the integrity of impression made by manifold natural objects" (p. 7)—that is, an integrity among parts of the Not Me—toward "an occult relation between man and the vegetable" (p. 8). The synthesis of soul and nature is revealed in the remark that "it is certain that the power to produce this delight does not reside in nature, but in man, or in a harmony of both" (p. 8); and the synthesis statement in the final paragraph is "Nature always wears the colors of the spirit" (p. 8).

This synthesis provides a new beginning point: having established a connection between soul and nature Emerson can now unfold that connection in terms of the "uses" of nature. The dialectical method of moving toward a synthesis is clearly evident in the first sentence of the second chapter, "Commodity": "Whoever considers the final cause of the world will discern a multitude of uses that enter as parts of that result" (p. 10). Nature as "commodity" is that material nature that ministers to man's lowest needs by its "prodigal provision" (p. 10); but, in providing for man, nature comes to be seen in terms of ecological process in which external nature is not only the beginning but also the end of the cycle. "Nature, in its ministry to man, is not only the ma-[392] terial, but is also the process and the result" (p. 10). Thus the "commodity" of nature cannot be considered objectively, except in a preliminary way; eventually we must consider it subjectively, until the objective and subjective views are synthesized in a higher third. At this point commodity is understood as a transaction: Nature ministers to man and man ministers to nature. This is implied in what I consider the synthesis sentence, the final one in the chapter: "A man is fed, not that he may be fed, but that he may work" (p. 11).

This dialectical structure may be visualized, using Emerson's earlier metaphor, as a "specular mount" up which the soul ascends. At each stopping place, corresponding to chapters in *Nature*, a new horizon appears: Nature presents to the soul a new aspect of its Not-Me-ness. After this new aspect has been assimilated by the soul the process of ascent begins again (see Diagram).

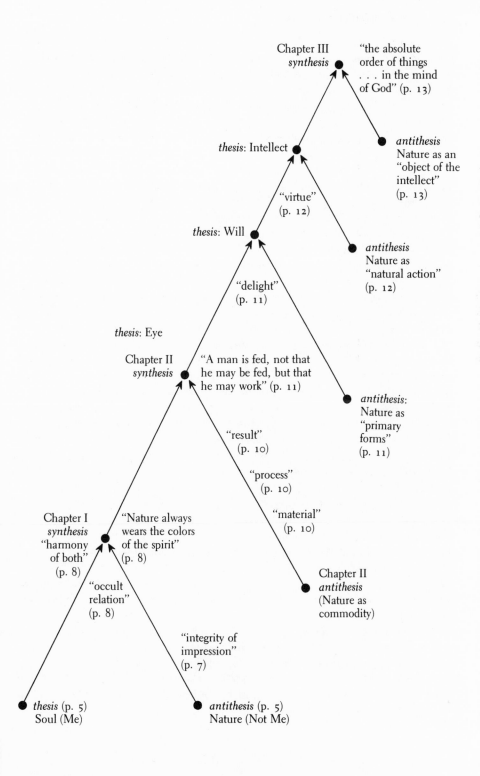

The third chapter, "Beauty" (pp. 11–14), begins again with nature seen as antithetical to soul, and then examines its beauty under three aspects. The first, based on the forms of nature seen objectively, "seems to lie on the confines of commodity and beauty." At this level beauty results from "the simple perception of natural forms"; and the close relation of this perception to commodity is suggested by words like "medicinal" and "health" (p. 11). The word "delight" describes the subjective response to this aspect of beauty. Second, Emerson deals with beauty that results when objects are "found in combination with the human will. Beauty is the mark God sets upon virtue" (p. 12). Citing a number of examples in which beauty results from the relation between the soul and its surroundings, he leads to a definition: "A virtuous man is in unison with her [nature's] works, and makes the central figure of the visible sphere" (p. 13). The third and highest kind of beauty results when "the beauty of the world . . . becomes an object of the intellect." Here beauty resides in "the absolute order of [393] things as they stand in the mind of God" (p. 13). Since "the creation of beauty is Art," Emerson finds it appropriate here to add a definition: "a work of art is an abstract or epitome of the world . . . in miniature" (p. 14). He might well have said a work of art is a synthesis of the world, for "the poet, the painter, the sculptor, the musician, the architect, seek each to concentrate this radiance of the world on one point" (p. 14).

Having reached his third major synthesis in *Nature*—the relation of nature to intellect—Emerson appropriately turns to the creative tool of intellect, language. Again, Nature is considered as antithetical to soul; and the synthesis occurs with the soul's perception of nature as the symbol of spirit. In the course of moving toward this synthesis Emerson again advances by preliminary steps, signified by his three principles of language (p. 15). The first, that "words are signs of natural facts," establishes a minor antithesis in which the "material" meaning of a word, when combined with intellect, "express[es] a moral or intellectual fact." Emerson's examples—"*Right* . . . means *straight*; *wrong* means *twisted*"—imply that language operates by dialectical synthesis where the thesis (the intellect) combined with the antithesis (straight, twisted, etc.) produces a meaning or synthesis (right, wrong, etc.). His second principle advances this dialectic to things themselves: "Particular natural facts are symbols of particular spiritual facts." Thus "every appearance in nature corresponds to some state of the mind, and that state of the mind can only be described by presenting that natural appearance." Consequently, the mind (thesis), by presenting or describing a lamb (antithesis), can convey its own idea of innocence (synthesis). Emerson's third principle— "Nature is the symbol of spirit"—advances the dialectic to the point where "the universe becomes transparent, and the light of higher laws than its own shines through it" (p. 18).

The use of each ascending synthesis as a new beginning point is clearly articulated at the beginning of the fifth chapter, "Discipline": "In view of this significance of nature," Emerson writes, referring to the sign-making function of nature as language, "we arrive at once at a new fact, that nature is a discipline." The purpose of the dialectical method is, of course, to reach higher or larger degrees of synthesis; thus "this use of the world includes the preceding uses, as parts of itself" (p. 19). The chapter as a whole presents an ascending dialectic with two steps: Nature is, first, a discipline of the understanding (pp. 19–20) and, second, a discipline of reason (pp. 20–23). As a discipline of the understanding, nature presents itself as orderly, continuous, and arranged according to a principle of progression, which is what Coleridge means by the term "method." [5] As Emerson describes it, Nature presents itself under the categories of space and time, providing man with "constant exercise in the necessary lessons of difference, of likeness, of order, of being and seeming, of progressive arrangement; of ascent from particular to general; of combination to one end of manifold forces" (p. 19). As a discipline of reason, however, nature presents itself as "Unity in Variety," in which each particle "faithfully renders the likeness of the world" (pp. 21–22). Thus disciplined, reason is sensitive to correspondences, resemblances, or what Emerson calls the "central Unity" (p. 22).

With the sixth chapter, "Idealism" (pp. 23–28), the dialectical method reveals its power, taking Emerson across the major chasm in his work. In the composition of *Nature* this point in the argument gave him trouble. On August 27, 1836, Emerson received the first proof sheet of *Nature* (*JMN*, V, 190), yet as recently as August 8 he had written to his brother William that the book still had "one crack in it not easy to be soldered or welded" (*L*, II, 32). No further mention of this problem or its solution occurs in Emerson's writings, but the nature of the solution is evident in the first few lines of the chapter. The celebrated "noble doubt"—so often singled out as the weak point in the book—turns out to be the crucial stepping-stone.

The first two sentences note the "unspeakable . . . meaning" conveyed to man, understood as "the immortal pupil," by nature, understood as discipline (p. 23). "All parts of nature conspire": the words are perfectly chosen, not only to suggest the totality of the conveyance but also to undercut the logic of the understanding upon which the argument so far has been strung. Then, as if to explain the conspiracy: "A noble doubt perpetually suggests itself, whether this end be not the Final Cause of the Universe." Here, in brief, is Emerson's confession that the "crack" in *Nature* was primarily epistemological, a chasm be-[394]yond which the mind (and the author) apparently

---

[5] In *The Friend* Coleridge writes: "Method implies a *progressive transition*, and it is the meaning of the word in the original language. The Greek Μεθοδος, is literally *a way*, or *path of Transit*. . . . without continuous transition, there can be no Method. . . . The term, Method, cannot therefore, otherwise than by abuse, be applied to a mere dead arrangement, containing in itself no principle of progression" (*Works*, IV, 457). Coleridge's treatment of Method begins with methodical thought (or its absence) in various Shakespearean characters. Thus, in 1831, Emerson wrote: "I read Shakspeare last ev.g & admired with all the fine minds his singular power. . . . His poetry never halts, but has what Coleridge defines [as] Method, viz. progressive arrangement. Another thing strikes me in the sonnets . . . and that is the assimilating power of passion that turns all things to its own nature" (*JMN*, III, 299). The term "progressive arrangement," occurring in the section of *Nature* under discussion, derives from Coleridge's "Preliminary Treatise on Method"; see also Emerson's January, 1836, entry, used in "Spiritual Laws," —"A man is a method; a progressive arrangement; a selecting principle gathering his like to him wherever he goes" (*JMN*, V, 114; W, II, 144)—which links the notion of method to the gathering, assimilative power of the soul.

could not go without simply writing another book. And, in fact, as late as June 28, Emerson had talked about his second book, *Spirit* (L, II, 26), at which time he did not think of it as welded to *Nature*, but simply between the same covers.

Here it should be noted, in the exact economy of Emerson's phrasing, that the "noble doubt" concerns primarily whether discipline for the mind is the highest purpose of nature, and only secondarily "whether nature outwardly exists." But the two are intimately related, rhetorically and dialectically. For it is precisely the totality of the "world conveyed"—the fact that *all* parts of nature "conspire"—that introduces the antithesis for further argument: doubt. Up to this point in *Nature* Emerson's argument had expressed his faith in the immense assimilative power of the soul: its power to effect a "transformation" (p. 15) or, as he would put it in later essays, the power of the mind to "dispose of" the abyss, "vanquish" the wilderness, "convert" experience into thought (CW, I, 59), or "flux" the universe (W, VI, 43). Here indeed was the miracle of the human mind. Yet the antithetical side of that miracle was that "doubt" about the adamantine reality of a world which *could be fluxed*. Thus, unable to posit his next antithesis according to the logic of understanding, as he had done till now, Emerson found the antithesis to his faith thrust upon him in a doubt which "suggests itself," yet suggests itself within the context of "unspeakable . . . meaning" conveyed to man as "the immortal pupil." The meaning seems clear: the soul capable of assimilating a world produces faith; the world that can be completely assimilated produces doubt. From this polarity, impossible to reconcile on its own level, Emerson simply soars to a new synthesis: "It is a sufficient account of that Appearance we call the World, that God will teach a human mind, and so makes it the receiver of a certain number of congruent sensations. . . . What difference does it make, whether Orion is up there in heaven, or some god paints the image in the firmament of the soul?" (p. 23).[6] Emerson was able to join *Spirit* (his second book) to *Nature* (his first) precisely because he found the soul capable of synthesizing his faith in and doubt about nature into spirit. "Idealism," then, culminates in a synthesis so exalted that nature seems to be left entirely behind. The implication of the synthesis in a dialectical process, however, as well as of the fine tuning of Emerson's language, suggests that nature—Coleridge's "objectively Real"—is subsumed to a higher unity; that is, transcended.

Emerson begins the argument at a very low level of perception with the effect of motion or change in point of view upon our idea of nature (pp. 24–25). This is the first of five steps in an ascending dialectic. The second (pp. 25–26) centers on the power of the poet to delineate things "lifted from the ground and afloat before the eye" (p. 25). The third (pp. 26–27) deals with the way in which the philosopher approaches nature, until "the solid seeming block of matter has been pervaded and dissolved by a

---

[6] My reading of this section of *Nature* is done against the background of Warner Berthoff's superb commentary on this paragraph in his introduction to *Nature: A Fascimile of the First Edition* (San Francisco: Chandler, 1968), pp. xlvi–lvi. Berthoff concludes flatly and I think accurately that "Emerson is in fact being solidly philosophical here, as precise about the mind's relation to the phenomenal world as anybody had learned to be by 1836" (p. lii).

thought" (p. 26). The fourth step (p. 27) describes the approach of pure "intellectual science" which concentrates solely on ideas; the result of this approach is that "we think of nature as an appendix to the soul" (p. 27). "Religion and ethics, which may be fitly called,—the practice of ideas," comprise Emerson's fifth example (pp. 27–28); for "they both put nature under foot" (p. 27). Each of these steps in the dialectical argument starts with nature as "objectively Real" and then shows what happens to it when approached by the "subjectively Real"; in each case the resulting synthesis suggests that nature dissolves into, or is assimilated by, the soul. It is this assimilation that "tend[s] to affect our convictions of the reality of the external world. . . . For, seen in the light of thought, the world always is phenomenal; and virtue subordinates it to the mind" (p. 28).

The final synthesis to which the whole chapter on idealism leads is spirit, which forms the topic of the seventh chapter. "All the uses of nature admit of being summed in one, which yields the activity of man an infinite scope" (p. 30). This synthesis occurs at the metaphorical summit of the "specular mount" and it represents the Archimedean point at the center from which the soul can balance the universe. Since no further dialectic is possible, there can be no antithesis to spirit; hence "that essence refuses to be recorded in propositions" (p. 30). At this high point of the dialectical ascent nature has been fully assimilated into spirit:

Following the invisible steps of thought . . . many truths arise to us out of the recesses of consciousness. We learn that the highest is present to the soul of man; [395] that the dread universal essence, which is not wisdom, or love, or beauty, or power, but all in one, and each entirely, is that for which all things exist, and that by which they are; that spirit creates; that behind nature, throughout nature, spirit is present; that spirit is one and not compound; that spirit does not act upon us from without, that is, in space and time, but spiritually, or through ourselves. Therefore, that spirit, that is, the Supreme Being, does not build up nature around us, but puts it forth through us, as the life of the tree puts forth new branches and leaves through the pores of the old. (pp. 30–31)

The image of the tree, combined with the opening phrase, suggests that Emerson understood the "steps of thought" in terms of organic process, as Coleridge had before him.

"Build therefore your own world" (p. 35), he writes in "Prospects," and the exhortation points toward self-reliance. Setting forth his final injunctions, Emerson casts the final chapter in terms of a visual metaphor, perhaps to complete the image of the "transparent eye-ball." But "Prospects" also underlines the continuing visual metaphor adopted a decade earlier for conveying the assimilative action of the self-reliant soul. Emerson's dialectical method in this work emphasizes how he was able, paradoxically, to reject the authority of the past while at the same time taking account of it. For, if the present was simply the terminus of the past, only the past could explain the present; Emerson, however, was able to synthesize a self-reliant present by adding the *future* as antithesis into his equation. This is clear when the argument of *Nature* is closed with the future-looking metaphor of "prospects," which exactly balances the opening assertion that "our age is retrospective" (p. 5). Emerson would argue that a "prospective" age is as limited as a "retrospective" age. Thus the dialectic of *Nature* unfolds between these poles, and the *present* is a synthesis of them, a union of opposites in a higher third. Such a present is akin to eternity; accordingly, idealism "beholds the whole circle of persons and things, of actions and events, of country and religion, not as painfully accumulated, atom after atom, act after act, in an aged creeping Past, but as one vast picture which God paints on the instant eternity for the contemplation of the soul" (p. 28).

Emerson's use of the dialectical method in *Nature* points directly toward his major purpose in the work. This may be stated in two ways, depending on whether we emphasize the "objectively Real" pole of experience (nature) or the "subjectively Real" (soul). Objectively, the work details the progressive "uses" that can be made of nature by the soul; subjectively, it outlines the possibilities for the growth of the soul through a methodical use of nature. For Emerson, as for Coleridge, dialectical logic was organic logic, for it duplicated the process of the mind during its organic assimilation of the universe. From one point of view, then, nature *is* the "Not Me" standing in antithetical opposition to the soul; but from another point of view God puts nature "forth through us" as the life of a tree is put forth through leaves and branches.

Which view is Emerson's? The answer must be both. Indeed, this is the answer of the transcendentalists, whose mature perspective on the world is grounded at a point where both views are possible. Geometrically, this is the Archimedean point at the center from which the world is visually balanced. From this point polarities are not obliterated, but instead synthesized. The difference between synthesis and obliteration is, in essence, what sets the transcendentalist apart from the idealist.[7] That Emerson is often described as an idealist—or that his transcendentalism is often misperceived as idealism—is continuing proof that the *method* of the transcendentalist is largely misunderstood. If the basic dialectic of that method is grasped, however, a good many of Emerson's other ideas are clarified.[8] The radical paradox of self-reliance in which one moves toward the world by apparently moving away, and the mature sense of compensation—not as do-goodism rewarded, but as balanced wholeness—are resolved in the notion of a method that duplicates the process of growth itself.

[7] In July, 1836, Emerson defined man as a synthesis or a "marriage" of matter and spirit and made this the basis of his distinction between the idealist and the spiritualist (or transcendentalist): "Man is the point wherein matter & spirit meet & marry. The Idealist says, God paints the world around your soul. The spiritualist saith, Yea, but lo! God is within you. The self of self creates the world through you, & organizations like you" (*JMN*, V, 187). The figure of marriage for the synthesis of transcendental vision recurs in November, 1836: "The world is full of happy marriages of faculty to object, of means to end; and all of Man marries all of Nature, & makes it fruitful. Man may be read therefore, if you choose, in a History of the Arts, or in a history of Sciences" (*JMN*, V, 236).

[8] Emerson adopted the dialectical method 8 years later in "Experience" (*W*, III, 43–86). Here the antithetical elements of experience which the soul must progressively assimilate—symbolized as the "lords of life" in the introductory poem—are conveniently listed in the final section of the essay: "Illusion, Temperament, Succession, Surface, Surprise, Reality, Subjectiveness" (*W*, III, 82).

The Instructed Eye:
Emerson's Cosmogony in "Prospects"
by Barbara Packer

For the Eye altering alters all—Blake

What does Emerson mean by the words he uses in the "axis of vision" formula? What *is* an axis of vision? What does he mean by the words "transparent" and "opake"? The curious schematism of Emerson's formula suggests that its deepest affinities are with something very like Blake's visionary cosmology:

> What is Above is Within, for every-thing in Eternity
>   is translucent:
> The Circumference is Within; Without, is formed the
>   Selfish Center
> And the Circumference still expands going forward to
>   Eternity.[1]

In other words, Emerson's formula is neither an attempt to record a particular experience of exhilaration nor a program for reconciling the perceiving subject with the object-world (its deliberately paradoxical mechanics make as little sense if interpreted according to the laws that govern a world of objects as Blake's notions of an internal circumference and an external center do); it is instead a condensed or reduced version of a complete cosmogony—a formula which, properly expanded, generates a unified and highly original myth of creation, fall, redemption, and apocalypse. The existence of a separate object-world is, for Emerson as for Blake, the product of a Fall or Dislocation, and the "axis of vision" formula is Emerson's laconic story of that Fall: *Jerusalem* as it might have been written by Calvin Coolidge.

"How few cosmogonies have we," Emerson muses in his journal. "A few have got a kind of classical character & we let them stand, for a world-builder is a rare man. And yet what ghosts & hollow formless dream-gear these theories are; how crass & inapplicable! how little they explain; what a poor handful of facts in this plentiful Universe

"The Instructed Eye" by Barbara Packer will appear in another form in her forthcoming book, *The Altering Eye: An Interpretation of Emerson*, to be published by Seabury Press/Continuum Books in 1979. All rights reserved.

[1] William Blake, *Jerusalem*, Plate 71, 6–8, in *The Poetry and Prose of William Blake*, edited by David V. Erdman, with a commentary by Harold Bloom, 4th printing, rev. (New York: Doubleday, 1970), pp. 222–223.

they touch. . . . And yet every man is master of the whole Fact & shall one day find himself so" (*JMN*, VII, 352–353). The cosmogonies we have do nothing to explain the paradox of our relationship to nature—a curious blend of kinship and estrangement. If nature were wholly Other, how could we account for the "radical correspondence" we perceive between "visible things and human thoughts" (*Nature*, p. 16)? On the other hand, if nature is somehow related to us, what accounts for our painfully evident alienation from it? "The fox and the deer run away from us; the bear and tiger rend us" (*Nature*, p. 31).

We need a new cosmogony, or, as Emerson calls it in *Nature*, a "theory of creation," that will explain both how nature came to resemble us and why it presently holds itself aloof from us—is permeated with human meaning, yet not subject to human will. The chant of the Orphic poet in "Prospects," Emerson's first attempt to solve the riddle of the world in a single fable, accounts for the "occult relation" (*Nature*, p. 8) between man and nature by positing their common origin in a divine ancestor, a giant form like Blake's Albion. Originally, the Orphic poet tells us, man was not only a god but a cosmos: what we now call nature was his perpetual emanation. All "Time" was human time; the laws of man's mind externized themselves into days, years, seasons. But something stopped this continuing outward flow of world-creating spirit; man began to ebb, to shrink, leaving the body of nature surrounding him like a vast shell. That shell still bears his impress, but instead of "fitting" him like a garment it now merely "corresponds" to him, and he worships it with timid adoration (*Nature*, pp. 33–34).

The Orphic poet's myth of contraction accounts beautifully for the "facts" Emerson considered most perplexing: the coexistence of our feelings of omnipotence with the undeniable evidence of our limited powers, our sense of an occult relation between the forms of nature and the ideas of the mind. But though the Orphic poet tells us *how* we fell, he fails to tell us *why*. The chant breaks off just when we expect it to give a reason for that first catastrophic shrinkage, the sudden ebb of spirit that left matter behind like an outcast corpse.

Emerson's reluctance to include a description of the causes for the Fall within the Orphic poet's chant may stem from his ambivalent attitude toward fable itself. In one way, fable appealed to him as an attractive compromise, a way for the Reason to present its truths to the limited comprehensive powers of the time-bound Understanding. In a journal passage written in 1835, Emerson praises fable for its economy and its universal appeal:

> Why must always the philosopher mince his words & fatigue us with explanation? He speaks from the Reason & being of course contradicted word for word by the Understanding he stops like a cogwheel at every notch to explain. . . .
> Fable avoids the difficulty, is at once exoteric and esoteric, & is clapped by both sides. (*JMN*, V, 31)

But he was also aware of the dangers of fable. The Understanding exhibits an exasperating tendency to forget the fictiveness of fable, to confuse apologue with chronicle.

And this habit is particularly dangerous when applied to fables about the Fall, since there it has the peculiar effect of *inverting* the meaning of the stories—at least as Emerson understood them. In a journal passage written around the time of the Divinity School Address he elaborates irritably upon the theme:

> What means all the monitory tone of the world of life, of literature, of tradition? Man is fallen Man is banished; an exile; he is in earth whilst there is a heaven. What do the apologues mean? These seem to him traditions of memory. But they are the whispers of hope and Hope is the voice of the Supreme Being to the Individual[.]
> We say Paradise was; Adam fell; the Golden Age; & the like. We mean man is not as he ought to be, but our way of painting this is on Time, and we say *Was*. (*JMN*, V, 371)

Emerson's own cosmogony is meant to inspire, not to depress. Hence when he reaches its central point he forsakes the language of fable for a mode of representation which, though forbidding in itself, is at least less easy to distort into a gospel of discouragement:

> The problem of restoring to the world original and eternal beauty, is solved by the redemption of the soul. The ruin or the blank, that we see when we look at nature, is in our own eye. The axis of vision is not coincident with the axis of things, and so they appear not transparent but opake. The reason why the world lacks unity, and lies broken and in heaps, is, because man is disunited with himself. (*Nature*, p. 34)

The passage is difficult to explicate for a number of reasons—unlike Emerson's first myth of the Fall, it makes few concessions to the Understanding. We cannot even begin to construe it unless we notice that Emerson is both drawing upon and revising his earlier cosmogony. This new formula depends upon an implicit assumption that the mind is a center from which nature radiates, yet it differs from the Orphic chant in assigning the cause of the mind's alienation to an error in vision rather than a failure of energy.

The first and last sentences of the passage, taken alone, could pass for a mere précis of the preceding Orphic chant—as though Emerson at last felt confident of asserting in bare formula what his Orphic poet has advanced as fable. "The problem of restoring to the world original and eternal beauty, is solved by the redemption of the soul. . . . The reason why the world lacks unity, and lies broken and in heaps, is, because man is disunited with himself." But the middle sentences introduce a new idea. To say, as the Orphic chant does, that nature is a shell from which we have shrunk is very different from arguing that the "ruin or blank" of nature is in our own eye. The former places the Fall in some mythical past; the latter places it in the present. Moreover, the latter hints that this Fall is really nothing more than a mis-seeing, an optical illusion. The problem is not so much in nature as in the way we see nature: "The axis of vision is not coincident with the axis of things, and so they appear not transparent but opake."

In order to explain what this striking and peculiar sentence means, it is necessary to examine in some detail a transformation that took place in Emerson's thought during the early 1830's. Two journal passages help to estimate the magnitude of this transformation. The first is a scrap of autobiographical verse from the 1827 journal:

> He is a man who tho' he told it not
> Mourned in the hour of manhood, while he saw
> The rich imagination that had tinged
> Each earthly thing with hues from paradise
> Forsake forever his instructed eye.
> Bewailed its loss, & felt how dearly bought
> Was wisdom, at the price of happiness.
>
> (*JMN*, III, 84)

The second is a brief entry in the 1833 journal: "To an instructed eye the universe is transparent. The light of higher laws than its own shines through it" (*JMN*, IV, 96).

The verse-fragment is pure pastiche, a blatant imitation of Wordsworth's "Ode: Intimations of Immortality." But Emerson's deviations from that poem are as significant as the evidence of his subservience to it. In the "Ode" Wordsworth laments the loss of the visionary gleam, yet consoles himself with "what remains behind": primal sympathy, faith, the philosophic mind. Nothing can bring back the original radiance that the child once saw in nature, but the mature eye learns to find a different sort of satisfaction in the "sober colouring" with which it now invests the landscape.

No trace of this consoling fiction remains in Emerson's version. He professed to be a great believer in the doctrine of Compensation, but the loss of paradisal imagination was one misfortune for which this doctrine could locate no answering benefit. The "instructed eye" sees nothing in nature but a ruin or blank.

The exaggerated bleakness of the 1827 passage makes the about-face of 1833 all the more surprising. Here the "instructed eye" is not only capable of perceiving the "visionary gleam" Wordsworth considers lost; it is incapable of perceiving anything else. Emerson turns the phenomenology of Wordsworth's "Ode" inside out. In the "Ode" the particulars of sense-experience—meadow, grove, and stream—are only *appareled* in light, and that light becomes gradually fainter as the child grows up. "At length the man perceives it die away/ And fade into the light of common day." But to Emerson's instructed eye it is the natural world itself that fades into light—the visionary light of higher laws.

What occasioned this reversal? We know that the years between 1830 and 1833 were years of crisis for Emerson. His first wife died in 1831; in 1832 he resigned his ministry at the Second Church. Stephen Whicher locates Emerson's intellectual awakening— his discovery of "the god within"—during this period, and argues that "the coincidence of this change with his renewed reading in Coleridge is so striking as to put beyond question who the catalyst was for this transformation."[2]

But there were more recondite influences operating also. The editors of Emerson's early lectures note that "a correlation of the *Journals* in the early crisis months of 1832 with Kenneth W. Cameron's lists of his withdrawals of books from the Boston Athenaeum and the Harvard libraries suggests an upsurge of interest in science at that

---

[2] *Freedom and Fate: An Inner Life of Ralph Waldo Emerson* (Philadelphia: University of Pennsylvania Press, 1953), p. 19.

time" (*EL*, I, 1). And though Coleridge may have been the catalyst for Emerson's inner transformation, these popularizing scientific works provided the patterns of imagery into which his thought ultimately crystallized.

The book which seems to have been the stimulus for Emerson's "axis of vision" passage is a *Life* of Newton written by the English astronomer David Brewster and published in 1831.[3] Brewster's book is largely concerned with presenting summaries of Newton's scientific and mathematical discoveries in a form intelligible to the layman. Chapters Three through Ten contain accounts of the various experiments on light and color that Newton describes in his *Opticks*. But Brewster does not merely paraphrase the *Opticks*: he also attempts to furnish hypotheses for phenomena Newton left unexplained, and he details the changes in optical theory that had taken place since Newton's time. Chapter Six of Brewster's work, which deals with Newton's experiments on the colors of thin plates, contains the passage which probably suggested Emerson's "axis of vision" formula; Chapter Seven, which deals with the colors of natural bodies, may have suggested the related images of transparence and opacity.

In the second book of his *Opticks* Newton discusses a number of puzzling optical phenomena. What causes the interference rings produced when a beam of light is shined through a very thin, curved, transparent medium?[4] Or the rings of colors on soap bubbles? Why do the surfaces of all thick transparent bodies reflect part of the light incident upon them and transmit the rest? The chief thing these rather disparate phenomena have in common is that they cannot be accounted for by the purely corpuscular theory of light which Newton attempted to establish in the first book of the *Opticks*. If light really is composed of small material particles identical in size and shape and propagated in straight lines, why should some of the particles bounce off the surface of a transparent medium while others bend through it?

In order to account for this phenomenon Newton is forced to introduce an undulatory principle somewhere in his theory. At first he tries to restrict the undulatory motion to the medium alone. The undulatory motion excited in the medium by the impinging light-particles (Newton usually calls them "rays") puts the particles into "Fits of Easy Transmission and Reflexion." He explains the process this way:

Those that are averse from assenting to any new Discoveries, but such as they can explain by an Hypothesis, may for the present suppose, that as stones by falling upon Water put the Water into an undulating motion . . . so the Rays of Light, by impinging on any refracting or reflecting surface, excite vibrations in the refracting or reflecting Medium or Substance . . . that the vibrations thus excited are propagated in the refracting or reflecting Medium or Substance, much after the manner that vibrations are propagated in the Air for causing Sound, and move faster than the Rays so as to overtake them; and that when any Ray is in that part of the vibration which

[3] *The Life of Sir Isaac Newton* (London: John Murray, 1831). Carl M. Lindner, in an article on "Newtonianism in Emerson's *Nature*," *Emerson Society Quarterly*, XX (1974), 260–269, discusses the influence of Brewster's book upon Emerson's metaphoric vocabulary; see esp. pp. 264–266.

[4] Such as the curved plate of air obtained by pressing a double convex lens against the flat surface of a plano-convex object-glass (Brewster, p. 71).

conspires with its motion, it easily breaks through a refracting Surface, but when it is in the contrary part of the vibration which impedes its Motion, it is easily reflected; and, by consequence, that every Ray is successively disposed to be easily reflected, or easily transmitted, by every vibration which overtakes it.[5]

This hypothesis, which accounts for the behavior of the particles by attributing undulatory movement to the medium, not the particle, explains the interference rings produced by thin transparent bodies. But even thick transparent bodies reflect some light and refract the rest; hence Newton is finally forced to conclude that "Light is in Fits of easy Reflexion and easy Transmission, before its Incidence on transparent Bodies. And probably it is put into such fits at its first emission from luminous Bodies, and continues in them during all its progress."[6] Newton does not even begin to offer an hypothesis for this "property," since it is pure supposition. But Brewster feels called upon to attempt one:

We may form a very intelligible idea of it by supposing, that the particles of light have two attractive and two repulsive poles at the extremities of two axes at right angles to each other, and that the particles revolve round their axes, and at equidistant intervals bring one or the other of the axes into the line of the direction in which the particle is moving. If the attractive axis is in the line of the direction in which the particle moves when it reaches the refracting surface, the particle will yield to the attractive force of the medium, and be refracted and transmitted; but if the repulsive axis is in the direction of the particle's motion when it reaches the surface, it will yield to the repulsive force of the medium, and will be reflected from it.[7]

And in the following chapter he gives Newton's explanation of the phenomena of transparence and opacity—recording Newton's belief that "the least particles of almost all natural bodies are in some measure transparent."

The details of this theory may seem rather recondite for Emerson to have bothered mastering. But his own eye troubles may have given him a more than casual interest in the science of optics,[8] and in any case his readings in scientific works during the crisis years of the early 1830's were undertaken to satisfy spiritual needs of peculiar

---

[5] *Opticks: or a Treatise of the Reflections & Colours of Light* (London: G. Bell and Sons, 1931; rpt. New York: Dover, 1952), p. 280.

[6] *Ibid.*, p. 282.

[7] Brewster, p. 75.

[8] In 1825 and 1826, when he was just beginning his studies in the Theological School at Harvard, Emerson suffered from eye trouble serious enough to prevent reading or writing; Aunt Mary consoled him at the time by suggesting that he might become a second Milton. The episode is discussed in Ralph L. Rusk, *The Life of Ralph Waldo Emerson* (New York: Columbia University Press, 1949), pp. 110–114. Even as late as 1835–36 we find Emerson complaining in his journal of weak and painful eyes, an affliction which he himself seems to have regarded as at least partially psychosomatic. See *JMN*, V, 26, and especially *JMN*, V, 180, where Emerson lists "self healing as weak eyes" as an example of "Reason's momentary grasp of the sceptre." The journal passage later became part of "Prospects" (*Nature*, p. 34), though there Emerson deletes the overly personal reference and writes merely of "self-healing." Both Emerson's preference for visual metaphors, and his insistence that vision was at least partially under the control of the will, seem to have had deeper roots in his own experience than has perhaps been recognized.

urgency. As Whicher remarks: "Newly severed from the authority of the Bible, this reminiscent Puritan sought to read a new gospel from nature, God's perpetual revelation."[9] But if nature were to replace Scripture as a source of truth and a guide to conduct, the exegete of nature must be prepared to master the complexities of her vocabulary, just as the divinity student mastered his Hebrew or Greek. Accordingly, we find Emerson, in his journal, recording a resolve "to learn the law of the diffraction of a ray, because when I understand it it will illustrate, perhaps suggest, a new truth in ethics" (*JMN*, IV, 322).

Apparently Emerson did learn that law, for Brewster's terms blended in his mind with material he had assimilated from Coleridge and the Swedenborgians to form the basis of a complex symbolic system that he retained to the end of his life. "Axis," for instance, comes from Brewster's book, but "coincidence" does not, despite its vaguely scientific ring (cf. "the angle of incidence is equal to the angle of reflection"). Emerson probably adopted the term from Coleridge or from Sampson Reed, who both employ it in discussions of epistemology. In *The Growth of the Mind* (a book Emerson greatly admired) Reed argues that a man who aspires to true philosophy must "bring his mind into coincidence with things as they exist, or in other words, with the truth."[10] And in the *Biographia Literaria* Coleridge asserts, "all knowledge rests on the coincidence of an object with a subject."[11]

Whatever Emerson took from other sources, though, Brewster's book seems to have been the primary stimulus behind his development of a coherent symbolic system. References to transparence and opacity, coincidence and dislocation (in the peculiar sense they bear in the axis of vision passage) do not occur in the journals before 1831, the year Brewster's book was published. But they are frequent after then.

The world becomes transparent to wisdom. Every thing reveals its reason within itself. (*JMN*, III, 280)

Whenever a man comes, there comes revolution. . . . When a man comes, all books are legible, all things transparent, all religions are forms. (*JMN*, V, 492)

If *I see*, the world is visible enough, clothed in brightness & prismatic hues. If again I see from a deeper energy,—I pierce the gay surface on all sides, & every mountain & rock & man & operation grows transparent before me. (*JMN*, VII, 435)

Every body, I think, has sublime thoughts sometimes. At times they lie parallel with the world or the axes coincide so that you can see through them the great laws. (*JMN*, V, 506)

Do something, . . . whether it be in the way of what you call your profession or not, so it be in the plane or coincident with the axis of your character. (*JMN*, VII, 297)

There is a certain fatal dislocation in our relation to nature, distorting all our modes of living and making every law our enemy. . . . Poetry and prudence should be coincident. (W, II, 230–231)

[9] *Freedom and Fate*, p. 87.
[10] *Observations on the Growth of the Mind*, new edition, with a biographical preface by James Reed (Cambridge: Riverside Press, 1886), p. 50.
[11] Edited by J. Shawcross, 2 vols. (Oxford: Clarendon Press, 1907), I, 174.

Why should these pairs of images appeal so strongly to Emerson? He himself could not have explained it, but he was content to accept their significance in the belief that "the soul's emphasis is always right" (W, II, 145). In "Spiritual Laws" he argues that a man is "a selecting principle, gathering his like to him wherever he goes." From the multitude of images offered to him by life or by books a man selects only what belongs to his "genius." "Those facts, words, persons, which dwell in his memory without his being able to say why, remain because they have a relation to him not less real for being unapprehended. They are symbols of value to him as they can interpret parts of his consciousness which he would vainly seek words for in the conventional images of books and other minds" (W, II, 144). With uncharacteristic patience Emerson declares his willingness to wait upon his genius' revelation of its own nature, secure in the faith that salient images held in the mind's solution will someday precipitate out into intelligible form.

Then if "coincidence" and "dislocation," "transparence" and "opacity" were symbols of value to Emerson, what traits of consciousness did they interpret? The periodicity that Newton had discovered in the behavior of light matched Emerson's own discovery of the periodicity of vision. At times he could invoke Newton in a relatively trivial context, as when he notes that "there is . . . in moon gazing something analagous to Newton's fits of easy transmission & reflection. You catch the charm one moment, then it is gone, then it returns to go again" (JMN, V, 189). But Newton's law also appears in an important passage from the 1833 journals, where it is used as the scientific counterpart of Wordsworth's lines from *The Excursion* on the impermanence of vision, lines which haunted Emerson all his life:

As the law of light is fits of easy transmission & reflexion such is also the soul's law. She is only superior at intervals to pain, to fear, to temptation, only in raptures unites herself to God and Wordsworth truly said

> Tis the most difficult of tasks to keep
> Heights which the soul is competent to gain.
> (JMN, IV, 87)

If Newton's hypothesis was the scientific, and Wordsworth's couplet the poetic expression of the law that governs the discontinuity of vision, then Coleridge's version of the German Idealist distinction between the Reason and Understanding was its philosophic equivalent. It helped account for a puzzling yet centrally important feature of the inner life—polarity. "Every body perceives the greatest contrasts in his own spirits and powers," he writes. "Today he is not worth a brown cent—tomorrow he is better than a million" (JMN, IV, 34). Again, he could assert "I am a God in nature, I am a weed by the wall" (W, II, 307). "I write laboriously after a law, which I see, and then lose, and then see again" (J, IX, 468).

It was predictable, then, that Emerson should try to assimilate his system of contraries to his favorite philosophical distinction. (Coleridge himself may have suggested the blending: in *The Friend* he speaks of "that eternal Reason whose fulness hath no opacity, whose transparency hath no vacuum."[12]) Reason, transparence, and coincidence versus Understanding, opacity and dislocation: the six terms became a kind of shorthand for recording the discontinuous splendors of the inner life.

Each pair of terms in this triad of contraries expresses a slightly different aspect of the central fact of discontinuity. The distinction between the Reason and the Understanding accounts for a dualism within consciousness itself (and so represents an advance upon more conventional dualisms, like the Christian or Cartesian). The distinction between transparence and opacity transfers the characteristics of that primary dualism from consciousness to the phenomenal world that is its shadow. Finally, the distinction between coincidence and dislocation indicates with great precision the statistical rarity of visionary moments: there is an infinite number of possible dislocations, but only one possible position of coincidence for the diameters of two concentric circles. There is a good deal more Understanding than Reason in the operation of our minds; a good deal more opacity than transparence in the world we perceive around us. "Our faith comes in moments," Emerson notes, "our vice is habitual" (W, II, 267).

But if visionary moments are rare, they are also surprisingly effortless. Vision always takes us by surprise. When we least expect it, the axis of vision suddenly snaps into place, and the universe dissolves in light. "But suddenly, in any place, in the street, in the chamber, will the heaven open, and the regions of wisdom be uncovered, as if to show how thin the veil, how null the circumstances" (JMN, V, 275). Notice that Emerson uses the language of traditional apocalyptic in describing the moment of vision—the uncovering of heaven, the rending of the veil—yet insists upon the unremarkable nature of its surroundings.

If one can begin to understand why the terms from Newton and Coleridge became primary symbols of value to Emerson, it is not hard to understand why he should have decided to employ them in constructing a believable cosmogony. They were the most resonant words in his private vocabulary. "As a man thinketh so is he, and as a man chooseth so is he and so is nature" (W, II, 144). His set of contraries had already proved to be convenient calipers for taking the dimensions of the universe. But if the "law of light" could furnish metaphors of frustration, it might also be made to yield prescriptions for apocalypse. With formulaic terseness Emerson offers the theory that explains all phenomena: "The ruin or the blank, that we see when we look at nature, is in our own eye. The axis of vision is not coincident with the axis of things, and so they appear not transparent but opake."

Perhaps the easiest way to characterize this theory, which attempts to blend scientific objectivity and religious enthusiasm, would be to say that Emerson conceived the startling idea of treating the "inner light" of the radical Protestant tradition as though it behaved according to Newton's laws. In this project he may have been encouraged by

[12]*The Friend*, edited by Barbara E. Rooke, 2 vols. (London: Routledge and Kegan Paul, 1969), I, 522.

some sentences in Guillaume Oegger's *Le Vrai Messie* (Paris, 1829), a manuscript translation of which he read during the summer of 1835. Oegger, a French Swedenborgian, is the "French philosopher" quoted in the "Language" chapter of *Nature* (p. 18); his influence on Emerson's theory of language has long been recognized. But the axis of vision passage, too, may owe something to Oegger's short "dictionary" of correspondential terms. Natural or "dead" light, according to Oegger, always corresponds to "some variety of truth": "All the phenomena of reflected light, all the colors, preserve some distant relation to the moral world; from white, which represents complex truths, to black, which recalls the darkness of absolute ignorance. . . . *And this amazing comparison of dead light with spiritual light, may be carried into the mysteries of refraction and transmission.*"[13]

One might wish to object that even Emerson could hardly have hoped to explain the structure of the universe in two sentences. But in "Idealism" he implies that a certain laconism is a sign of the highest reasoning. In physics, once man "has penetrated the vast masses of nature with an informing soul, and recognized itself in their harmony, that is, seized their law" then "the memory disburthens itself of its cumbrous catalogues of particulars, and carries centuries of observation in a single formula" (*Nature*, pp. 26–27). By the time Emerson ventures the axis of vision formula his memory has disburdened itself not only of cumbrous particulars but of any subsidiary propositions upon which that formula was based. Let us try to supply them:

1. Emerson uses the term "inner light" as a synonym for soul or Reason; he also identifies the soul with vision. "In the highest moments," he says, "we are a vision" (*JMN*, V, 467). It follows then, that the soul may also be spoken of—by metonymy— as an Eye. Oegger calls man's eye "the emblem of his soul,"[14] and Coleridge, in *Aids to Reflection*, calls it "the *micranthropos* in the marvellous microcosm."[15]

2. This Eye, or spherule of inner light, resembles a Newtonian particle in having "poles" or "axes." In his journal Emerson records an anecdote told him by a friend about a "boy that was cross eyed when ever he lied, but the axes of the eyes parallel when he spoke truth" (*JMN*, V, 102). Of Swedenborg's attempt to formulate a science of correspondences Emerson wrote: "It required such rightness of position that the poles of the eye should coincide with the axis of the world" (*W*, IV, 117).

3. This Eye is the center of the visible world. Emerson begins the essay "Circles" with the statement that "The eye is the first circle; the horizon which it forms is the second; and throughout nature this primary emblem is repeated without end" (*W*, II, 301). And he hints at the Eye's possible transcendence by associating this "emblem"

---

[13] G. Oegger, *The True Messiah: or The Old and New Testaments, examined according to the Principles of the Language of Nature*, reprinted in Kenneth Walter Cameron, *Young Emerson's Transcendental Vision* (Hartford: Transcendental Books, 1971), p. 338 (emphasis added).

[14] *Ibid.*

[15] *Aids to Reflection*, with a Preliminary Essay by James Marsh, D.D., from the fourth London edition, with the author's last corrections, edited by Henry Nelson Coleridge (1840; rpt. Port Washington, N.Y.: Kennikat Press, 1971), p. 342.

with the mighty paradox whose literary metamorphoses Georges Poulet has traced:[16] "St. Augustine describes the nature of God as a circle whose center was everywhere and its circumference nowhere" (W, II, 301).

4. All natural objects are opaque, but they may become, or be made, transparent. That "transparence" and "opacity" denote spiritual rather than physical states is apparent from a charming sentence in "The Poet": "I shall mount above these clouds and opaque airs in which I live,—opaque, though they seem transparent" (W, III, 12). Opacity is the condition Blake called Mystery: the threatening and unknowable otherness of the material world. Transparence is Revelation or Apocalypse, the state in which the mute characters of nature become wholly intelligible, like hieroglyphics translated by Champollion.[17]

Coleridge, significantly, resorts to a similar metaphor in his influential Essays on Method in *The Friend*. A man who studies nature without method is like the "rude yet musing Indian" who has come into possession of an illuminated manuscript of the Bible. If he studies it diligently, he may begin to notice that the symbols on the page fall into recurrent patterns; but he can get no farther until the helpful missionary arrives to translate the book for him. "Henceforward, the book is unsealed for him; the depth is opened out; he communes with the spirit of the volume as a living oracle. *The words become transparent, and he sees them as though he saw them not.*"[18]

When Emerson calls the world transparent, then, he is referring not to its appearance but to its intelligibility. Behind Emerson's assertion that "the ruin or the blank, that we see when we look at nature, is in our own eye" lies Milton's moving complaint that in his blindness the "Book of knowledge fair" is now a "Universal blanc/ Of Nature's works to me expung'd and ras'd" (*Paradise Lost*, III, 47–49).

In Milton's lines the blankness of the book of knowledge is a metonymy of effect for cause. But in Emerson the question of figuration is less easily resolved. On one level the axis of vision formula functions perfectly well as a striking though rather peculiar figure of speech. To say that we see a ruin or blank when we look at nature is, on the face of it, a hyperbolic protest against the gloom of the Christian or the emptiness of the Cartesian vision of nature; to say that this ruin or blank is in our own eye identifies perception with projection.

But in another sense the formula is not figurative at all. If the Orphic poet is right, then projection *is* the cause of nature. "Perhaps these subject-lenses have a creative power; perhaps there are no objects," Emerson muses in "Experience" (W, III, 76).

---

[16]*The Metamorphoses of the Circle*, trans. Carley Dawson and Elliott Coleman (Baltimore: Johns Hopkins Press, 1967).

[17]John T. Irwin, in an article on "The Symbol of the Hieroglyphics in the American Renaissance," *American Quarterly*, XXVI (1974), 103–126, discusses the significance of Champollion's work (he deciphered the Rosetta Stone in 1822) for Emerson and for figures who taught or influenced him: Edward Everett, Sampson Reed, Oegger. The Swedenborgians were particularly quick to point out the resemblance between their system of interpretation and Champollion's.

[18]*The Friend*, I, 512–513 (emphasis added).

But if there are no objects, then what is "the great apparition, that shines so peacefully around us" (*Nature*, p. 5)? Only a hieroglyphic text that we wrote, then lost the key to; only a kind of giant parapraxis, a slip or dislocation of the mind. "Nonsense is only sense deranged, chaos is paradise dislocated" (*JMN*, X, 40).

From these principles, or something like them, Emerson derives his cosmological formula. If the poles of the eye, the first circle, were coincident with the poles of the second, the horizon which it makes, the particulars of the natural world would dissolve into the transparency of pure significance. One cannot really call the formula a program for uniting subject and object, since it denies, at least implicitly, that what we call "objects" really exist, just as it denies the existence of any essential difference between the inner light and the light of higher laws, the god within and the God without. "The simplest man who in his integrity worships God becomes God, at least no optics of the human mind can detect the line where man the effect ceases, and God the cause begins" (*JMN*, IV, 385). The Transparent Eye-ball is a circle whose center is everywhere and its circumference nowhere.

We are now in a position to understand why Emerson cast his formula in such oddly negative terms. I have been attempting to describe the state of Coincidence; Emerson would have denied that any such description is possible. Discursive language is the language of the Understanding: it can hint at the truths of Reason only through fable, paradox, or negation. The Orphic chants are fables; the transparent eye-ball passage is chiefly composed of paradoxes ("I am nothing, I see all").[19] Here Emerson approaches the subject through negation. "The axis of vision is not coincident with the axis of things, and so they appear not transparent but opake." He cannot say that the problem of restoring original and eternal beauty to the world would be solved if the axis of vision *were* coincident with the axis of things, because in the state of Coincidence there are no separate things. The object-world is the product of dislocation, and will vanish when the dislocation is remedied. But the question then arises: what is the nature of this dislocation? If there is no "axis of things" in the state of perfect Coincidence, then what is it the "axis of vision" deviates *from*? I think we have to say (with some violence both to language and to sense, as Dr. Johnson might remark) that it deviates from it-

[19] In *Aids to Reflection* Coleridge argues that it is in fact a "test and character" of a truth affirmed by the Reason "that in its own proper form it is inconceivable. For to conceive is a function of the understanding, which can be exercised only on subjects subordinate thereto. And yet to the forms of the understanding all truth must be reduced, that is to be fixed as an object of reflection, and to be rendered expressible. And here we have a second test and sign of truth so affirmed, that it can come forth out of the moulds of the understanding only in the disguise of two contradictory conceptions. . . . Examples: Before Abraham *was*, I *am*.—God is a circle, the center of which is every where, and its circumference nowhere" (footnote to p. 223). The notion of an eye-ball wholly transparent is itself a paradox: if we try to picture Emerson's eye-ball we can imagine either a transparent globe or a giant eye (as in Cranch's drawing; see *Nature*, p. 9), but not both at once. For a discussion of another aspect of the paradoxicality of the figure, see James M. Cox, "R. W. Emerson: The Circles of the Eye," in *Emerson: Prophecy, Metamorphosis, and Influence*, edited by David Levin (New York: Columbia University Press, 1975), p. 61.

self. Geoffrey Hartman notes Blake's belief that "all myths are creation myths and tell of man's self-alienation." [20] Emerson's creation myths, too, are myths of self-alienation; and the "dislocation" of the axis of vision formula, like the "contraction" of the first Orphic chant, is a way of describing man's lapse from his own divinity. But the axis of vision formula does something the Orphic chant cannot. It evades temporality.

Remember Emerson's objections to most myths of the Fall: they express differences between states as differences between times, and thus obscure or pervert the meanings they were supposed to convey. In his journal Emerson tries to explain the causes of this persistent misrendering: "Reason, seeing in objects their remote effects, affirms the effect as the permanent character. The Understanding listening to Reason, on one side, which saith *It is*, & to the senses, on the other side, which say, *It is not*, takes middle ground and declares *It will be*. Heaven is the projection of the ideas of Reason on the plane of the Understanding" (*JMN*, V, 272–273). In other words, the Reason can see in the acorn a full-grown oak: the senses can see only the acorn: and the Understanding works out the compromise formula, "This acorn will grow into an oak." Or, the Reason can see paradise in the world: the senses see only the world: and the Understanding asserts that the world will someday become a paradise.

In the Orphic chants that surround the axis of vision formula, Emerson is willing to make concessions to the time-bound Understanding: "*Once* [man] was permeated and dissolved by spirit." "*Then* shall come to pass what my poet said." But in the axis of vision formula itself Emerson speaks uncompromisingly from his Reason to ours. "The problem of restoring original and eternal beauty to the world *is* solved. . . . The ruin or the blank . . . *is* in our own eye. The axis of vision *is* not coincident with the axis of things, and so they *appear* not transparent but opake." The word "restoring," it is true, seems to admit the fallacy Emerson wished to deny, but the rest of the formula is temporally noncommittal. The myth of dislocation neatly avoids locating perfection either in a remote past or a distant future. It is a spatial rather than a temporal image, a formula rather than a plot. If the kingdom of man over nature does not seem to be in any hurry to establish itself, its postponement is accidental rather than necessary: "it is only the feebleness and dust of the observer that makes it future, the whole *is* now potentially in the bottom of his heart" (*JMN*, IV, 87).

[20] *Wordsworth's Poetry 1787–1814* (New Haven: Yale University Press, 1964), p. 193.

SELECTED BIBLIOGRAPHY

There being no better commentary on a work by Emerson than other works by Emerson, the most immediately rewarding area for further reading may well be Emerson's other writings, particularly those composed shortly before and after *Nature*. In addition to entire volumes of the correspondence, lectures, and journals (*CEC, EL, JMN, L*), see (1) the selection of his early sermons edited by Arthur C. McGiffert, Jr., under the title *Young Emerson Speaks* (Boston: Houghton Mifflin Company, 1938); (2) "The American Scholar" (1837) and the Divinity School Address (1838); and (3) such later writings as "The Method of Nature" (1841), "Experience" (in *Essays, Second Series*, 1844), and "Fate" (in *The Conduct of Life*, 1860).

Among secondary materials, the standard biography is Ralph L. Rusk, *The Life of Ralph Waldo Emerson* (New York: Charles Scribner's Sons, 1949). For general orientation in Emerson scholarship and criticism, see (1) Frederic I. Carpenter, *Emerson Handbook* (New York: Hendricks House, 1953); (2) Robert E. Spiller, "Ralph Waldo Emerson," in *Literary History of the United States*, ed. Spiller, Thorp, Johnson, and Canby, 3 vols. (New York: The Macmillan Company, 1948), I, 358–387; (3) Floyd Stovall, "Emerson," in *Eight American Authors: A Review of Research and Criticism*, edited by Stovall (New York: The Modern Language Association of America, 1956), pp. 47–99; Revised Edition, edited by James Woodress (New York: W. W. Norton & Company, Inc., 1971), pp. 37–83; (4) *Emerson: A Collection of Critical Essays*, edited by Milton R. Konvitz and Stephen E. Whicher (Englewood Cliffs, N.J.: Prentice-Hall, Inc., 1962); (5) *The Recognition of Ralph Waldo Emerson: Selected Criticism Since 1837*, edited by Milton R. Konvitz (Ann Arbor: The University of Michigan Press, 1972).

In addition to the articles, books, and reviews drawn upon for the present volume, the following specialized studies bearing upon *Nature* will prove useful:

Allen, Gay Wilson. "A New Look at Emerson and Science," *Literature and Ideas in America: Essays in Memory of Harry Hayden Clark*, edited by Robert Falk. Athens: Ohio University Press, 1975, pp. 58–78.

Berthoff, Warner. Introduction to *"Nature" by Ralph Waldo Emerson: A Facsimile of the First Edition*. San Francisco: Chandler Publishing Company, 1968, pp. vii–lxxiv.

Cameron, Kenneth Walter. "Emerson and Swedenborgism: A Study Outline," *Emerson Society Quarterly*, No. 10 (I Quarter, 1958), 14–20.

———. *Emerson the Essayist*. 2 vols. Raleigh, N.C.: The Thistle Press, 1945. A detailed study of the sources of Emerson's thought.

————, ed. *Nature (1836) by Ralph Waldo Emerson*. Edited with an Introduction, Index-Concordance and Bibliographical Appendices. New York: Scholars' Facsimiles & Reprints, 1940.

Provides a facsimile of the 1836 text and a census of copies of the first edition.

————. *Young Emerson's Transcendental Vision: An Exposition of His World View with an Analysis of the Structure, Backgrounds, and Meaning of "Nature" (1836)*. Hartford, Conn.: Transcendental Books, 1971. Also published as Nos. 64–65 of *ESQ: Journal of the American Renaissance* (Summer–Fall, 1971).

Clark, Harry Hayden. "Emerson and Science," *Philological Quarterly*, X (July, 1931), 225–260.

Written before the publication of Emerson's lectures on natural history, but still valuable: see Gay Wilson Allen, "A New Look at Emerson and Science."

D'Avanzo, Mario L. "Emerson's 'Scoriae,'" *American Notes & Queries*, XIII (May, 1975), 141–143.

On Emerson's symbolic use (in *Nature*, p. 18) of a figure from Oegger.

Feidelson, Charles, Jr. "Toward Melville: Some Versions of Emerson," in *Symbolism and American Literature*. Chicago: The University of Chicago Press, 1953, pp. 119–161.

On ramifications of Emerson's dialectic method.

Fletcher, Richard M. "Emerson's *Nature* and Goethe's *Faust*," *American Notes & Queries*, XII (March, 1974), 102.

Emerson's reference to "a canal" in the Introduction to *Nature* (p. 5) may be "a consciously-intended allusion" to *Faust*, Part II.

Hansen, Chadwick C. "Ralph Waldo Emerson's *Nature*; Gospel of Transcendentalism," in *American Renaissance, the History of an Era: Essays and Interpretations*, edited by George Hendrick. Frankfurt: Diesterweg, 1961, pp. 39–51.

Analysis and explication.

Hedges, William L. "A Short Way Around Emerson's Nature," *Transactions of the Wisconsin Academy of Sciences, Arts and Letters*, XLIV (1955), 21–27.

A neo-classical approach to Emerson's concept of "nature."

Hopkins, Vivian C. "Emerson and Bacon," *American Literature*, XXIX (January, 1958), 408–430.

Considers Bacon's influence on *Nature*.

————. "Emerson and Cudworth: Plastic Nature and Transcendental Art," *American Literature*, XXIII (March, 1951), 80–98.

Notes parallels between *Nature* and Cudworth's *The True Intellectual System of the Universe* (1678).

Hotson, C. P. "Emerson and the Doctrine of Correspondence," *New-Church Review*, XXXVI (January, April, July, October, 1929), 47–59, 173–186, 304–316, 435–448.

————. "Emerson and Swedenborg," *New-Church Messenger*, CLX (September, 1930), 274–277.

————. "Emerson and the Swedenborgians," *Studies in Philology*, XXVII (July, 1930), 517–545.

La Rosa, Ralph C. "Emerson's Sententiae in *Nature* (1836)," *Emerson Society Quarterly*, No. 58 (I Quarter, 1970), 153–159.

Lauter, Paul. "Truth and Nature: Emerson's Use of Two Complex Words," *ELH, A Journal of English Literary History*, XXVII (March, 1960), 66–85.

Lindner, Carl M. "Newtonianism in Emerson's *Nature*," *ESQ: A Journal of the American Renaissance*, XX (4th Quarter, 1974), 260–269.

Matthiessen, F. O. "The Word One with the Thing," *American Renaissance: Art and Expression in the Age of Emerson and Whitman*. New York: Oxford University Press, 1941, pp. 30–44.

Provocative commentary on Emerson's use of language at the time of *Nature*.

Miller, F. DeWolfe. *Christopher Pearse Cranch and His Caricatures of New England Transcendentalism*. Cambridge: Harvard University Press, 1951.

For commentary on Cranch's several illustrations of *Nature*, see pp. 38–44.

Miller, Perry. "From Edwards to Emerson," *New England Quarterly*, XIII (December, 1940), 589–617. Reprinted in Miller, *Errand into the Wilderness*. Cambridge: The Belknap Press of Harvard University Press, 1956, pp. 184–203.

"What is persistent . . . is the Puritan's effort to confront, face to face, the image of a blinding divinity in the physical universe, and to look upon that universe without the intermediacy of ritual, of ceremony, of the Mass and the confessional" (*Errand into the Wilderness*, p. 185).

Neufeldt, Leonard N. "The Law of Permutation—Emerson's Mode," *American Transcendental Quarterly*, No. 21 (Winter, 1971), pp. 20–30.

Discusses the language of *Nature* (pp. 20–26).

Packer, Barbara. "Uriel's Cloud: Emerson's Rhetoric," *Georgia Review*, XXXI (Summer, 1977), 322–342.

Includes a comment on the "transparent eye-ball" passage (pp. 327–328).

Pochmann, Henry A. "Ralph Waldo Emerson," in his *German Culture in America: Philosophical and Literary Influences 1600–1900*. Madison: The University of Wisconsin Press, 1957, pp. 153–207.

Includes a concise review of Emerson's intellectual development and an analysis of *Nature*, emphasizing Platonic and Germanic elements (pp. 153–192).

Poirier, Richard. "Is There an I for an Eye?: The Visionary Possession of America," in his *A World Elsewhere*. New York: Oxford University Press, 1966, pp. 50–92.

Includes an examination of the first chapter of *Nature* (pp. 56–70) as the point of departure for treatment of later American authors and works.

Pollock, Robert C. "A Reappraisal of Emerson," *Thought*, XXXII (Spring, 1957), 86–132. Reprinted as "Single Vision" in *American Classics Reconsidered: A Christian Appraisal*, edited by Harold C. Gardiner, S.J. New York: Charles Scribner's Sons, 1958, pp. 15–58.

Regan, Earlene Margaret. "A Literary Introduction to Emerson's *Nature*," *American Transcendental Quarterly*, No. 30 (Spring, 1976), Part 3, pp. 1–20.

Thompson, F. T. "Emerson and Carlyle," *Studies in Philology*, XXIV (July, 1927), 438–453.

———. "Emerson's Indebtedness to Coleridge," *Studies in Philology*, XXIII (January, 1926), 55–76.

Tuerk, Richard. "Emerson's *Nature*: Miniature Universe," *American Transcendental Quarterly*, No. 1 (I Quarter, 1969), 110–113.
  On the "poetic character" of *Nature*.

Wahr, F. B. *Emerson and Goethe*. Ann Arbor: George Wahr, 1915.

Woodberry, George Edward. "'Nature' and Its Corollaries," in his *Ralph Waldo Emerson*. New York: The Macmillan Company, 1907, pp. 44–63.

For additional bibliographical listings through 1961, see (1) Lewis Leary, *Articles on American Literature 1900–1950* (Durham, N.C.: Duke University Press, 1954), and (2) Jackson R. Bryer and Robert A. Rees, *A Checklist of Emerson Criticism 1951–1961 with a Detailed Index* (Hartford: Transcendental Books, 1964). For listings since 1961, see (1) "Articles on American Literature Appearing in Current Periodicals" in successive issues of *American Literature*; (2) the annual bibliographical numbers of *PMLA*; (3) "Recent Emerson Bibliography" in *The Emerson Society Quarterly* through volume 17 (1971); and (4) the chapters on "Emerson, Thoreau, and Transcendentalism" in successive volumes of *American Literary Scholarship: An Annual / 1963–*, variously edited by James Woodress and J. Albert Robbins (Durham, N.C.: Duke University Press, 1965–).